HEGEL

HIGHLIGHTS: AN ANNOTATED SELECTION

HEGEL

HIGHLIGHTS:
AN ANNOTATED SELECTION

WANDA ORYNSKI

PHILOSOPHICAL LIBRARY
New York

 Type set in Times Roman at The Polyglot Press, New York. Printed in the United States of America.

Dedicated in loving friendship to
Edith Harris Schultz
granddaughter of William Torrey Harris
America's foremost Hegelian Scholar
The Teacher of the great Hegelian
Dr. Edward Elliott Richardson
The late Professor Emeritus of Philosophy
The George Washington University
Washington, D. C.

PREFACE

Few names in the history of western philosophy have evoked as many contradictory feelings running the gamut from adulation to utter derision, as has that of Hegel. Lips curl in vilipending jeers and with hauteur and a smirk his system is dispensed with by some who probably never studied or, if they did so, miserably failed to comprehend it. The associations which Hegel himself would have emphatically shunned, such as with men of violence, unsanctified spirits and faithless revolutionaries, are inevitably brought in when his name is mentioned, ill concealing the suggestion that he might be at the bottom of attitudes and thoughts reprehensible to free and democratic minds. At best, his thoughts are adjudged incomprehensible and vague, far removed from reality. Though a gracious critic will cede Hegelianism antithetical value in discussions with materialism, many nevertheless are inclined to dispose of it as visionary. And yet there are those who believe that in Hegel the profoundest thoughts of God became articulated in man.

Greatness, of course, can never be subject to impartial evaluation. We first have to determine on what eminence, if any, we ourselves are ensconced, what is the fathom of our own thought, what capabilities are ours intellectually, and what the range of our charity and sympathy is. We have heard Shakespeare called trite, Kant pedantic, and Aristotle banal, wondering not only what the censor read, but what, intelligencewise, his candle footage is.

We may be sure of this: If not all books are lost in the holocaust of which some have dark forebodings, men whose sense of value is not completely whelmed by the exigencies of immediacy and thought-destitute living, will dig with their bare hands for Plato's works, for Lao-tse's *Tao Te Ching,* for Sankara's comments on the *Brahmasutras,* for gems like Boëthius' *Consolation of Philosophy,* Pascal's *Pensées,* Spinoza's *Ethics*, or Fichte's *Vocation of Man*; but the discriminating will search for Hegel fragments to reassure themselves by these as they could never do by anything else, that spirituality, freedom and God ultimately and absolutely, not only will but must triumph. When all faith has left man and he has lost all sense of value and grace has fled his life, it is then that spirit begins to vibrate with intensity, for God is beginning to be reborn.

We readily acknowledge that in Hegel's hands logic becomes mystical and mysticism turns to rationality. The true pupil of Hegel condemns nothing, he endeavors to comprehend all. Even would the universe yield all its secrets to science and men mock God who has completely hidden himself from view, Hegel will perceive him in all his grandeur still and wonder at the sceptic's obtuseness. Thought is not the end product of evolution: It is *sui generis,* and stood at the cradle of the world. When all is relative, the Absolute celebrates its greatest victory and in the very act of self-contradiction achieves its own fullness and being.

The method of Hegel is unique. The position which he took was never before him taken so daringly and uncompromisingly as a fulcrum for philosophic, religious, historic and scientific thought combined. Existentialism today is preparing us for a "leap," for paradox, yes for absurdity. It thrives on crises and perplexities, and discovers its answers in irrationalism. It leaves us with despair, fear and trembling. Its alienation or estrangement technique is not predicated upon an original over-riding unity and hence incapable of producing eleusinian solutions.

Hegel likewise made a leap, not after having experienced despondency but while in the best of mental health, with capabilities fully intact for insight, enthusiasm and daring. He led the falcade into the lucid spheres of intelligence. His reason is not romantic search but the unshakable conviction that thought is not only the primary concern of man but that Nature is mute without intelligent response. All phases of being, becoming, essence are not simply antithetical. In spiritual clarity there is light, life and generosity, God, truth and Being, and all things are in safe-keeping. No other system before or since is so liberal without being paternal.

There may be plenty of scintillation in the split thinking of existentialists, but there is luminosity and beauty in Hegel. This thinker does not uproot men from nature, does not deny the urgency which stuff or matter may impose on living, thinking substance, and picks no quarrel with science, neither does he deny divinity in the most devious, nor fail to point without rancor to the pretentiousness in the sanctified. His motive is not indifference, not sentimentality, not social necessity, not tolerance however pressing. Divine ensphering intelligence places all for him in proper perspectives.

In these days of doubt, uncertainty, frustration, forsakenness of God and man, Hegel posits the unquestioned certainty of the Absolute—not as a stale and stable existence, or merely as a living reality. It is rather one vast dialectically unfolding idea alienating itself from itself, becoming reconciled, and reinterpreting itself in endless variation.

To get away from the commonplace and trifling there is no greater refuge than the vast domain of Hegel's thinking whose basic theme is God's idea as it appears in the world dramatically and profoundly. It is doubtful whether anyone has probed the possibilities of Hegel's suggestions to the full. Hegel, the man, was fallible without a doubt, but the idea he espoused remains grand and momentous. Certainly, concern is voiced over the alleged deduction of empirical reality from the movement of thought, and the equation of logic and being. The fact that the originator of dialectical materialism who, with great consistency interpreted the development of economic and social events, used Hegel's dialectical method is proof that even the opposition bowed to the master. How otherwise than by exploring the profundity of thought can reality be understood? Man, nature, the multifariousness of the world is interesting and quite entertaining, but only principles of structure, relation, evolution give substance and meaning to the grand show, while history remains agonizing, tantalizing without a universal concinnity.

Wanda Orynski has accomplished with indefatigable courage a labor of love in this digest of Hegel's writings upon which she is to be heartily congratulated. She has done the work competently and in scholarly fashion, as only one, with proper philosophic preparation, and one who truly understands a most difficult and at times obscure master, could have done. To have accomplished the epitome of Hegel in the compass of these pages is a feat worthy of highest commendation.

In congratulating her we must not forget to congratulate ourselves in that we are the recipients of this illuminating and concise presentation. For now Hegel becomes accessible to those who cannot devote the hours necessary to comprehend this encyclopedic comprehender. And it has, indeed, become necessary that wider circles know Hegel and pass from hearsay and superficial and inadequate knowledge of his system to a true understanding of it.

Hegel's name is well-known enough, to be sure, but the circumstances surrounding the mention of his name breathe an ill wind and are such as make a garbled view of his work and intention almost inevitable. For Hegel was neither the official Prussian State Philosopher, though unofficially he may with human pride have considered himself that, nor was he in any sense responsible for the Marxian dialectic. We must absolve the master from responsibility if a later generation pupil, such a Marx, assuredly understood him yet undertook to twist and reapply his theory to the very opposite of what he tried to prove, that not God but matter is the primary substance of the world. It is, in fact, meaningless to still talk about a dialectic at all if Hegel's presuppositions are taken away and even the synthesis is treated as a farce. That Hegel is expurgated and only cursorily referred to in the literature of dialectical materialism is surely proof that Hegel is in a different "class" from Marx altogether and will not bear comradery.

The present *Digest* makes a major contribution, thus, to enlightenment about Hegel's main theses and an appreciation of the depth of his thought. It is important that this has been accomplished at this juncture in history when the forces of antithetical thinking and material contradictions are loosed on a scale unprecedented. In this connection it may be noted that events have moved the so-called abstractions of Hegel into a new light. Men's minds are about saturated with empirical reality and the avalanche of economic demands is displacing man's finer sensibilities. The remedy or cure, however, does not lie in orthodoxy, in a return to anything in the past. For, not only are the ages of faith recorded indelibly on Clio's scroll, but the present age, well prodded by logical positivism, psychoanalysis, existentialism, Zen and beat, is rather sophisticated. The simple-minded will have to shift for themselves in a world with which they are out of tune. It will be found, however, that Hegel satisfies the intellectual gourmet as much today as he did a century and a half ago. Beyond that, the relevancy of his contemplative doctrine of God—as which Iwan Iljin characterizes Hegel's philosophy—will be received with acclaim by ever wider circles of thinkers who want to leave the shoals in search of spiritual turbulence and dynamic thought. More exquisite patterns are in store for those possessed of a maturer religious consciousness.

Wanda Orynski's book is, hence, appearing at a fit time when minds need an adult guide to mundane problems and, in addition, the support of philosophy and metaphysics to undergird the visible complexity. And if, as is the case with Hegel, the logical patterns are also distinguishable in the empirical realm, and actual being accrues to both, a decisive interpretation of man, nature and universe will be arrived at which is utterly destructive of the Marxian hypothesis. Hegel hits the material dialectics where it matters most, at its roots, and does the job more effectively than thought rambling without benefit of system. If there should be no other virtue in Hegel's philosophy than this, it will have served the world well. However, there is immense treasure beyond. May this *Digest* prepare the way and lead the appreciative reader to greater ventures of the spirit.

Mary Washington College of the University of Virginia

Kurt F. Leidecker

CONTENTS

FOREWORD

This book has two objects—namely to serve as a wedge into the profundity of the Hegelian philosophy and to present that philosophy in this abbreviated form against the background of the world of today. A period of over one hundred and fifty years has elapsed since Hegel wrote.

Three main works are made the fulcrum that it is hoped will raise the comprehension of Hegel's whole system into a higher, clearer atmosphere. These are *The Phenomenology of Mind, The Science of Logic,* and *The Philosophy of History*.

The first named is Hegel's voyage of discovery. Because of this, Hegel's own words will be brought to bear on all matters of importance. It is thought that such a method will meet the needs of students more satisfactorily. *The Logic* is digested without quotations. *The Philosophy of History* is rendered by a combination of these two methods. The references throughout the latter are quoted from the translation of J. Sibree, M.A., The Colonial Press, N. Y., 1900. The references to *The Phenomenology of Mind* are quoted from the translation of J. B. Baillie, Unwin Brothers, London; The Macmillan Company, N. Y., Revised Edition, 1931.

In the introduction to his translation of the *The Phenomenology of Mind*, Professor Baillie has the following to say: "So exhaustive an analysis of the life history of the human spirit; so sustained an effort to reduce its varied and involved forms of expression to their simple leading principles and to express these controlling ideas in an orderly, connected system, had certainly never before been compressed within the compass of a single treatise . . ." (Translator's Introduction, page 13.) And further: "The argument of *The Phenome-*

nology presents unusual difficulties even to the trained student of philosophy. It has been said that a great man lays the world under the obligation to understand him. This obligation is not easily fulfilled when a man of genius of the highest order produces a philosophical interpretation of experience so novel in its design, so subtle in the texture of its thought, so comprehensive in its range, and penetrating in its vision." (Translator's Introduction, page 19.)

It will be noticed that Hegel makes no reference to the Unnameable Unconditioned Absolute—carefully distinguished in the ancient systems of philosophy. He does not include the recognition of these systems, but rather he lets them play their roles unheralded as he delineates the historic process.

Acknowledgment and gratitude are hereby expressed to the New World pioneer Hegelian, Dr. William Torrey Harris. His many writings on the Hegelian philosophy lighted the way for the comprehension of the perfect whole which Hegel's system brings to birth in Speculative Conception. Also to Dr. Kurt F. Leidecker for his wise Hegelian counsel and his help throughout the years.

W. O.

HEGEL

A Digest

Introduction

Hegel's system of philosophy becomes important as a study by reason of the fact that Hegel was the first philosopher to unite all systems into one self-moving whole. This one system embodies all phases of experience as well as all phases of thought. In fact, as Professor Baillie points out, ". . . the drama of history is shown to be the progressive march of unfolding principles in the Spirit of Man." Systems of thought but mark the ebb and flow of advancement and seeming recession, as man moves onward toward a final realization of himself. This final efflorescence of the Spirit in Man constitutes the goal of attainment. It is "Absolute Knowledge" in which Philosophy, Religion and Science are understood in their co-relationship. The outcome of the whole process gives a unified, purposeful world behind the apparent differences.

To show forth this basic world with its philosophical *raison d'être,* Hegel has delivered a system framed in a rigid logic. He has endeavored to unfold pure thought genetically. This logical genesis of pure thought by Hegel marks the most distinctive attainment of the Western mind. Also it forms the necessary complement to the genius of the East. The Eastern mind has concentrated on "Being." These two in mutual relation will form a unified consciousness for the world of the future.

It is in order that the Western mind may the better understand its share in philosophic thought that this résumé of the Hegelian Philosophy is attempted.

In the past, various systems of philosophy have been evolved to explain the universe and man. Each has been a ray of light from the mind that evolved it. Perhaps it was a faint light such as is seen in the early dawn before the full glory of the risen sun. Perhaps a stronger, more central light. One ancient philosopher, in search of the Real, out of which all things come, named *water*. This he concluded was the underlying reality. Another named *fire*. Still another named *air*. Then later came the idea of atoms, or monads, which were sparks of light and life. Yet, as these philosophers reasoned in this way, there was a greater reality at work in their own power of reason than lay in any of the partially inert elements. These material elements were moved by some extraneous force in comparison to reason which is "self-moving." With this consideration, philosophy came into an expanded position. The idea brings with it implications. There is duality. There is mind and matter. There is subject and object. We have here a question which is vexing to men's minds. It existed in the past and it is with us today. There is a world within of thought and ideas. There is a world without. Which is the Real One? Which is the greater?

At one extreme, we have the philosopher trying by means of abstract reasoning to fathom the meaning of existence. At the other, we have the scientist trying by means of sense perception to find the answer. Yet all the while the bodies and minds of men are using the elements of nature to furnish and maintain these bodies and minds which are the instruments of thought and inspiration. There must be a link of deep significance. There must be inter-action internally at work.

As Manly P. Hall suggests, "May not the time arrive when the consciousness of man will evolve the perfection necessary to bridge this gap. When the relation of the parts of existence to their sum total in the whole will be comprehended." When the parts of existence, with which science deals, and the whole of existence with which philosophy deals, will be seen as inter-acting in an eternal drama for the production of heroes of Light—those who are the Knowers of Truth, the Doers of Good and the Creators of Beauty.

For ages, the elements of earth have been at work in cyclic periodicity. The races of men have each in turn reached a high water mark in the production of great thinkers, seers, and geniuses. Each of these as he appeared was unique in his individuality. Yet, he was in a sense the résumé of all that had gone before. The philosophical insight that came with our present philosopher bears this out. Hegel made wholly his own the light shed by his predecessors. He attained the insight of Plato. He was guided yet more fully by the light shed by the insight of Aristotle. He comprehended Thomas Aquinas. He reviewed and exhausted the systems of Kant, Fichte, and Schelling. In fact, his deeper penetration saw the generic relation of these systems and showed up this relation as a progressive evolution. By a complete mastery of the portends and place of each, he beheld their underlying unity. To the strength in diversity—which characterizes the West—was added the realization of unity, which characterizes the East. We see then a unity evolving into diversity and a diversity involving to unity.

The purpose of this treatise is to review and summarize the delivery of the one who first made it possible for man to see all that there is in himself and in his world and to formulate such knowledge scientifically. George Wilhelm Friedrich Hegel lived at a time when this insight was made possible by that which had gone before. He was a product of the West. He had his incubation in the race that was the first to assert an independent spirit when most other races were under mandate. He saw his way clearly. He saw the logical unfoldment of his system, but he had much to consider in his endeavor to state it. There were several contending expositions of philosophy current in Hegel's time to which reference must be made. In order to make his meaning stand out against these systems, Hegel felt obliged to interpolate explanations and various refutations along the way. Added to this, his years as an instructor gave to his style a quality of repetition that halts the onward flow of mental concepts. These features tend to clutter the main stream of thought. This fact has made for discouragement among neophytes who found themselves overwhelmed at the outset. Even lion-hearted veterans have declared their trials heavy. But the time has come when the light that shines through the insight of this genius in speculative thinking is brought into bright relief by the developments since his day. Not only historical development, but the development in human consciousness itself—which is the theme of Hegel's stupendous treatise. For that reason, this era seems an auspicious one in which to put out a clear-cut series of expositions after the manner of headline summaries which will finally deliver the philosophy in its entire scope and place within the power of those who possess this key a surer approach to the Master himself. It will be found that the present age will help to open to view a better perspective.

An attempt will be made to bring together under one cover a comprehensive digest of that which is contained in Hegel's three main works, The Phenomenology of Mind, The Science of Logic, and The Philosophy of History.

The first of these—The Phenomenology of Mind—deals through-out, with the ways in which experience appears. It is here shown that the forms of experience are a continuous connected series, which constitute the life of mind as a whole, moving toward the Self-Comprehension of Spirit. When this ground is completely covered and the Logic is reached, it is seen in the light of Self-Comprehension. In the Logic however, all the findings are formulated according to the scientific method. The results are delivered in the rigid genesis of pure thought. And, lastly, in The Philosophy of History, the movement is delineated as it evolves in the world, through the races of men as the unfoldment of the historic process. We have in the system of the Hegelian Philosophy one that is strictly scientific, one that meets logical demands, yet one which embodies all phases of experience, of being and of thought.

THE PHENOMENOLOGY OF MIND

That part of Hegel's philosophy which will have the initial review, namely, *The Phenomenology of Mind,* constitutes a systematic survey of the ways in which experience appears. It is the introductory part to a comprehensive philosophical system. It lays the foundation by showing that Absolute Knowledge, as a mode of Spiritual life, has its roots in experience. That it is the cause and the consummation of the whole process of life. The elaboration of Absolute Knowledge as such, comes later.

The Phenomenology of Mind—as has been said, takes up the general subject of the stages through which experience passes. These stages are six in number. First, there is the stage of Consciousness. The second to be developed is Self-consciousness. The third is Reason. The fourth is Spirit. The fifth is Religion. The sixth is Absolute Knowledge. (Hegel puts Reason, Spirit, and Religion under the general heading of Concrete Mind.) Each of these, except the last, has subdivisions or phases.

1. Consciousness
    - (a) Sense Certainty
    - (b) Perception
    - (c) Understanding (i.e. force and understanding)
2. Self-consciousness
    - (a) Independence and Dependence
    - (b) Freedom of Self-consciousness
3. Reason
    - (a) Observation as a Mode of Reason
    - (b) Realization of Rational Self-Consciousness
    - (c) Individuality
4. Spirit
    - (a) The Objective Spirit

(b) Spirit in Self-estrangement
(c) Spirit certain of Itself—morality

5. Religion
   (a) Natural Religion
   (b) Religion in the Form of Art
   (c) Revealed Religion
6. Absolute Knowledge
   Three distinctions are made under Absolute Knowledge:
   (a) The ultimate content of the Self which knows itself as all existence;
   (b) Philosophical Science as the Self-comprehension of Spirit;
   (c) The Return of Spirit so comprehended, to immediate existence

This survey constitutes, according to Hegel, the whole scope of the evolution of Consciousness. It is the journey that Consciousness takes on the way from its most meager aspect to its full consummation. The Law evolves in the same manner for humanity as a whole, for a race, and for each individual. The way of this journey is the way of Self-knowledge.

It might be well to point out here that, on this journey, Hegel employs a certain vocabulary of his own. In fact, Philosophy has ever found this necessary in its function of grasping unity and the diversity arising within it. In *The Phenomenology of Mind*, there are two usages which stand out above all others because of their constant repetition. These are *The Notion* and *The Moment*. The latter is more or less familiar and may be said to refer to the phases in the stages of realization. Regarding Hegel's use of *The Notion*, a volume might be required to exhaust the subject. However, as a makeshift raft on which to cling, one may adopt a simple concept until such time as acquaintance with Hegel and experience in his method bring full satisfaction. *The Notion*, in its supreme sense, would be self-conscious mind come full circle as enlightenment. Hence, it may be said that Hegel uses this term, *The Notion*, to designate this general function of Self-conscious Mind—Reason—*par excellence*. But he likewise uses this term, *The Notion*, to express the stages in realization of the movements of Self-Moving-Mind in its differences, which are the externalization of itself in diversity. Because whether it operates as the whole or in the whole, whether it operates as the part or in the part, it is the same. Hence, wherever individuality possesses it, by realization, there you deal with *The Notion*. With this meager indication to guide us, we shall proceed to the consideration of The Phenomenology of Mind.

I

CONSCIOUSNESS

Starting now with the initial phase of the six stages of experience which have been named as Consciousness, Self-Consciousness, Reason, Spirit, Religion and Absolute Knowledge, we have first of all Consciousness. This lowest form of experience shows itself in three grades, namely: Sense Certainty, Perception and Force or Understanding. The first grade is that of Sense Certainty. It is the most elementary and in reality the poorest kind of truth. Yet at first it seems to be the richest and most reliable. By sense certainty is meant the report which the senses give to consciousness. I, this particular I, am certain of this tree before me. The I in this case does not deliberate. It merely reports the fact of a tree here and now. The first item for us to note is that the experience at once breaks up into two factors which are not distinct and therefore they are not determined and are not immediate. Neither factor can exist alone. They are mediated the one through the other. The I feels certainty through the other, likewise the other exists through the I. All the elements which constitute the sense-certainty of the fact "I see a tree here and now," can be shown to be universals which are only held together momentarily on account of their relationship. The now is no sooner named than it is already another now. "Here is a tree" with but a turn of the head becomes "a not-tree," and "a not-here." A simple entity of this sort which is neither this nor that, but is constantly vanishing according to its relation is called "A Universal." The "I" seems to be the store house that holds all of these in validity, but this *I* can be shown to be a Universal also, as far as sense-certainty is concerned. For a hundred I's could assert as many distinct verdicts all equally true. Yet, sense-certainty itself remains unaware that its essence is the empty abstraction of pure being. It thinks, on the contrary, that it has to do with solid material and content. This in meagre outline is sense-certainty.

The next movement of consciousness characterized by Hegel is Perception. In Sense-Certainty, we had a series of "acts of apprehending," each act certain of itself—each instantly annulled—as consciousness did nothing more than "merely sense". But in the next phase of the operation of consciousness, where the mind realizes also the fact of its own operation in grasping what the senses furnish, we rise one step in our function to perception. Hegel gives the example of salt, which is white, hard, cubical and of distinct taste. These qualities are kept distinct by the mind and also held together by the mind as characteristic of salt. Thus all the wealth of sense knowledge belongs to perception, but besides there is distinction, negation, and multiplicity. For instance, the mind distinctly negates the fact that these different properties of the salt are isolated and separate. The mind can see them in their multiplicity, yet it holds them in their relationship. To quote Hegel: "In this way, we have in the case of perception as happened in the case of sensuous certainty, the aspect of consciousness being forced back upon itself; but, in the first instance, not in the sense in which this took place in the former case, i.e., not as if the truth of perception fell within it. Rather consciousness is aware that the untruth, that comes out there, falls within it. By knowing this, however, consciousness is able to cancel and supersede this untruth. It distinguishes its apprehension of the truth from the untruth by its perception, corrects this untruth, and, so far as itself takes in hand to make the correction, the truth . . . of perception, certainly falls within its own consciousness. The procedure of consciousness, which we have now to consider, is thus so constituted that it no longer merely perceives but is also conscious of its reflection into self, and keeps this apart from the simple apprehension proper." (169)

And further: "These pure determinations appear to express the essential nature itself; but they are merely a self-existence which is fettered at the same time with existence for another. Since, however, both essentially exist in a single unity, we have before us now unconditioned absolute universality; and it is here that consciousness first truly passes into the sphere of Understanding, of Intelligence." (175)

Before proceeding with a consideration of the Understanding, there will be a pause, in order to make a few comments regarding Hegel's characteristic method of treating his theme. It is made at this point because the reader has now been led into the shallow waters at the edge of this ever widening and deepening ocean of thought. He has also experienced Hegel at first hand in the quoted paragraphs. As Hegel advances in this unfoldment, the play of thought becomes more subtle and more intricate. Hence a few words to prepare the way for this journey. As a matter of fact, it is a journey in which one goes no-where. Instead, one stays at home and from that center known as consciousness, attempts an expansion of insight until there is established the realization of free Enlightened Reason. This journey is a long one. It may be said to reach the distance of man's evolutionary span, or the distance between two declarations of the simple statement of "I am". The first is that of the infant, or the infantile mind of primitive man. He vaguely senses the statement "I am", in the mere fact of being alive. The second statement is the "I am", of Enlightenment. This statement of "I am", far from being meagre, holds within it a knowledge of its universality and its universal power. Between these extremes travels the eternal pilgrim—humanity. It is the mission of Philosophy to explain this way. In summarizing Hegel's findings, Dr. W. T. Harris epitomized in words to this effect: "The world is not divine but it has a divine mission to perform in the creation of immortal souls who forever emerge into the consciousness of freedom."

According to Hegel, philosophy portrays this journey of

expansion. It is accomplished on the ocean of consciousness. The reason Hegel's text is difficult to follow is because he renders a painstaking account of every phase of the movement of mind as it makes this expanse from the meagre affirmation of sense-certainty to the highest efflorescense of Enlightened Reason. He starts with the first ripple on the Ocean of Being. From there, it is as if he pointed out each succeeding ripple, as it arose, swelled to initiate a second—then both collapsed into the Ocean, only to begin again in greater volume. Thus, we have the expanse and the reason for it. This is followed by its augmentation to a second and the reason for it. Then comes the inevitable inadequacy that causes a collapse. So it goes, on and on, to a third, a fourth, a fifth; each time Hegel delineates with elaborate detail, how the mind takes hold of these advancing concepts, establishes them in their positive and negative aspects, and then must needs let them collapse into the great ocean of the unconditioned universal as they prove inadequate to answer the quest which will be the perfect fulfillment for consciousness. All the while, it is consciousness alone with which we deal as it was when we began with sense certainty and perception. These Hegel had characterized. We had seen them collapse and we were left in the unconditioned universal. Here we shall resume our analysis of the journey of consciousness.

Now, in coming to this next phase of Mind, which is Understanding, Hegel says it has an objective counterpart, namely, Force. Force is a unity; the differences are expressions of force. In like manner does understanding explain differences in the unity of itself.

To expand the idea of force as Hegel sees it, and at the same time get a clear example of the dialectical necessity that carries through the whole system which his insight penetrated, let the words of the originator make clear the facts. To quote: "The difference between force proper, withdrawn into itself, and force unfolded and expressed in independent constituent elements would at the same time have no being at all if they had no subsistence; i.e., force would have no being, if it did not exist in these opposite ways. But to exist in this way as opposite aspects means nothing else than that both moments are themselves at the same time independent. It is this process we have now to deal with —the process by which both moments get themselves fixed as independent and then cancel their independence again." (184) More on the same. Says Hegel: "When we thus keep both moments in this immediate unity, it is Understanding to which the conception of force belongs, that is, properly speaking the principle which carries the different moments . . . (as) different. For, *per se,* they are not to be different; the distinction consequently exists only in thought (183) . . . Consciousness takes up a mediated relation to the intervening play of forces into the real and true background of things. The middle term combining the two extremes, understanding and the inner of things, is the explicitly evolved being of force, which is now and henceforth a vanishing process for understanding. Hence it is called Appearance." (190)

"Within this inner truth, this absolute universal which has got rid of the opposition between universal and particular, and become the object of understanding, is a supersensible world which henceforth opens up as the true world lying beyond the sensuous world which is the world of appearance. Away remote from the changing vanishing present (*Diesseits*) lies the permanent beyond (*Jenseits*) an immanent, inherent reality (*ein Ansich*), which is the first and therefore imperfect manifestation of Reason, i.e., it is merely the pure element where the truth finds its abode and its essential being.

"Our object henceforth has thus the form of a syllogistic inference (*Schluss*), whose extremes are in the inner being of things and understanding, and its middle term the sphere of appearance." (191)

"The relation of understanding to the inner world through mediation is, however, its own process, by which the inner world will be found to receive fullness of content."

"The play of forces is what understanding has directly to

do with; but the real truth for it is the inner world bare and simple. (193-194)

"But change, when planted in the inner reality as it (change) truly is, forthwith is taken up into that (reality) as equally absolute universal difference at peace with itself, and remaining at one with itself. In other words, negation is an essential moment of the universal; and negation or mediation in what is universal is universal difference. This difference is expressed in the law, which is the stable presentment or picture of unstable appearance. The supersensible world is in this way a quiescent 'kingdom of laws', no doubt beyond the world of perception—for this exhibits the law only through incessant change—but likewise present in it, and its direct immovable copy or image.

"This kingdom of laws is indeed the truth for understanding; and that truth finds its content in the distinction which lies in the law." (195)

"So far, however, as it is not *law* in general, but *a* law, it has determinateness within it; and as a result there are found an indeterminate plurality of laws. But this plurality is rather itself a defect; it contradicts the principle of understanding, for which, since it is consciousness of the simple inner being, truth is the inherently universal unity. It must, therefore, let the many laws coalesce into a single law, just as, e.g., the law by which a stone falls, and that by which the heavenly bodies move have been conceived as one law. When the laws thus coincide, however, they lose their specific character. . . . The unification of all laws in universal attraction expresses no further content than just the bare concept of the law itself, a concept which is therein set down as existing. Universal attraction says merely that everything has a constant distinction for anything else. Understanding pretends by that to have found a universal law which gives expression to universal reality as such; but, in point of fact, it has merely found the conception of law itself, although in such a way that it at the same time thereby declares all reality to be in its very nature conformed to law. The idea of universal attraction has, therefore, to this extent great importance, that it is directed against that unthinking way of representing reality, to which everything appears in the shape of accident and chance, and for which determinateness, specificity, takes the form of sensuous independence.

"In contrast then, with determined law stands universal attraction or the bare conception of law." (196-197)

Hegel goes on to say that in like manner as we see the unity, force, expressing itself in repeated manifestations of force which return to the universal store, so we have in the kingdom of laws the endless process of change which was formerly the play of force, with the rise of appearance constantly coming to be, and as constantly annulled. The specific laws belong to the sphere of appearance, to the sphere of sensible existence. The inner being is the implicit universal out of whose permanence arises universal difference. This thought brings to birth the idea of infinity.

"This bare and simple infinity, or the absolute notion may be called the ultimate nature of life, the soul of the world, the universal life-blood, which courses everywhere, and whose flow is neither disturbed nor checked by any obstructing distinction, but is itself every distinction that arises, as well as that into which all distinctions are dissolved; pulsating within itself, but ever motionless, shaken to its depth, but still at rest. It is self-identical for the distinctions are tautological; they are distinctions that are none." (208)

"Infinitude, this absolute unrest of pure self-movement, such that whatever is determined in any way, e.g., as being, is really the opposite of this determinateness—has from the start been no doubt the very soul of all that has gone before; but it is in the inner world that it has come out explicitly and definitely. The world of appearance, or the play of forces shows its operation; but it is in the first instance as Explanation that it comes openly forward. And since it is at length an object for consciousness, and consciousness is aware of it as what it is, consciousness is in this way Self-Consciousness." (209-210)

"This self identical reality stands, therefore in relation solely to itself. *To Itself*; which means this is an other, to which the relation points; and relation to itself is, more strictly, breaking asunder; in other words, that very self-identity is internal distinction. These sundered factors have, hence, each a separate being of their own; each is an opposite,—of another; and thus with each the other is herein *ipso facto* expressly given; or it is not the opposite of an other, but only the pure opposite; and thus each is therefore, in itself the opposite of itself." (208)

The world of appearance, the play of forces—Law, Understanding cancelling these distinctions in the concept of Infinitude which Hegel designates as the absolute unrest of pure self-movement—we have, as stated, here come to consciousness as Self-Consciousness. Hegel says, "In that this notion of infinitude is its object, it is thus a consciousness of the distinction as one which at the same time is at once cancelled. Consciousness is for itself and on its own account, it is a distinguishing of what is undistinguished, it is Self-Consciousness. I distinguish myself from myself; and herein I am immediately aware that this factor distinguished from me is not distinguished. I, the self-same being, thrust myself away from myself; but this which is distinguished, which is set up as unlike me, is immediately on its being distinguished no distinction for me. Consciousness of another, of an object in general, is indeed itself necessarily self-consciousness reflected into self; consciousness of self in its otherness. The necessary advance from the previous attitudes of consciousness which found their true content to be a thing, something other than themselves, brings to light this very fact that not merely is consciousness of a thing only possible for a self-consciousness, but that this self-consciousness alone is the truth of those attitudes. But it is only for us (who trace this process) that this truth is actually present; it is not yet so for consciousness immersed in the experience. Self-consciousness has in the first instance become a specific reality on its own account (für sich), has come into being for itself; it is not yet in the form of unity with consciousness in general." (211-212)

Hegel says, "This curtain (of appearance) therefore hanging before the inner world is withdrawn, and we have here the inner being (the ego) gazing into the inner realms—the vision of the undistinguished self-same reality, which repels itself—affirms itself as a divided and distinguished inner reality, but as one for which at the same time the two factors have immediately no distinction; what we have here is Self-consciousness. It is manifest that behind the so-called curtain, which is to hide the inner world, there is nothing to be seen unless we ourselves go behind there, as much in order that we may thereby see, as that there may be something behind there which can be seen. But it is clear at the same time that we cannot without more ado go straightway behind there. For this knowledge of what is the truth of the idea of the realm of appearance and of its inner being, is itself only a result arrived at after a long and devious process in the course of which the modes of consciousness, 'meaning', 'perception', and 'understanding' disappear. And it will be equally evident that to get acquainted with what consciousness knows when it is knowing itself, requires us to fetch a still wider compass. . . ." (212)

With this analysis of Consciousness which we traced through the stages of its phases,—(A) Sense-certainty; (B) Perception; (C) Understanding (force, appearance, law, infinitude;)—we are now truly face to face with the second of the major divisions, namely—Self-Consciousness.

Arrived at Self-Consciousness, let us see it unfold—under Hegel's guidance.

II

SELF-CONSCIOUSNESS

The Truth of Self-Consciousness

We are now ready to give ourselves over to the consideration of Self-Consciousness. Up to the point that we had reached, consciousness had first of all to deal with an objective world which seemed outside of itself—something other than consciousness. It was dealing with appearance, with the play of force, and with the operation of law. There was a process of movement, of instability. It was here that we saw Understanding come to birth. We saw it experience itself for the first time as it unified diversity within itself. It found the notion of infinitude to be its object. It found itself existing on its own account. These are the facts that bring us to the consideration of Self-consciousness. Hence we have a fresh starting point for further analysis. Self-consciousness now comes forth into a position of Supremacy. It assumes different distinctions. It realizes itself in relation to nature, in relation to other selves, and in relation to the ultimate Being of the world. The final outcome is that Self-consciousness realizes itself throughout reality. Later, it emerges into the next category of itself, namely, Reason. But, it is first this arm of the journey that we shall now traverse under Hegel's leadership. Self-consciousness will reveal to us the new phase of consciousness in a state of Desire—which leads to life as living in the Genus.

This Self-consciousness has different degrees. As stated it passes through a realization of itself in relation to nature—which had at first seemed different from the mind aware of it. This difference breaks down under analysis and consciousness finds itself in unity and identity with its object, also "certain of itself in its object". As consciousness experiences itself at this higher level it must, beside realizing itself in relation to nature, realize itself also in relation to other selves which are similar to it.

"But in reality" says Hegel, "self-consciousness is reflection out of the bare being that belongs to the world of sense and perception, and is essentially the return out of otherness. As self-consciousness, it is movement. But when it distinguishes only itself as such from itself, distinction is straightway taken to be superseded in the sense of involving otherness. The distinction *is* not, and self-consciousness is only motionless tautology. Ego is Ego. I am I. When for self-consciousness the distinction does not also have the shape of *being,* it is *not* self-consciousness." (219) Again, "And, consequently, the sensible world is regarded by self-consciousness as having a subsistence which is, however, only appearance, or forms a distinction from self-consciousness that *per se* has no being. This opposition of its appearance and its truth finds its real essence, however, only in the truth—in the unity of self-consciousness with itself. This unity must become essential to self-consciousness, i.e., self-consciousness is the state of *Desire* in general. Consciousness has, *qua* self-consciousness, henceforth a two-fold object—the one immediate, the object of sense-certainty and of perception, which, however, is here found to be marked by the character of negation; the second, viz., itself, which is the true essence, and is found in the first instance only in the opposition of the first object to it. Self-consciousness presents itself here as the process in which this opposition is removed, and oneness or identity with itself established." (220)

"For us or implicitly, the object, which is the negative element for self-consciousness, has on its side returned into itself, just as on the other side consciousness has done. Through this reflection into itself, the object has become life." (220)

"The determination of the principle of life, as obtained from the conception or general result with which we enter this new sphere, is sufficient to characterize it, without its nature being evolved further out of that notion. Its circuit is completed in the following moments. The essential element (*Wesen*) is infinitude as the supersession of all distinctions, the pure rotation on its own axis, itself at rest while being absolutely restless infinitude, the very self-dependence in which the differences brought out in the process are all dissolved, the simple reality of time, which in this self-identity has the solid form and shape of space. The differences, however, all the same hold as differences in this simple universal medium; for this universal flux exercises its negative activity merely in that it is the sublation of them; but it could not transcend them unless they had a subsistence of their own. Precisely this flux is itself, as self-identical independence, their subsistence or their substance, in which they accordingly are distinct members, parts which have being in their own right." (221)

Hegel says: "Life in the universal fluid medium, quietly, silently shaping and moulding and distributing the forms in all their manifold detail, becomes by that very activity the movement of those forms or passes into life *qua Process*. The mere universal flux is here the inherent being; the outer being, the "other", is the distinction of the forms assumed. But this flux, this fluent condition, becomes itself the other in virtue of this very distinction; because now it exists "for" or in relation to that distinction, which is self-conditioned and self-contained (*an und für sich*), and consequently is the endless, infinite movement by which that stable medium is consumed—is life as living." (223)

"This simple substance of life, therefore, is the diremption of itself into shapes and forms, and at the same time the dissolution of these substantial differences; and the resolution of this diremption is just as much a process of diremption, of articulating. Thus both the sides of the entire movement which were before distinguished, viz., *the setting up of in-*

dividual forms lying apart and undisturbed in the universal medium of independent existence, and the *process* of life—collapse into one another. The latter is just as much a formation of independent individual shapes, as it is a way of cancelling a shape assumed; and the former, the setting up of individual forms, is as much a cancelling as an articulation of them. The fluent, continuous element is itself only the abstraction of the essential reality, or it is actual only as a definite shape or form; and that it articulates itself is once more a breaking up of the articulated form, or a dissolution of it. The *entire* circuit of this activity constitutes Life. It is neither what is expressed to begin with, the immediate continuity and concrete solidity of its essential nature; nor the stable, subsisting form, the discrete individual which exists on its own account; nor the bare process of this form; nor again is it the simple combination of all these moments. It is none of these; it is the *whole* which develops itself, resolves its own development, and in this movement simply preserves itself." (223-224)

"Since the object is in its very self negation, and in being so is at the same time independent, it is Consciousness. In the case of life, which is the object of desire, the negation *either* lies in another, namely, in desire, *or* takes the form of determinateness standing in opposition to an other external individuum indifferent to it, or appears as its inorganic general nature. The above general independent nature, however, in the case of which negation takes the form of *absolute* negation, is the genus as such, or as self-consciousness. Self-consciousness attains its satisfaction only in another self-consciousness." (226)

"The object of self-consciousness, however, is still independent in this negativity of itself; and thus it is for itself genus, universal flux or continuity in the very distinctiveness of its own separate existence; it is a living self-consciousness." (226)

"A self-consciousness has before it a self-consciousness. Only so and only then *is* it self- consciousness in actual fact;

for here first of all it comes to have unity of itself in its otherness. Ego which is the object of its motion, is in point of fact not "*object*." The object of desire, however, is only independent, for it is the universal, ineradicable substance, the fluent self-identical essential reality. When a self-consciousness is the object, the object is just as much ego as object." (227)

"With this we already have before us the notion of *Mind* and *Spirit*. What consciousness has further to become aware of, is the experience of what mind is—this absolute substance, which is the unity of the different self-related and self-existent self-consciousnesses in the perfect freedom and independence of their opposition as component elements of that substance; Ego that is "we", a plurality of Egos, and "we" that is a single Ego. Consciousness first finds its self-consciousness—the notion of mind—its turning point, where it leaves the parti-coloured show of the sensuous immediate, passes from the dark void of the transcendent and remote supersensuous and steps into the spiritual daylight of the present." (227)

Lordship and Bondage

The truth of self consciousness takes its rise in the fact it has another self-consciousness before it. The same process is repeated which we saw in the case of the play of forces. Here the middle term is self-consciousness and the two extremes are determinateness. Hegel says: "*Consciousness* finds that it immediately is and is not another consciousness, as also that this other is for itself only when it cancels itself as existing for itself, and has self-existence only in the self-existence of the other. Each is the mediating term to the other, through which each mediates and unites itself with itself; and each is to itself and to the other an immediate self-existing reality, which, at the same time, exists thus for itself only through this mediation. They recognize themselves as mutually recognizing one another". (231)

Hegel goes on to develop the fact that, to quote: "The relation of both self-consciousnesses is in this way so constituted that they prove themselves and each other through a life-and-death struggle. They must enter into this struggle for they must bring their certainty of themselves, the certainty of being for themselves, to the level of objective truth, and make this a fact both in the case of the other and in their own case as well. And it is solely by risking life that freedom is obtained; only thus is it tried and proved that the essential nature of self-consciousness is not bare existence, is not the merely immediate form in which it at first makes its appearance, is not its mere absorption in the expanse of life. Rather it is thereby guaranteed that there is nothing present but what might be taken as a vanishing moment—that self-consciousness is merely pure self-existence, being-for-self. The individual, who has not staked his life, may, no doubt, be recognized as a Person; but he has not attained the truth of this recognition as an independent self-consciousness." Through a life and death struggle there comes this recognition.

In this Hegel sees the "breaking up into extremes with opposite characteristics—the middle term collapses into a lifeless unity—which is broken up into lifeless extremes, merely existent and not opposed. And the two do not mutually give and receive one another back from each other through consciousness; they let one another go quite indifferently, like things. Their act is abstract negation, not the negation characteristic of consciousness, which cancels in such a way that it preserves and maintains what is sublated, and thereby survives its being sublated." (234)

"In this experience self-consciousness becomes aware that *life* is as essential to it as pure self-consciousness. In immediate self-consciousness the simple ego is absolute object, which however, is for us or in itself absolute mediation, and has as its essential moment substantial and solid independence. The dissolution of that simple unity is the result of the first experience; through this there is posited a pure self-consciousness, and a consciousness which is not purely for itself, but for another. . . . The one is independent, and its essential nature is to be for itself; the other is dependent, and its essence is life or existence for another. The former is the master, or Lord, the latter is the Bondsman." (234)

In this distinction between Master and Bondsman Hegel is pointing to the difference in degrees of self-consciousness. In the case of the Master there is more of free self-maintenance —more of self-assertion. But the very fact of servitude in human history shows it to be a principle in the development of consciousness. Hegel says: "The feeling of absolute power, however, realized both in general and in the particular form of service, is only dissolution implicitly; and albeit the fear of the Lord is the beginning of wisdom, consciousness is not therein aware of being self-existent. Through work and labor, however, this consciousness of the bondsman comes to itself. In the moment which corresponds to desire in the case of the master's consciousness, the aspect of the nonessential relation to the thing seemed to fall to the lot of the servant, since the thing there retained its independence. Desire has reserved to itself the pure negating of the object and thereby unalloyed feeling of self. This satisfaction, however, just for that reason is itself only a state of evanescence, for it lacks objectivity or subsistence. Labor, on the other hand, is desire restrained and checked, evanescence delayed and postponed; in other words, labor shapes and fashions the thing. The negative relation to the object passes into the form of the object, into something that is permanent and remains; because it is just for the labourer that the object has independence. This negative mediating agency, this activity giving shape and form, is at the same time the individual existence, the pure self existence of that consciousness which now in the work it does is externalized and passes into the condition of permanence. The consciousness that toils and serves accordingly attains, by this means the direct apprehension of that independent being as its self." (238)

Stoicism: *Scepticism*: *The Unhappy Consciousness*

From this stage, brought about through the attitude of master and bondsman, we move on under Hegel's guidance through three other forms, namely *Stoicism, Scepticism* and the *Unhappy consciousness* to the freedom of self-consciousness. Although Stoicism and Scepticism appeared most prominently in Greece and Rome they can be shown to be modes of consciousness found throughout human experience. In speaking of Stoicism Hegel says, "In this way we have a new attitude or mode of consciousness brought about: a type of consciousness which takes on the form of infinitude, or one whose essence consists in unimpeded movement of consciousness. It is one which *thinks* or is free self consciousness. For thinking does not mean being an abstract ego, but an ego which has at the same time the significance of inherently existing in itself; it means being object to itself or relating itself to objective reality in such a way that this connotes the self-existence of that consciousness for which it is an object." (242-43)

"This freedom of self-consciousness, as is well known," says Hegel, "has been called Stoicism, in so far as it has appeared as a phenomenon conscious of itself in the course of the history of man's spirit. Its principle is that consciousness is essentially that which thinks, is a thinking reality, and that anything is really essential for consciousness, or is true and good, only when consciousness in dealing with it adapts the attitude of a thinking being." (243-44)

"This consciousness in consequence takes a negative attitude towards the relation of lordship and bondage. Its action, in the case of the master, results in his not simply having his truth in and through the bondsman; and, in that of the bondsman, in not finding his truth in the will of his master and in service. The essence of this consciousness is to be free, on the throne as well as in fetters, throughout all the dependence that attaches to its individual existence, and to maintain that stolid lifeless unconcern which persistently withdraws from the movement of existence, from effective activity as well as from passive endurance, into the simple essentiality of thought. Stubbornness is that freedom which makes itself secure in a solid singleness and keeps within the sphere of bondage. Stoicism, on the other hand, is the freedom which ever comes directly out of that sphere, and returns back into the pure universality of thought. It is a freedom which can come on the scene as a general form of the world's spirit only in a time of universal fear and bondage, a time, too, when mental cultivation is universal, and has elevated culture to the level of thought." (244-5)

Hegel continues: "*Scepticism* is the realization of that of which Stoicism is merely the notion, and is the actual experience of what freedom of thought is; it is in itself and essentially the negative, and must so exhibit itself. . . ." (246)

"In Stoicism, self-consciousness is the bare and simple freedom of itself. In Scepticism, it realizes itself, negates the other side of determinate existence, but in so doing, really doubles itself, and is itself now a duality. In this way the duplication, which previously was divided between individuals, the lord and the bondsman, is concentrated into one. Thus we have here that dualizing of self-consciousness within itself, which lies essentially in the notion of mind; but the unity of the two elements is not yet present. Hence the *Unhappy Consciousness*, the Alienated Soul which is the consciousness of self as a divided nature, a double and merely contradictory being." (250-51)

"This unhappy consciousness, divided and at variance within itself, must, because this contradiction of its essential nature is felt to be a single consciousness, always have in the one consciousness the other also; and thus must be straightway driven out of each in turn, when it thinks it has therein attained to the victory and rest of unity. Its true return into itself, or reconciliation with itself, will, however, display the notion of mind endowed with a life and existence of its own, because it implicitly involves the fact that, while being an undivided consciousness, it is a double-consciousness. It is itself the gazing of one self-consciousness into another, and itself is both, and the unity of both is also its own essence; but objectively and consciously it is not yet this essence itself —it is not yet the unity of both." (251)

Hegel continues: "in this process, however, consciousness experiences just this appearance of particularity in the unchangeable and of the unchangeable in particularity. Consciousness becomes aware of particularity *in general* in the immutable essence, and at the same time it there finds its own particularity. For the truth of this process is precisely that the double consciousness is one and single. This unity becomes a fact to it, but in the first instance the unity is one in which the diversity of both factors is still the dominant feature. Owing to this, consciousness has before it the threefold way in which particularity is connected with unchangeableness. In one form it comes before itself as opposed to the unchangeable essence, and is thrown back to the beginning of that struggle, which is, from first to last, the principle constituting the entire situation. At another time it finds the unchangeable appearing in the form of particularity; so that the latter is an embodiment of unchangeableness, into which in consequence, the entire form of existence passes. In the third case, it discovers *itself* to be this particular fact in the unchangeable. The first unchangeable is taken to be merely the alien, external Being, which passes sentence on particular existence; since the second unchangeable is a form or mode of particularity like itself, it, i.e. the consciousness, becomes in the third place spirit (Geist), has the joy of finding itself therein, and becomes aware within itself that its particularity has been reconciled with the universal." (253) Hegel continues:

"But although the 'unhappy consciousness' does not possess this actual presence, it has, at the same time, transcended pure thought, so far as this is the abstract thought of Stoicism, which turns away from particulars altogether, and again the merely restless thought of Scepticism—so far, in fact, as this is merely particularity in the sense of aimless contradiction and the restless process of contradictory thought. It has gone beyond both of these; it brings and keeps together pure thought and particular existence, but has not yet risen to that level of thinking where the particularity of consciousness is harmoniously reconciled with pure thought itself. It rather stands midway, at the point where abstract thought comes in contact with the particularity of consciousness *qua* particularity. Itself *is* this act of contact; it is the union of pure thought and individuality; and this thinking individual or pure thought also exists as object for it, and the unchangeable is essentially itself an individual existence. But that this its object, the unchangeable, which assumes essentially the form of particularity, is *its own self,* the self which is particularity of consciousness—this is *not* established *for it.*" (256-7)

"In the first condition, consequently, in which we treat it as pure consciousness, it takes up toward its object an attitude which is not that of thought; but rather (since it is indeed in itself pure thinking particularity and its object is just this pure thought, but pure thought is not their relation to one another as such), it, so to say, merely gives itself up to thought, devotes itself to thinking (*geht an das Denken hin*), and is the state of Devotion (*Andacht*). Its thinking as such is no more than the discordant clang of ringing bells, or a cloud of warm incense, a kind of thinking in terms of music, that does not get the length of notions, which would be the sole, immanent, objective mode of thought. This boundless pure inward feeling comes to have indeed its object; but this object does not make its appearance in conceptual form, and therefore comes on the scene as something external and foreign. Hence we have here the inward movement of pure emotion (Gemuth) which feels itself in the bitterness of soul-diremption. It is the movement of an infinite yearning, which is assured that its nature is a pure emotion of this kind, a pure thought which thinks itself as particularity—a yearning that is certain of being known and recognized by this object, for the very reason that this object thinks itself as particularity. At the same time, however, this nature is the unattainable "beyond" which, in being seized, escapes or rather has already escaped. The "beyond" has already escaped, for it is in part the unchangeable, thinking itself as particularity, and consciousness, therefore, attains itself therein immediately,—attains itself, but as something opposed to the unchangeable; instead of grasping the real nature consciousness merely *feels,* and has fallen back upon itself— . . . Consciousness, therefore, can only come upon the *grave* of its life. But because this is itself an actuality, and since it is contrary to the nature of actuality to afford a lasting possession, the presence even of that tomb is merely the source of trouble, toil, and struggle, a fight which must be lost. But since consciousness has found out by experience that the grave of its actual unchangeable Being has no concrete *actuality* that the vanished particularity *qua* vanished is not true particularity, it will give up looking for the unchangeable particular existence as something actual or will cease trying to hold on to what has thus vanished. Only so is it capable of finding particularity in a true form, a form that is universal." (257-58-59)

Hegel continues: "In that the unchangeable consciousness condemns its specific shape and form, and abandons it entirely, while on the other hand, the individual consciousness "gives thanks", i.e. denies itself the satisfaction of being conscious of its independence, and refers the essential substance of its action to the "beyond" and not to itself: by these two movements, in which both parts give themselves up the one to the other, there certainly arises in consciousness a sense of *its own* unity with the unchangeable." (261)

After an elucidation of the stages through which consciousness passes, Hegel goes on to say, "Through these moments—the negative abandonment first of its own right and power of decision, then of its property and enjoyment, and finally the positive moment of carrying on what it does not understand—it deprives itself, completely and in truth, of the consciousness of inner and outer freedom, or reality in the sense of its own existence for itself. It has the certainty of having in truth stripped itself of its Ego, and of having turned its immediate self-consciousness into a "thing," into an objective external existence." (265-66)

"It could ensure its self-renunciation and self-abandonment solely by this real and vital sacrifice (of its self). For only thereby is the deception got rid of, which lies in inner acknowledgment of gratitude through heart, sentiment and tongue—an acknowledgment which indeed disclaims all power of independent self-existence, and ascribes this power to a gift from above, but in this very disclaimer retains for itself its own proper and peculiar life, outwardly in the possession it does not resign, inwardly in the consciousness of the decision which itself has resolved upon and in the consciousness of its own self-constituted content, which it has not exchanged for a content coming from without and filling it with meaningless ideas and phrases." (266)

"But in the sacrifice actually accomplished, while consciousness has cancelled the action as its own act, it has also implicitly demitted and put off its unhappy condition." (266)

And further and in conclusion to this phase of being Hegel says: "But for itself, action and *its own* concrete action remain something miserable and insignificant, its enjoyment pain, and the sublation of these, positively considered, remains a mere "beyond." But in this object, where it finds its own action and existence, *qua* this particular consciousness, to be inherently existence and action as such, there has arisen the idea of Reason, of the certainty that consciousness is, in its particularity, inherently and essentially absolute, or is all reality." (267)

III

REASON

With the arrival at the stage of reason we come to where consciousness has laid hold of the fact that it is inherently absolute reality. This must not be taken in the sense of a one-sided Idealism. It must rather be understood as meaning "That existence and self-consciousness are the same being, the same not as a matter of comparison," says Hegel, "but really and truly in and for themselves. It is only a one-sided, unsound idealism which lets this unity again appear on one side as consciousness, with a reality *per se* over against it on the other. (276).

"But now this category, or simple unity of self-consciousness and being, has differences within it; for its very nature consists just in this—in being immediately one and identical with itself in otherness or in difference. Difference there *is*, but completely transparent, a difference that is at the same time none." (276) Hegel continues:

"Now because, in this way, the pure essential being of things, as well as their aspect of difference, belongs to reason, we can, strictly speaking, no longer talk of things at all, i.e. of something which would only be present to consciousness by negatively opposing it. For the many categories are species of the pure category, which means that the pure category is still their genus or essential nature, and not opposed to them. But they are indeed that ambiguous being which contains otherness too, as opposed to the pure category in its plurality. They, in point of fact, contradict the pure category by this plurality, and the pure category must sublate them in itself, a process by which it constitutes itself the negative unity of the different elements." (277) Hegel continues:

"We see pure consciousness here affirmed in a twofold form. In one case it is the restless activity which passes hither and thither through all its moments, seeing in them that otherness which is sublated in the process of grasping it; in the other case it is the imperturbable unity certain of its own truth. That restless activity constitutes the "other" for this unity, while this unity is the "other" for that activity; and within these reciprocally determinating opposites consciousness and object alternate. Consciousness thus at one time finds itself seeking about hither and thither, and its object is what absolutely exists *per se,* and is the essentially real; at another time consciousness is aware of being the category bare and simple, and the object is the movement of the different elements. Consciousness, however, *qua* essential reality, is the whole of this process of passing out of itself *qua* simple category into individuality and the object, and of viewing this process in the object, cancelling it as distinct, appropriating it as its own and declaring itself as this certainty of being all reality, of being both itself and its object." (279) Continuing Hegel says,

"Reason sets out to know the truth, to find in the form of a *Notion* what, for "meaning" and "perceiving," is a "thing"; i.e., it seeks in thinghood to have merely the consciousness of its own self. Reason has, therefore, now a universal interest in the world, because it is certain of its presence in the world or is certain that the actual present is rational. It seeks its "other," while knowing that it there possesses nothing else but itself; it seeks merely its own infinitude." (281)

In doing this Hegel says that the free concrete mind in the stage of reason begins the study of the world in which it finds itself. This study gives rise to scientific observation with its characteristic spheres of organic and inorganic nature. But there are steps along the way. To quote Hegel for his guidance:

"Observation, which confines itself in this way to what is simple, or restricts the sensuously dispersed elements by the universal, thus finds its principle confused by its object, because what is determined, must by its very nature get lost in its opposite. Reason, therefore, must pass from that inert characteristic which had the semblance of stability, and go on to observe it as it really is in truth, viz., as relating itself to its opposite. What are called essential marks are passive characteristics, which, when expressed and apprehended as simple do not bring out what constitutes their real nature—which is to be vanishing moments of its process of withdrawing and betaking into itself. Since the instinct of reason now arrives at the point of looking for the characteristic in the light of its true nature—that of essentially passing over into its opposite and not existing apart by itself and for its own sake—it seeks after the *Law* and the notion of Law. It seeks for them, moreover, as existing reality; but this feature of concrete reality will in point of fact disappear before reason, and the aspects of the law will become for it mere moments or abstractions, so that the law comes to light in the nature of the notion, which has destroyed within itself the indifferent subsistence of sensuous reality." (288) Further says Hegel,

"Consciousness thus finds in experience the objective being of the law, but has it there in the form of a notion as well; and only because of both factors together is the law true for consciousness. The law, therefore is accepted as a law because it presents itself in the sphere of appearance and is, at the same time, in its very nature a notion." (291)

Hegel continues: "Matter, on the contrary, is not a thing that exists, it is being in the sense of universal being, or being in the way the concept is being. Reason, still instinctive, correctly draws this distinction without being conscious that it (reason), by this very fact of its testing the law in every sense-particular, cancels the merely sensuous existence of the law; and when it construes the moments of the law as forms of matter, their essential nature is taken to be something universal, and specifically expressed as a non-sensuous element of sense, an incorporeal and yet objective existence." . . . "As the outcome and truth of this experimentation we find *pure law,* which is freed from sensuous elements; we see it as a concept, which, while present in sense, operates there independently and unrestrained, while enveloped in sense, is detached from it and is a concept bare and simple. This, which is in truth result and essence, now comes before this consciousness itself, but as an object; moreover, since the object is not exactly a result for it and is unrelated to the preceding process, the object is a specific kind of object, and the relation of consciousness to it takes the form of another kind of observation." (293)

This is the observation of organic nature. Of this Hegel says that, "such an object which sustains the procedure in the simple activity of the notion is an organism." (294)

"The organic substance *qua* inner is the Soul simply, the pure notion of purpose or the universal which in dividing into its discrete elements remains all the same a universal fluent continuity, and hence in its being appears as activity or the movement of vanishing reality; while, on the other hand, the outer, opposed to that existing inner, subsists in the passive being of the organic. The law, as the relation of that inner to this outer, consequently expresses its content, now by setting forth universal moments, or simple essential elements, and again by setting forth the realized essential nature or the form and shape actually assumed. Those first simple organic properties, to call them so, are Sensibility, Irritability, and Reproduction. These properties, at least the two first, seem indeed to refer not to any and every organism, but merely to the animal organism. Moreover, the vegetable level of organic life expresses in point of fact only the bare and simple notion of an organism, which does not develop and evolve its moments. Hence in regard to those moments, so far as observation has to take account of them, we must confine ourselves to the organism which presents them existing in developed form.,,(302)

"As to these moments, then, they are directly derived from the notion of self-purpose, of a being whose end is its own self. For Sensibility expresses in general the simple notion of organic reflexion into itself, or the universal continuity of this notion. Irritability, again, expresses organic elasticity, the capacity to exercise the function of reacting simultaneously with self-reflection, and expresses, in contrast to the previous state of being passively and inertly within itself, the condition of being explicitly actualized—a realization, where that abstract existence for its own sake is an existence for something else. Reproduction, however, is the operation of this entire self—reflected organism, its activity as having its purpose in itself, its activity *qua* genus, wherein the individual repels itself from itself, where in procreating it repeats either the organic parts or the whole individual. Reproduction, taken in the sense of self—preservation in general, expresses the formal principle or conception of the organic, or the fact of Sensibility; but it is, properly speaking, the realized notion of organic existence, or the whole, which either *qua* individual returns into itself through the process of producing individual parts of itself, or *qua* genus does so through the production of distinct individuals." (303)

"The other significance of these organic elements, viz. as outer, is their embodiment in a given shape; here they assume the form of actual but at the same time universal parts, or appear as organic systems. Sensibility is embodied in the form, for instance, of a nervous system, irritability, of a muscular system, reproduction, of an intestinal system for the preservation of the individual and the species." (303)

"Laws peculiar to organic life, accordingly, concern a relation of the organic moments, taking account of their twofold significance—viz. of being in one respect a part of definite organic formation or embodiment, and in another respect a continuous universal element of a determinate kind, running through all those systems. ....Both aspects of such a law can be observed." (303)

And further: "Here, then, law appears as the relation of an element to the formative process of the organic being which at one moment has the element over against itself, at another exhibits it within its own self—determining organic structure." (294)

"Observation of nature finds the notion realized in inorganic nature, laws, whose moments are things which at the same time are in the position of abstractions. But this notion is not a simplicity reflected into self. The life of organic nature, on the other hand, is only this self—reflected simplicity. The opposition within itself, in the sense of the opposition of universal and individual, does not make its appearance in the essential nature of this life with one factor apart from the other. Its essential nature is not the genus, self—sundered and self—moved in its undifferentiated element, and remaining at the same time for itself undifferentiated in its opposition. Observation finds this free notion, whose universality has just as absolutely within it developed individuality, only in the notion which exists as notion, i.e., in self—consciousness." (329)

"When observation now turns in upon itself and directs itself on the notion which is real *qua* free notion, it finds to begin with, the *Laws of Thought*. This kind of individuality, which thought is in itself, is the abstract movement of the negative, a movement entirely introverted into simplicity; and the laws are outside reality." (329)

At this point Hegel takes up a logical course to show that the laws of thought under the guidance of observation cannot be relied upon to furnish an adequate account of mind itself. This is because it is impossible for observation to be separated from the mind which is observing. Thought and environment cannot be explained apart from each other in the case of observation. Hegel says:

"In the active practical reality of consciousness, observation thus finds opened up before it a new field. Psychology contains the collection of laws in virtue of which the mind takes up the different attitudes towards the different forms of its reality given and presented to it in a condition of otherness. The mind adopts these various attitudes partly with a view to receiving these modes of its reality into itself, and conforming to the habits, customs, and ways of thinking it thus comes across, as being that wherein mind is reality and as such object to itself; partly with a view to knowing its own spontaneous activity in opposition to them, to follow the bent of its own inclinations, affections, and emotions, and carry off thence what is merely of particular and special moment for itself, and thus make what is objective conform to itself. In the former it behaves negatively towards itself as single and individual mind, in the latter negatively towards itself as the universal being." (331-332)

Hegel further explains: "To take up again thus the different concrete individualities, and to describe how one man has more inclination for this, the other for that, how one has more intelligence than the other—all this is, however, something much more uninteresting than even to reckon up the species of insects, mosses, and so on. For these latter give observation the right to take them thus individually and disconnectedly (begrifflos), because they belong essentially to the sphere of fortuitous detailed particulars. To take conscious individuality, on the other hand, as a particular phenomenal entity, and treat it in so wooden a fashion, is self—contradictory, because the essential nature of individuality lies in the universal element of mind. Since, however, the process of apprehending it causes it at the same time to pass into the form of universality, to apprehend it is to find its laws, and seems in this way to have a rational purpose in view, and a necessary function to fulfill." (333)

"The moments constituting the content of the law are on the one hand individuality itself, on the other its universal inorganic nature, viz, the given circumstances, situation, habits, customs, relation and so forth; from these the determinate individuality is to be understood and comprehended. They contain something specific, determinate, as well as universal, and are at the same time something lying at hand, which furnishes material for observation and on the other side expresses itself in the form of individuality." (333)

"The law of this relation of the two sides has now to contain and express the sort of effect and influence these determinate circumstances exert on individuality. This individuality, however, just consists both in being the universal, and hence in passively and directly assimilating and blending with the given universals, the customs, habits, etc., thus becoming conformed to them, as also in taking up an attitude of opposition towards them and thus transforming and transmuting them; and again in behaving towards them in its individual character with complete indifference, neither allowing them to exert an influence over it, nor setting itself actively against them. On that account *what* is to have an influence on individuality, and what *sort* of influence it is to have—which properly speaking mean the same thing—depend entirely on individuality itself." (334) And further—"It is the world of the individual either in so far as this individual was merely fused and blended with it, had let that world, just as it is, pass into its own nature, and had taken up towards it merely the attitude of a formal consciousness; or, on the other hand, it is the world of the individual in the sense in which the given has been transformed and transmuted by that individual." (335) And further, Hegel says, "Herewith drops out of account that existence which was to be something all by itself, and was meant to constitute one aspect, and that the universal aspect, of a law. Individuality is what its world, in the sense of its own world, is. Individuality itself is the cycle of its own action, in which it has presented and established itself as reality and is simply and solely a unity of what is given and what is constructed—a unity whose aspects do not fall apart, as in the idea of psychological law, into a world given *per se* and an individuality existing for itself." (336)

The foregoing sums up what Hegel has to say about individuality and its relation to reality. The next thing for observation to take up is the relation of mind to its own physical embodiment. Here follow discussions dealing with Physiognomy and Phrenology or Cranioscopy—prevalent in Hegel's time, but now looked upon as insufficient and more adequately supplanted by present day psychology and its allies.

However the philosophical implication holds good equally now as then. And for a summary of Hegel's delivery on the subject the last few paragraphs of his lengthy discussion will be quoted verbatim in order to have his conclusions. Says Hegel:

"Observation has thus reached the point of explicitly expressing what our notion of observation was at the outset, viz. that rational certainty means objectivity of reason, that the certainty of reason seeks itself as an objective reality." (369)

"One does not, indeed, suppose that mind, which is represented by a skull, is defined as a thing. There is not meant to be any materialism, as it is called, in this idea; mind rather must be something very different from these bones of the skull. But that mind *IS, means* nothing else than that it is a *thing*. When being as such, or thingness, is predicated of the mind, the true and genuine expression for this is, therefore, that mind is such an entity as a bone is. Hence it must be considered as supremely important that the true expression has been found for the bare statement regarding mind, that it *is,* has a being, is a thing, an individual reality. Mind, that *is,* has a being, is a thing. But by this, we do not *mean it is something we can see, or knock about,* or take in our hands, and so on, but that is what we say, and what the statement really amounts to is consequently conveyed in the expression that the existence of mind is a bone." (369)

"This result has now a twofold significance: one is its true meaning, in so far as the result is a completion of the outcome of the preceding movement of self—consciousness. The unhappy self—consciousness renounced its independence, and wrested its distinctive self—existence out into the shape of a thing. By so doing, it left the level of self—consciousness and reverted to the condition of mere consciousness, i.e., to that phase of conscious life for which the object is an existence, a thing. But what is "thing" in this case is self—consciousness; "Thing" here is the unity of ego and being—the category. When the object before consciousness is determined thus, consciousness possesses reason. Consciousness as well as self—consciousness, is in itself properly reason in an implicit form; but only that consciousness can be said to *have* reason whose object has the character of being the category. From this however, we must still distinguish the knowledge of what reason *is*." (370)

"The category, which is the immediate unity of being and self (*Sein und Seinen*), must traverse both forms, and the conscious attitude of observation is just where the category is set forth in the form of being. In its results, consciousness expresses that, whose conscious implicit certainty it is, in the shape of a proposition—the proposition which lies in the very notion of reason. This proposition is the infinite judgment that the self is a thing—a judgment that cancels and transcends itself." (370)

"Through this result, then, the category gets the added characteristic of being this self—cancelling opposition. The "pure" category which is present to consciousness in the form of being or immediacy, is still an unmediated, a merely given object, and the attitude of consciousness is also direct, has no mediation in it. That infinite judgment is the moment which is the transition of immediacy into mediation or negativity. The given present object is therefore characterized as a negative object while consciousness in its relation towards it assumes the form of *self*—consciousness; or the category, which traversed the form of *being* in the process of observation, is now set up in the form of self—existence. Consciousness no longer seeks to find itself immediately, but to produce itself by its own activity. Consciousness itself is the purpose and end of its own action, as in the process of observation it had to do merely with things." (370)

"The other meaning of the result is the one already considered, that of unsystematic (*begrifflos*) observation. This has no other way of understanding and expressing itself than by declaring the reality of self—consciousness to consist in the skull bone, just as it appears in the form of a thing of sense, still retaining its character as an object for consciousness. In stating this it has no clear consciousness as to what the statement involves, and does not grasp the determinate character of the subject and predicate in the proposition and of their relation to one another, still less does it grasp the proposition in the sense of a self—resolving infinite judgment and a notion. Rather, in virtue of a deeper lying self—consciousness of mind, which has the appearance here of being an innate decency and honesty of nature, it conceals from itself the ignominiousness of such an irrational crude thought as that of taking a bone for the reality of self—consciousness; and the very senselessness of introducing all sorts of relations of cause and effect, "symbol," "organ," etc., which are perfectly meaningless here, and of hiding away the glaring folly of the proposition behind distinctions derived from them—all this puts a gloss on that thought and white washes its naked absurdity." (370-371)

"Brain—fibres and the like, looked at as forms of the being of mind, are already an imagined, a merely hypothetical actuality of mind—not its presented reality, not its felt, seen, in short not its true reality. If they are present to us, if they are seen, they are lifeless objects, and then no longer pass for the being of mind. But its objectivity proper must take an immediate, a sensuous form, so that in this objectivity *qua* lifeless—for the bone is lifeless so far as the lifeless is found in the living being itself—mind is established as actual." (371)

"The principle involved in this idea is that reason claims to be all thinghood, even thinghood of a purely objective kind. It is this, however, *in conceptu:* or, only this notion is the truth of reason; and the purer the notion itself is, the more silly an idea does it become, if its content does not take the shape of a notion (*Begriff*) but of a mere presentation or idea (*Vorstellung*)—if the self-superseding judgment is not taken with the consciousness of this its infinity, but is taken as a stable and permanent proposition, the subject and predicate of which hold good each on its own account, self fixed as self, thing as thing, while one has to be the other all the same." (372)

"Reason, essentially the notion, is immediately parted asunder into itself and its opposite, an opposition which just for that reason is immediately again superseded. But if it presents itself in this way as both itself and its opposite, and if it is held fast in the entirely isolated moment of this disintegration, reason is apprehended in an irrational form; and the purer the moments of this opposition are, the more glaring is the appearance of this content, which is either alone for consciousness, or alone expressed ingenuously by consciousness." (372)

"The 'depth' which mind brings out from within, but carries no further than to make it a presentation (Vorstellung), and let it remain at this level—and the "ignorance" on the part of this consciousness as to what it really says, are the same kind of connection of higher and lower which, in the case of the living being, nature naively expresses when it combines the organ of its highest fulfillment, the organ of generation, with the organ of urination. The infinite judgment *qua* infinite would be the fulfillment of life that comprehends itself, while the consciousness of the infinite judgment that remains at the level of presentation corresponds to urination." (372)

Realization of Rational Self-consciousness Through its own Activity.

We have traversed the way of Free Concrete Mind using Reason in observation of Nature, in observation of organic existence and of nature as an organic whole—finding life as Reason in contingent form. With lastly the observation of self—consciousness as purely self—consciousness,—which embraced the laws of thought, psychology and individuality, concluding with the relation of self—consciousness to actuality; i.e., the identity of thinghood and reason.

This ground covers what may be called the operation of theoretical reason. There is an other phase of reason where reason does not find its unity by observation but by actualizing an object after its own nature. This is the practical mode of reason. This experience expands to the phase of conscious purpose. It finally establishes this purpose in the general realm of the moral and social life. It is this ground which is designated under Hegel's caption—"The Realization of Rational Self—Consciousness Through Its Own Activity."

"Self-consciousness," says Hegel, "found the 'thing' in the form of itself, and itself in the form of a thing; that is to say, self-consciousness is explicitly aware of being in itself the objective reality. . ." (374)

"Self-consciousness is mind, which has the assurance of having, in the duplicity of its self-consciousness and in the independence of both, its unity with its own self. This certainty has to be brought out now before the mind in all of its truth; what self-consciousness holds as a fact, viz., that implicitly *in* itself and *in* its *inner* certainty it, *is,* has to enter into its consciousness and become explicit *for* it." (374)

Hegel goes into this phase of the subject with his characteristic completeness summarizing the results along the way. He says, "In point of fact the notion of the realization of self-conscious reason—of directly apprehending complete unity with another in his independence: of having for my object an other in the fashion of a "thing" found detached and apart from me, and the negative of myself, and of taking this as my own self-existence *(Fürmichsein)*—finds its complete reality in fulfillment in the life of a nation. Reason appears here as the fluent universal substance, as unchangeable simple thinghood which yet breaks up into many entirely independent beings, just as light bursts asunder into stars as innumerable luminous points, each giving light on its own account, and whose absolute self-existence *(für sich sein)* is dissolved, not merely implicitly *(an sich)* but explicitly for themselves (*für sich*), within the simple independent substance. They are conscious within themselves of being these individual independent beings through the fact that they surrender and sacrifice their particular individuality, and that this universal substance is their soul and essence—as this universal again is the action of themselves as individuals, and is the work and product of their own activity." (376) And further: "As the individual in his own particular work *ipso facto* accomplishes unconsciously a universal work, so again he also performs the universal task as his conscious object. The whole becomes in *its entirety* his work, for which he sacrifices himself, and precisely by that means receives back his own self from it." (377)

This unity in reciprocity utters itself in the customs and laws of a nation. "In a free nation," says Hegel, "reason is in truth realized. It is a present living spirit, where the individual not only finds his destiny *(Bestimmung)* i.e., his universal and particular nature (*Wesen*), expressed and given to him in the fashion of a thing, but himself is this essential being, and has also attained his destiny." (378) However all stages have their different phases. Therefore we find that reason must now leave this happy condition. In this specially determined ethical substance mind reaches higher and then casts off unity as a present limitation. The security experienced from the sense of the solid social order gives way as individuality reaches out to have the opposite experience of isolated independence. "Ethical substance," says Hegel, "has sunk to the level of a floating selfless adjective, whose living subjects are individuals, which have to fill up their universality through themselves, and to provide for their destiny out of the same source." (380)

Now the purpose which consciousness adopts in order to cancel this opposition between itself in sundered objectivity and the ethical substance is morality. In Hegel's words, "—if we bring this still inward and unevolved mind to light as the substance that has developed into its concrete existence —we shall find that in this notion there is opened up the realm of the Social Order, the Ethical World (*Sittlichkeit*). For this latter is nothing else than the absolute Spiritual unity of the essential substance (*Wesen*) of individuals in their independent reality; it is an inherently universal self-consciousness, that this latter has complete independence, is looked on as a "thing," and the universal self-consciousness is aware precisely therein of its unity with that "thing," and is only then self-consciousness, when thus in unity with this objective being (*Wesen*)." (376)

This consciousness finally learns the law of the heart in which the individual does not seek to preserve the particular self but rather, the good, through the sacrifice of the individual. In this attitude the individual no longer finds any resistance in a reality opposed to it.

However this subjective individualism brings to consciousness a sense of private satisfaction that becomes an end in itself. This private pleasure by means of a universal principle brings to the individual a sense of contrast—because he is usurping and pouring into himself as private pleasure that which is universal. To quote "It is not the seemingly divine spirit of universality in knowledge and action . . . that has passed into and fills this new level of self-consciousness; but the spirit of the earth, a spirit which holds that being alone as true reality which is the reality of individual consciousness . . . It plunges thus into life, and carries to its completion the pure individuality in which it appears. It does not so much make its own happiness as take it directly and enjoy it." (384)

Thus in a consciousness which appears independent it enjoys Pleasure. However the negative element shows up in these pleasurable objects, for consciousness is now self-realizing mind. Hegel says, "It is this firm unbending connection, because that which is connected consists in pure essentialities or empty abstraction. Unity, Difference and Relation are Categories, each of which is nothing as it stands by itself, but only in its relation to its opposite, and they therefore cannot come apart from one another. They are by their own notion related to each other, for they are the pure notions themselves; and this absolute relation and abstract process constitute Necessity. The merely particular individuality, which has in the first instance only the pure notion of reason for its content, instead of having escaped from dead theory and plunged into actual life, has thus only precipitated itself into consciousness of its own lifelessness, and enjoys itself merely as naked and alien necessity, *lifeless* actuality." (387)

"This reflection of consciousness into self, the knowledge that necessity is itself, is a new mode or attitude of consciousness." (389)

Now in this new attitude self-consciousness comes to regard itself as the necessary element and is filled with the weight of a high purpose in working for the welfare of mankind. When this law of the heart, this heart-throb for humanity becomes a driving personal force it passes into a fanatic conceit. Hegel says: "When consciousness therefore sets up the law of its heart, it finds itself resisted by others because it conflicts with the equally individual laws of their heart; and the latter in opposing it are doing nothing else but setting up in their turn and making valid their own law. The universal here presented, therefore, is only a universal resistance and struggle of all against one another . . ." (399)

"The other side is the universal in the sense of stable passive essence; but, for that very reason, the universal is only something inner, which is not indeed absolutely nonexistent, but still not an actual reality, and can itself only become actual by cancelling the individuality, that has presumed to claim actuality. This type of consciousness, which becomes aware of itself in the law; which finds itself in what is inherently true and good not as mere individual, but only as essentially real; and which knows individuality to be what is perverted and perverting, and hence feels bound to surrender and sacrifice individualism of consciousness—this type *of* consciousness is *Virtue*." (400)

The next phase that is brought forth to consciousness, as it adopts virtue, is, that consciousness makes a personal merit of it and comes to feel that a perverted world awaits its efforts to change its wicked course. This mood of moral strenuousness brings on a struggle in the course of which consciousness learns that the course of the world is not as bad as it seemed. "With the discovery of this," says Hegel, "it is seen that there is no way of producing the good through the sacrifice of individuality . . . for individuality is precisely the explicit actualization of what is implicitly and inherently real (i.e., the universal); and the perversion ceases to be looked at as a perversion of goodness, for it is just the transmuting of the good, *qua* bare purpose, into actual reality. The movement of individuality is the reality of the universal . . ." (411) And further, "Thus, then, the effort, the struggle the activity of individuality is inherently an end in itself; the use of powers, the play of their outward manifestations—that is what gives them life: otherwise they would be lifeless, potential, and merely implicit (*an sich*). The inherent, implicit nature is not an abstract universal without existence and never carried into effect; it is itself immediately this actual present and this living actuality of the process of individuality." (412)

The virtuous consciousness now reconciled to the course of the world takes up a new attitude toward it. Henceforth it finds the world sufficient and itself sufficient; both are adequate to justify the end. This becomes for consciousness simple self expression. This state is that where the individual seeks fulfillment through union with the universal and by this action the whole becomes actualized in and through the individual. Such a condition is moving towards a free spiritual community. Hegel calls this the individuality which takes itself to be real in and for itself. He says of it: "Self-consciousness has now grasped its own principle, which at first was only *our* notion of it, viz. the notion that, when consciously certain of itself, it is all reality. Its purpose and nature henceforth consist in the interpenetration of the universal (its "gifts" and "capacities") and individuality." (414) The individuality has cast away all limitation. It finds itself to be actuality.

But next this rational self-contained individuality comes to carry on its powers of self-expression in a way that is pursuing its own end only, without regard to any other connection—without having a purpose that includes others. This phase Hegel naively designates a "Society as a community of animals". The development that supersedes it, however, is one in which the co-existence with other individuals, under universal conditions, comes to light. For consciousness is now self-active reason and complete in itself. It therefore becomes self-differentiating individuality realizing that the distinctions within it are also the content of the universal. Hegel says, "The category is implicit (an sich) as the universal of pure consciousness; it is also explicit (für sich) for the self of consciousness is likewise its moment. It is absolute being, for that universality is the bare self-identity of being . . ." (440) "This 'fact' is therefore the *ethical substance*; and consciousness of it is *ethical* consciousness . . ." (440) "These laws or spheres (massen) of the substance of ethical life are directly recognized and acknowledged . . ." (441)

"Since self-consciousness knows itself to be a moment of this substance, the moment of self-existence (of independence and self-determination), it expresses the existence of the law within itself in the form: "The healthy natural reason knows immediately what is right and good." (441)

Hegel then takes up a number of the well-known ethical laws such as "Love thy neighbor as thyself"; "Everyone ought to speak the truth", and discusses them at length, bringing out various ethical distinctions. The important feature in this development of "reason as lawgiver" is the fact of the coming to light of the *ethical substance* and the *ethical* consciousness. These must be well understood and born in mind; since it is within these, and through these, that the movement revolves as it establishes itself in ever deeper realizations. As this ethical substance and ethical consciousness are not yet fully established for consciousness there is a period when consciousness perceives only individually. We next have reason seated in the capacity of "Testing the laws." Hegel gives a number of circumstances under which the law has different applications and states conclusions. To quote: "Spiritual reality (das geistige Wesen) is thus, in the first place, for self-consciousness in the shape of a law implicitly existing. The universality present in the process of testing, which was of a formal kind and not inherently existent, is transcended. The law is, too, an eternal law, which does not have its ground in the will of a given individual, but has a being all its own (an und für sich), the pure and absolute will of all which takes the form of immediate existence. This will is, again, not a command which merely *ought to be*; it *is* and has validity; it is the universal ego of the category, ego which is immediately reality, and the world is only this reality. Since, however, this existing law is absolutely valid, the obedience given by self-consciousness is not service rendered to a master, whose orders are mere caprice and in which it does not recognize its own nature. On the contrary, the laws are thoughts of its own absolute consciousness, thoughts which are its own immediate possession. Moreover, it does not [merely] *believe* in them, for belief, while it no doubt sees the essential nature, still gazes at an alien essence—not its own. The ethical self-consciousness is directly at one with the essential reality, in virtue of the universality of its own self. Belief, on the other hand, begins with an individual consciousness; it is a process in which this consciousness is always approaching this unity, without ever being able to find itself at home with its essential nature. The above consciousness, on the other hand, has transcended itself as individual, this mediating process is complete, and only because of this, is it immediate self-consciousness of ethical substance." (452)

"The distinction, then, of self-consciousness from the essential nature (Wesen) is completely transparent. Because of this the distinctions found within that nature itself are not accidental characteristics. On the contrary, because of the unity of essence with self-consciousness (from which alone discordance, incongruity, might have come), they are articulated groups (Massen) of the unity permeated by its own life, unsundered spirits transparent to themselves, stainless forms and shapes of heaven, that preserve amid their differences the untarnished innocence and concord of their essential nature." (452)

"Self-consciousness, again stands likewise in a simple and clear relation to those different laws. They *are* and nothing more—this is what constitutes the consciousness of its relation to them. Thus, Antigone takes them for the unwritten and unerring laws of the god. . . They are. If I ask for their origin, and confine them to the point whence they arose that puts me beyond them, for it is I who am now the universal, while they are the conditioned and limited. If they are to get the sanction of my insight, I have already shaken their immovable nature, their inherent constancy, and regard them as something which is perhaps true, but possibly may also be not true, so far as I am concerned. True ethical sentiment consists just in holding fast and unshaken by what is right, and abstaining altogether from what would move or shake it or derive it. (452) But whether this or the opposite determination is the right, that is settled just as it stands (an und für sich). I might, for my own part, have made the law whichever I wanted, and neither of them just as well, and am, by my beginning to test them, thereby already on an immoral track. That the right is there for me just as it stands—this places me within the substance of ethical reality: and in this way that substance is the essence of self-consciousness. But self-consciousness, again, is *its* actualization and its existence, its self, and its will." (453)

In order to sustain the meaning Hegel has here we will pause to give a particular emphasis to the three preceeding statements which pertain to the substance of ethical reality—for reason has now come into the insight of itself as ethical substance also as universal essence. Of it Hegel says "It is." "The right is there for me just as it stands." Then by consciousness realizing this, *that* substance becomes the essence of self-consciousness as well as the fact that it is self-consciousness that will give it its actualization. The thought is of a subtle fabric. We are dealing here with reason in its highest mode in the phase of free concrete mind. For these experiences the word *mind* is used. But the next higher, deeper level of experience is more adequately expressed by the word spirit,—The consideration of which will now engage our attention.

IV

SPIRIT

Spirit is mind at a higher level of existence than any realm so far considered, yet in all of them spirit has been present. Spirit was present in Consciousness in general with its stages of sense-certainty, perception and understanding. Spirit was present when consciousness became Self-consciousness; and it was also present in the stage of Reason; but in this phase of consciousness, Reason did not have the value of a category. In the next phase it does so. Hegel says. "Reason is spirit, when its certainty of being all reality has been raised to the level of truth, and reason is *consciously* aware of itself as its own world, and of the world as itself. The development of spirit was indicated in the immediately preceding movement of mind, where the object of consciousness, the category pure and simple, rose to be the notion of reason. When reason "observes", this pure unity of ego and existence, the unity of subjectivity and objectivity, of for-itself-ness and in-itself-ness—this unity is immanent, has the character of implicitness or of being; and consciousness of reason *finds itself*." (457) "Spirit is thus the self-supporting absolutely real ultimate being (Wesen)". (459)

"Its essential spiritual being (*Wesen*) has been above designated as the ethical substance; spirit, however, is concrete ethical actuality (*Wirklichkeit*). Spirit is the *self* of the actual consciousness, to which spirit stands opposed, or rather which appears over against itself, as an objective actual world that has lost, however, all sense of strangeness for the self, just as the self has lost all sense of having a dependent or independent existence by itself, cut off and separated from that world. Being substance and universal self-identical permanent essence (Wesen), spirit is the immovable irreducible basis and the starting point for the action of all and everyone; it is their purpose and their goal, because the ideally implicit nature *(an sich)* of all self-consciousness. This substance is likewise the universal product, wrought and created by the action of each and all, and constituting their unity and likeness and identity of meaning; for it is self-existence *(für sich sein)* the self, action." (458)

At this point of our progress it might be well to emphasize the fact that we have always to deal with a seeming duality which arises for consciousness and through the alternates of which consciousness travels and augments itself by the very fact of bringing these alternates together in itself. In the case of the ethical world, this is important to understand in connection with consciousness now risen to the level of Spirit—for Spirit is in fact the ethical life actually existent in its essential nature. Hegel says: "Spirit in its ultimate simple truth, is consciousness, and breaks asunder its moments from one another. An act divides spirit into spiritual substance on the one side, and consciousness of the substance on the other; and divides the substance as well as consciousness. The substance appears in the shape of a universal inner nature and purpose standing in contrast to itself *qua* individualized reality. The middle or mediating term, infinite in character, is self-consciousness, which, being *implicitly* the unity of itself and that substance, becomes so, now, explicitly (*für sich*), unites the universal inner nature and its particular realization, raises the latter to the former and acts *ethically*: and, on the other hand, brings the former down to the latter and carries out the purpose, the substance presented merely in thought. In this way it brings to light the unity of itself and the substance, and produces this unity in the form of its work." (462)

"When consciousness breaks up into these elements, the simple substance has in part acquired the attitude of opposition to self-consciousness; in part it thereby manifests in itself the very nature of consciousness, which consists in distinguishing its own content within itself—manifests it as a world articulated into its spheres. The substance is thus an ethical being split up into distinct elemental forms, a human and a divine law." (462)

It is in this substance that the individuals of the social whole move finding therein a pattern of human adjustments already established. For it is in fact the objectively embodied life of individuals containing all levels of realization. Here the function of creating distinctions and of uniting these distinctions again has full play. The order of the whole is maintained by the relation of these distinctions which have their union in the sex distinction and relation giving rise to the family, to generation and genus. The relation is one of inviolability and absoluteness seeming to have roots in Absolute Mind. Over against this there are the laws of the social order which are man made laws. These two forms exist side by side. We have in them the law of individuality and the law of universality, but in each the substance remains spirit in its entirety. "In the one case," says Hegel, "this spirit can be named Human Law, because it has its being essentially in the form of self-conscious actuality. In the form of universality, that spirit is the law known to everybody, familiar and recognized, and is the everyday Customary Convention.

"Over against this power and publicity of the ethical secular human order there appears, however, another power, The Divine Law." (467)

"Now in the one law as in the other there are differences and stages. For since these laws involve the element of consciousness in both cases, distinction is developed within themselves: and this is just what constitutes the peculiar process of their life." (473)

Hegel then takes up the consideration of the self-consciousness of the ethical world showing the universal principles of this ethical world in their actual operation.

It is in the community that the upper law has its validity in the form of government—for here government is an individual whole. In Hegel's words: "Government is concrete actual spirit reflected into itself, the self pure and simple of the entire ethical substance. This simple force allows, indeed, the community to unfold and expand into its component members, and to give each part subsistence and self-existence or its own (für sich sein). Spirit finds in this way its realization or its objective existence and the family is the medium in which this realization takes effect." (473)

Yet it must be understood that spirit is the force of the whole. In it the parts are unified; it is also the power by which they pursue personal ends. Then conversely, when these personal ends defy the unity of the whole, either singly or in assemblage, and this isolation tends to evaporate the common spirit, Government reestablishes itself by War. "By this means," says Hegel, "it confounds the order that has been established and arranged, and violates their right to independence, while the individuals (who, being absorbed therein, get adrift from the whole, striving after inviolable self-existence [*für sich sein*] and personal security), are made, by the task thus imposed on them by government, to feel the power of their lord and master, death. By thus breaking up the form of fixed stability, spirit guards the ethical order from sinking into merely natural existence, preserves the self of which it is conscious and raises that self to the level of freedom and its own powers. The negative essential being shows itself to be the might proper of the community and the force it has for self-maintenance. The community therefore finds the true principle and corroboration of its power in the inner nature of divine law, and in the kingdom of the nether world." (474)

"The divine law which holds sway in the family has also on its side distinctions within itself, the relations among which make up the living process of its realizations. Amongst the three relationships, however, of husband and wife, parents and children, brothers and sisters, the relationship of husband and wife is to begin with the primary and immediate form in which one consciousness recognizes itself in another, and in which each knows that reciprocal recognition. Being natural self-knowledge, knowledge of self on the basis of nature and not on that of ethical life, it merely represents and typifies in a figure the life of spirit, and is not spirit itself actually realized. Figurative representation, however, has its reality in another than it is. This relationship, therefore, finds itself realized not in itself as such, but in the child—an other, in whose coming into being that relationship consists, and with which it passes away. And this change from one generation onwards to another is permanent in and as the life of a nation." (475)

Hegel says of the brother and sister relationship that theirs is "an unmixed intransitive form of relationship." It is one in which the feminine element unconsciously shadows forth the nature of the ethical life while the masculine turns to the external in order to give concrete reality to the ethical order in the life of the community.

"'The distinction of the sexes and of their ethical content remains all the same within the unity of the ethical substance, and its process is just the constant development of that substance. The husband is sent forth by the spirit of the family into the life of the community, and finds there his self-conscious reality. Just as the family thereby finds in the community its universal substance and subsistence, conversely the community finds in the family the formal element of its own realization, and in the divine law its power and confirmation. Neither of the two is alone self-complete. Human law as a living and active principle proceeds from the divine, the law holding on earth from that of the nether world, the conscious from the unconscious, mediate from immediacy; and returns to whence it came. The power of the nether world, on the other hand, finds its realization upon earth; it comes through consciousness to have existence and efficacy." (479)

Thus we have "The universal elements of the ethical life, the ethical substance as universal and again that substance as particular consciousness." (479) Through these are brought out the nature of Duty, the nature of *Guilt*—which is the departure on the part of consciousness, by its own act from its own ethical substance or spiritual self. Since these forces ever seek their equilibrium there comes into operation Destiny.

Further from Hegel: "The whole is a stable equilibrium of all the parts, and each part is a spirit in its native element, a spirit which does not seek its satisfaction beyond itself, but has the satisfaction within itself for the reason that itself is in this balanced equipoise with the whole. This condition of stable equilibrium can, doubtless, only be living by inequality arising within it, and being brought back again to equipoise by Righteousness and Justice." (480)

"The ethical realm remains in this way permanently a world without blot or stain, a world untainted by any internal descension. So, too, its process is an untroubled transition from one of its powers to the other, in such a way that each preserves and produces the other. We see it no doubt divided into two ultimate elements and their realization; but their opposition is rather the confirming and substantiation of one through the other; and where they directly come in contact with each other as actual factors, their mediating common element is the immediate permeation of the one with the other. The one extreme, the universal spirit conscious of itself, becomes, through the individuality of man, linked together with its other extreme, its force and its element, with *unconscious* spirit. On the other hand, divine law is individualized, the unconscious spirit of the particular individual finds its existence, in woman, through the mediation of whom the unconscious spirit comes out of its unrealizedness into actuality, and rises out of the state of unknowing and unknown into the conscious realm of universal spirit. The union of man with woman constitutes the operative mediating agency of the whole, and constitutes the element which, while separated into the extremes of divine and human law, is, at the same time their immediate union. This union, again, turns both those first mediate connections (*Schlusse*) into one and the same synthesis, and unites into one process the twofold movement in opposite directions—one from reality to unreality, the downward movement of human law, organized into independent members, to the danger and trial of death, —the other, from unreality to reality, the upward movement of the law of the nether world to the daylight of conscious existence. Of these movements the former falls to man, the latter to woman." (482)

However, in coming now to an analysis of this ethical world with spirit as its truth and moving with it as it actualizes itself it must be noted, first of all, that the character is still abstract and its knowledge is of a formal kind which is occupied at the same time with the various content of existence. It is a particular individual who has the power to prescribe laws and possess knowledge—while from the side of substance this is seen to be self-contained. There must ensue a long series of stages and forms of development before this self-contained and self-sufficient spiritual reality has been made actual and presents itself to itself in Consciousness as Spirit, i.e., the real ultimate of all existence. It is then lived and breathed as an actuality to Consciousness.

The various phases of development along the way to this ultimate consummation are first when spirit gets sundered within itself in the realm of Culture and Civilization as over against the element of thought involved in Faith, or Belief. Both worlds get into confusion but are finally penetrated in their fullness and truth through individual insight risen to Enlightenment. The road traveled extends all the way from the idea of The Family—which is the simplest form of the social life—up to "Religion" which is the highest experience of universal mind. For it must be remembered that as consciousness extends into these higher and at the same time deeper realizations, they are not true for consciousness until consciousness makes them actualities in its life and in its world through the social order.

Now coming from this compact general unity in which immediate living individuality and ethical substance are comprehended, there comes to pass a level—a soulless community

—the universal being split into atomic units—as Persons—a sheer plurality of individuals. Hegel says: "What in the realm of the ethical life was called the hidden divine law has in fact come out of concealment to the light of actuality." It is Personality being manifested out of the active life of the ethical substance. Just as Lordship and Bondage rose out of the stoical phase of Self-consciousness—and proved to be the mode where it was existing immediately and was there implicit in an abstract way—is now explicit and concrete. It is now reduced to the abstract form—"independence devoid of the qualities of spirit." (502) "In fact," says Hegel, "it is simply the contradiction of consciousness claiming to be at once independent and yet devoid of independence." (503) This is the principle of legal status in its abstract form. It acquires actual power when it is given the significance of the entire content by the will of other personalities who delegate their rights thereto until there is established the universality of one person who becomes a master and lord of the world. He is "the universal might of actuality" . . . however, "in a merely negative relation, a relation of exclusion both of one another and to him." (505)

Hegel says, "The truth consists in the fact that this universal accepted objectivity of self-consciousness is reality estranged from it. This objectivity is the universal actuality of the self; but this actuality is directly the perversion of the self as well —it is the loss of its essential being. The reality of the self that was not found in the ethical world, has been gained by its reverting into a "person." What in the case of the former was all harmony and union, comes now on the scene, no doubt in developed form, but self-estranged." (506)

This brings us to Hegel's next designation as "Spirit in Self-estrangement"—wherein is delineated that way of calvary through which all consciousness passes on the road to full spiritual self-realization. For now at this phase of consciousness we have the rigid unity of an individual self. This legal personality rose out of the social whole. By the power of other free wills he became The Lord of the World actually.

But in the negative aspect. To be the true master of the essential essence as well as substance is the journey that lies ahead.

Starting with the social whole there has developed the personality risen to Lord of the World in the actual sense and controlling all. But this control is with actuality merely; the spiritual essence, "the essential," is lacking. We have therefore an actuality that is the direct perversion of the essential self. Because of this the actual personality is unable to tame the titanic forces arising from a perverted harmony. It is then given over to excessive measures and chaos is the final result. This is the outcome of the process by which the individual starts with the social whole and attains mastery in actuality. The other process starts with the individual and we have the movement by which the individual spirit secures full realization of spiritual existence in a universal order of absolutely free wills. Now it is because the contrast of these two states is essential for consciousness, destined to be complete, and because the contrast and the estrangement it involves are the most profound in the process of man's spiritual life, that it has been universally recognized as the way of sorrow.

For the individual spiritual existence which consciousness seeks to achieve, and the unified rigid personality of this established being are now in contrast—standing over against each other in an estrangement the deepest that spirit can possibly experience. In the course of its struggle for its true spiritual life it covers all the way of human travail. Its prolonged endeavor Hegel designates as Culture and Civilization. As Hegel says: "This world is a spiritual reality, it is essentially the fusion of individuality with being. This its existence is the work of self-consciousness, but likewise an actuality immediately present and alien to it, which has a peculiar being of its own, and in which it does not know itself. This reality is the external element and the free content of the sphere of legal right." (509)

And further: "Here, however, what is present means merely objective actuality, which has its consciousness in the beyond;

each single moment, as an essential entity, receives this, and thereby actuality, from another, and so far as it is actual, its essential being is something other than its own actuality. Nothing has a spirit self-established and indwelling within it; rather each is outside itself in what is alien to it. The equilibrium of the whole is not the unity which abides by itself, nor its inwardly secured tranquility, but rests on the estrangement of its opposite. The whole is, therefore, like each single moment, a self-estranged reality. It breaks up into two spheres: in one kingdom self-consciousness is actually both the self and its object, and in another we have the kingdom of pure consciousness, which, being beyond the former, has no actual present, but exists for Faith, is matter of Belief." (511)

"This world," says Hegel, "although it has come into being by means of individuality, is in the eyes of self-consciousness something that is directly and primarily estranged, and, for self-consciousness, takes on the form of a fixed, undisturbed reality. But at the same time self-consciousness is sure this is its own substance, and proceeds to take it under control. This power over its substance it acquires by culture, which, looked at from this aspect, appears as self-consciousness making itself conform to reality, and doing so to the extent permitted by the energy of its original character and talents."

"By means of the self *qua* inner soul of the process, the substance is so moulded and worked up in its various moments, that one opposite puts life into the other, each opposite, by its alienation from the other, gives the other stability, and similarly gets stability from the other. At the same time, each moment has its own definite nature, in the sense of having an insuperable worth and significance; and has a fixed reality as against the other." (517)

"We have here," says Hegel, "something like what we find in nature. Nature, we find, is resolved and spread out into separate and general elements—air, water, fire, earth. Of these air is the unchanging factor, purely universal and transparent; water, the reality that is forever being resolved and given up;

fire, their animating unity which is forever dissolving opposition into unity, as well as breaking up their simple unity into opposite constituents: earth is the tightly compact knot of this articulated whole, the subject in which these realities *are,* where their processes take effect, that which they start from and to which they return. In the same way the inner essential nature, the simple life of spirit that pervades self-conscious reality, is resolved, spread out into similar general areas or masses, spiritual masses in this case and appears as a whole organized world. In the case of the first mass it is the inherently universal spiritual being, self-identical; in the second it is the self-existent being, it has become inherently self-discordant, sacrificing itself, abandoning itself; the third which takes the form of self-consciousness is subject, and possesses in its very nature the fiery force of dissolution. In the first case it is conscious of itself, as immanent and implicit, as existing *per se*; in the second it finds independence, self-existence *(für sich sein)* developed and carried out by means of the sacrifice of what is universal. But spirit itself is the self-containedness and self-completeness of the whole which splits up into substance *qua* self-sacrificing, and which at the same time resumes substance again into its own unity; a whole which is at once a flame of fire bursting out and consuming the substance, as well as the abiding form of the substance consumed." (518)

This analogy is now carried forward in its application to the phase of consciousness under consideration—namely, culture and its realm of reality. The first state is that formed in pure consciousness and in its being the self-identical and unchanging—the nature of the Good. It is "the inherently existing or positive." (521) The other over against this is the passive spiritual being, the explicit self-existent and negative. It is characterized as the Bad. It represents a state of nothingness. The first of these looked at in its developed whole becomes the State. The second over against the state—inherently the opposite of itself—becomes Wealth or Resources.

"According to this aspect state-power expresses its essential nature: the power of the state is in part the quiet insistence of law, in part government and prescription, which appoints and regulates the particular processes of universal action. The one is the simple substance itself, the other its action which animates and sustains itself and all individuals. The individual thus finds therein his ground and nature expressed, organized, and exercised. As against this, the individual, by enjoyment of wealth, does not get to know his own universal nature: he only gets a transitory consciousness and enjoyment of himself *qua* particular and self-existing, and discovers his discordance, his want of agreement with his own essential nature. The conceptions of Good and Bad thus receive here a content the opposite of what they had before."(523, 524)

At this point Hegel goes into a thorough delineation of the different phases through which consciousness passes in its dialectic.

"State-power and wealth," says Hegel, "are the supreme purposes of its strenuous exertion, it is aware that through renunciation and sacrifice it is moulded into universal shape, that it attains universality, and in possessing universality finds general recognition and acceptance: state-power and wealth are the real and actually acknowledged forms of power. But its gaining acceptance thus is itself vain, and just by the fact that it gets the mastery over them it knows them to be not real by themselves, knows rather itself to be the power within them, and them to be vain and empty." (547)

In speaking of wealth he regards each one of the characteristics that accompany the process and its culmination. Finally we come to the end. "It (consciousness) stands directly in front of this abyss, cleaving it to the innermost, this bottomless pit, where every solid base and stay have vanished: and in the depths it sees nothing but a common thing, a play thing for its whims, a chance result of its own caprice. Its spirit consists in quiet unreal imagining, in being superficially forsaken of all true spiritual import." (539-540)

Further he continues "Looked at formally, everything is likewise in its external aspects the reverse of what it is internally for itself; and again it is not really and in truth what it is for itself, but something else that it wants to be; its existence on its own account is, strictly speaking, the loss of self, and alienation of self is really self-preservation." (542)

"That alone is true sacrifice of individuality, therefore, in which it gives itself up as completely as in the case of death, but all the while preserves itself in the renunciation. It comes thereby to be actually what it is implicitly—the identical unity of self with its opposite self. In this way, by the inner withdrawn and secret spiritual principle, the self as such, coming forward and abrogating itself, the state-power becomes *ipso facto* raised into a proper self of its own; without this estrangement of self the deeds of honor, the actions of the noble type of consciousness, and the counsels which its insight reveals, would continue to maintain the ambiguous character, which, as we saw, kept the secret reserve of private intention and self-will, in spite of its overt pretensions." (529)

"The means, then whereby an individual gets objective validity and concrete actuality here is the formative process of Culture. The estrangement on the part of spirit from its natural existence is here the individual's true and original nature, his very substance. The relinquishment of this natural state is, therefore, both his purpose and his mode of existence; it is at the same time the mediating process, the transition of the thought-conditioned substance to concrete actuality, as well as, conversely, the transition of determinate individuality to its essential constitution. This individuality moulds itself by culture to what it inherently is, and only by so doing is it then something *per se* and possessed of concrete existence. The extent of its culture is the measure of its reality and its power. Although the self, *qua* this particular self, knows itself here to be real, yet its concrete realization consists solely in counseling and transcending the natural self." Hegel says further: (514)

"That which, in reference to the single individual, appears as his culture, in the essential moment of spiritual substance as such, *viz.:* the direct transition of its ideal, thought-constituted, universality into actual reality; or otherwise put, culture is the single soul of this substance, in virtue of which the essentially inherent *(an sich)* becomes something explicitly acknowledged, and assumes definite objective existence. The process in which an individual cultivates itself is, therefore, *ipso facto* the development of individuality *qua* universal objective being; that is to say it is the development of the actual world." (516)

When individuality stands finally as this universal objective being it is in the power of expression that the efflorescence manifests. It is by Language that the actuality of culture comes to be established. There is in the union of thought and the spoken word a spiritual manifestation that takes place and stands as a unique divine accomplishment completely isolated. Of it Hegel says: "This estrangement, however, takes place in Language, in words alone, and language assumes here its peculiar role. Both in the sphere of the general social order (*Sittlichkeit*), where language embodies laws and commands, and in the sphere of actual life, where it appears as conveying advice, the content of what it expresses is the essential reality, and language is the form of that essential content. Here, however, it takes the form in which *qua* language it exists to be its content, and possesses authority, *qua* spoken word; it is the power of utterance *qua* utterance which, just in speaking performs what has to be performed. For it is the existence of the pure self *qua* self; in speech the self existent singleness of self-consciousness comes as such into existence, so that its particular individuality is something for others. Ego *qua* this particular pure ego is non-existent otherwise; in every other mode of expression it is absorbed in some concrete actuality, and appears in a shape from which it can withdraw; it turns reflectively back into itself, away from its act as well as from its physiognomic expression, and leaves such an incomplete existence . . . lying soulless behind. Speech, however, contains this ego in its purity; it alone expresses I, I itself. Its existence in this case is, *qua* existence, a form of objectivity which has in it its true nature. Ego is this particular ego, but at the same time universal; its appearing is *ipso facto* and at once the alienation and disappearance of this particular ego, and in consequence its remaining all the while universal. The I, that expresses itself, is apprehended as an ego; it is a kind of infection in virtue of which it established at once a unity with those who are aware of it, a spark that kindles a universal consciousness of self." (529-530)

After this exposition on Language as the actuality of culture Hegel says: "The spiritual substance comes as such into existence only when it has been able to take as its aspects those self-consciousnesses, which know this pure self to be a reality possessing immediate validity, and therein immediately knows, too, that they are such realities merely through the mediating process of alienation. Through that pure self the moments of substance get the transparency of a self-knowing category, and become clarified so far as to be moments of spirit; through the mediating process spirit comes to exist in spiritual form. Spirit in this way is the mediating term, presupposing those extremes and produced through their existence; but it is also the spiritual whole breaking out between them, which sunders itself into them, and, solely in virtue of that contact, creates each into the whole in terms of its principle." (531)

"The state of things brought about here, then, is that all moments execute justice on one another all around, each is just as much in a condition of inherent self-alienation as it moulds itself into its opposite, and in this way reverses the nature of that opposite." (542)

"Spirit truly objective, however, is just this unity of absolutely separate moments, and in fact comes into existence as the common ground, the mediating agency, just through the independent reality of these self-less extremes." (542)

State-power and wealth were shown as these extremes. They constituted the goal for the pursuit of consciousness as the forms of its power. But the gaining of these goals proves to consciousness that they are not the ultimate. In this acknowledgment consciousness comes into a new realization. The estrangement that brought this realization to consciousness was the estrangement which characterizes the realm of culture and civilization. We now pass on to the consideration of Belief as over against Pure Insight.

Belief and Pure Insight

Consciousness experiences estrangement in the realm of culture. It therefore moves toward the realm that lies beyond —the non-actual realm of pure consciousness. It is a realm of thought that does not know itself as thought—but rather where thoughts appear in the form of presentations—ideas with the form of objects elevated to another element. There comes thus to consciousness a phase of Religion—which is the pure consciousness of substance. Hegel says:

"But at the stage we are now considering, religion is in part the outcome of substance, and is the pure consciousness of that substance; in part this pure consciousness is alienated from its concrete actual consciousness, the essence from its existence. It is thus doubtless no longer the insubstantial process of consciousness; but it has still the characteristic of opposition to actuality *qua* this actuality in general, and of opposition to the actuality of self-consciousness in particular. It is essentially, therefore, merely a *belief*." (551)

This pure consciousness is undifferentiated for the reason that the distinction it makes is really no distinction. In this belief, spirit has the character of universality—although this pure consciousness of Absolute Being is a consciousness in estrangement. To quote:

"Forced back upon itself away from this unsubstantial world whose being is mere dissolution, spirit when we consider its true meaning is in undivided unity, at once the absolute movement, the ceaseless process of negating its appearance, as well as the essential substance thereof satisfied within itself, and the positive stability of that process. But, bearing as they inherently do the characteristic of alienation, these two moments fall apart in the shape of a twofold consciousnesses. The former is pure Insight, the spiritual process concentrated and focussed in self-consciousness, a process which has over against it the consciousness of something positive, the form of objectivity or presentation, and which directs itself against this presented object. The proper and peculiar object of this insight is, however, merely pure ego. The bare consciousness of the positive element, of unbroken self-identity, finds its object, on the other hand, in the inner reality as such." (552)

"Pure insight has, therefore, in the first instance, no content within it, because it exists for itself by negating everything in it; to belief, on the other hand, belongs the content, but without insight." (553)

Both of these attitudes, however, constitute the mind's return from the sphere of culture with its concrete aspect. Here the pure consciousness as Belief and the pure self-consciousness as Insight regard consciousness and actuality in three aspects which give rise to the three persons of the Trinity. "In one aspect," to quote Hegel, "each is outside every relation and has a being all its own; in another each takes up an attitude towards the concrete actual world standing in antithesis to pure consciousness; while in the third form each is 'related to the other'—inside pure consciousness." (554)

"These forms in answer to the demands of reason involve a series whose movement constitutes a necessity. But for belief," says Hegel, "their distinction is a static diversity, and their movement simply a historical fact." (554)

"To deal shortly with the external character of their form: as in the world of culture state-power or the good was primary, so here the first and foremost moment is Absolute Being, spirit absolutely self-contained, so far as it is simple eternal substance." This refers to the first person of the Trinity—God as Substance, God the Father. Hegel continues and takes up next the Second Person of the Trinity, The Godman Christ. And lastly the Third Person of the Trinity—God as Absolute Spirit—God the Holy Ghost. The first designated was the Absolute Being, eternal substance. In Hegel's words: "But in the process of realizing its constitutive notion, which consists in being spirit, that substance passes over into a form where it exists for an other; its self-identity becomes actual Absolute Being, actualized in self-sacrifice; it becomes a self, but a self that is transitory and passes away. Hence the third stage is the return of self thus alienated, the substance thus abased, into its first primal simplicity. Only when this is done is spirit presented and manifested as Spirit." (555) Hegel continues:

"These distinct ultimate Realities, when brought back by thought into themselves out of the flux of the actual world, are changeless, eternal spirits, whose being lies in thinking the unity which they constitute. While thus torn away from self-consciousness, these Realities all the same lay hold on it; for if the Ultimate Reality were to be fixed and unmoved in the form of the first bare and simple substance, it would remain alien to self-consciousness. But the laying aside, the "emptying," of this substance, and afterwards its spirit, involves the element of concrete actuality, and thereby participates in the believing self-consciousness, or the believing attitude of consciousness belongs to the real world." (555)

It is this fact that belief and pure insight have each grasped in different ways. Hegel goes through the phases of this stage of consciousness showing how service, in prayer and communion, tend to produce a sense of unity with the self-complete, self-existing Being, although the essential notion remains an inner principle which never comes to light for belief—only for insight risen to enlightenment.

"In the case of pure insight, however, the concept, the essential notion (Begriff) is alone the real; and this third aspect of belief—that of being an object for pure insight—is the specific relation in which belief here appears. Pure insight itself has like belief to be considered partly by itself (*an und für sich*), partly in relation to the real world—so far as the real world is still present in positive shape, viz., in the form of a vain consciousness—and lastly in that relation to belief just mentioned." (556)

"We have already seen what pure insight by itself is. Belief is unperturbed pure consciousness of spirit as the essentially real; pure insight is the self-consciousness of spirit as the essentially real; it knows the essentially real, therefore, not *qua* essence but *qua* Absolute Self. Its aim thus is to cancel every kind of independence which falls without self-consciousness, whether that be the independence of the actually objective or of the inherently real, and to mould it into conceptual form. It not merely is the certainty of self-conscious reason assured of being all truth; it knows that it is so." Hegel continues: (557)

"Pure insight, therefore, is the simple ultimate being undifferentiated within itself, and at the same time the universal achievement and result and a universal possession of all. In this simple spiritual substance self-consciousness gives itself and maintains for itself in every object the sense of this its own individual being or of action, just as conversely the individuality of self-consciousness is there identical with itself and universal."

"This pure insight is, then, the spirit that calls to every consciousness: be for yourselves what you are in yourselves—rational." (558)

Enlightenment

"The peculiar object against which pure insight directs the active force of the notion is belief, this being a form of pure consciousness like itself and yet opposed to it in that element. But at the same time pure insight has a relation to the actual world, for, like belief, it is a return from the actual world into pure consciousness." (559)

"The various negative forms which consciousness adapts, the attitude of scepticism, and that of theoretical and practical idealism, are inferior attitudes compared with that of pure insight and the expansion of pure insight—enlightenment; for pure insight is born of the substance of spirit, it knows the pure self of consciousness to be absolute, and enters into conflict with the pure consciousness of the Absolute Being of all reality. (561)

"Since belief and insight are the same pure consciousness but in form are opposed—the reality in the case of belief being a thought, not a notion, and hence something absolutely opposed to self-consciousness, while the reality in the case of pure insight is the self—they are such that *inter se* the one is the absolute negation of the other." (561)

"As appearing the one against the other, all content falls to belief; for in its unperturbed element of thought every moment obtains definite subsistence. Pure insight, however, is in the first instance without any content; it is rather the sheer disappearance of content; but by its negative attitude towards what it excludes it will make itself real and give itself a content." (561)

In the philosophical consideration of these terms it must be remembered that "what is not rational has no truth"—to continue in Hegel's words "or what is not comprehended through a notion, conceptually determined, *is* not. When reason thus speaks of some other than itself, it in fact speaks merely of itself; it does not therein go beyond itself." (566)

"This struggle with the opposite, therefore, combines in its meaning the significance of being insight's own actualization. This consists just in the process of unfolding its moments and taking them back into itself. One part of this process is the making of the distinction in which the insight of reason opposes itself as object to itself; so long as it remains in this condition it is at variance with itself. *Qua* pure insight it is without any content; the process of its realization consists in itself becoming content to itself; for no other can be made its content, because it is the category become self-conscious. But since this insight in the first instance thinks of the content as in its opposite, and knows the content merely as a content, and does not as yet think of it as its own self, pure insight misconceives itself in it. The complete attainment of insight therefore, has the sense of a process of coming to know that content as its own, which was to begin with opposite to itself. Its result, however, will be thereby neither the reestablishment of the errors it fights with, nor merely its original notion, but an insight which knows the absolute negation of itself to be its own proper reality, to be its self, or an insight which is its self-understanding notion." (566)

Now since this world is the fusion of individuality and the substance of being its work is done by self-consciousness. But this self-consciousness feels that it has a being all of its own different from the universal world. As it develops deeper levels of its self-consciousness, this difference is mitigated and in the stage of pure insight it is overcome. Insight has been looking at the essence of itself that it realizes is in truth its very own. Belief does this also, but in the case of Belief there is content and this content is held in thought as the Absolute Being, just as in the case of enlightenment, the essence is at first over against consciousness. (567)

"Enlightenment that seeks to teach belief this new wisdom does not, in doing so, tell it anything new. For the object of belief itself is just this too, viz., a pure essential reality of its own peculiar consciousness; so that this consciousness does not put itself down for lost and negated in that object but rather puts trust in it; and this just means that it finds itself there as this particular consciousness, finds itself therein to be self-consciousness." (568)

"In the notion of insight there lies not merely this that consciousness knows itself in the object it looks at, and finds itself directly there without first quitting the thought element and then returning into itself; the notion implies as well that consciousness is aware of itself as being also the mediating process, aware of itself as active, as the agency of production. Through this it gets the thought of this unity of self as self and object. (568)

"Belief also is this very consciousness. Obedience and action make a necessary moment, through which the certainty of existence in Absolute Being comes about. This action of belief does not indeed make it appear as if Absolute Being is itself produced thereby. But the Absolute Being for belief is essential not the abstract being that lies beyond the believing consciousness; it is the spirit of the religious communion, it is the unity of that abstract being and self-consciousness. The action of the communion is an essential moment in bringing about that it is this spirit of the communion. That spirit is what it is by the productive activity of consciousness, or rather it does not exist without being produced by consciousness. For essential as this process of production is, it is as truly not the only basis of Absolute Being; it is merely a moment. The Absolute Being is at the same time self-complete and self-contained (an und für sich selbst)." (569)

Now we come to a very important part of Hegel's Phenomenology of Mind, namely, the relation of particular beings to the Asbolute Being. We have made the road clear by delineating the way that the two types of consciousness designated as Belief and Insight have approached this problem. Belief signified that which had its reality in thought while Insight had its reality in the Self. Belief has all content. Insight is without content but by its negative attitude to content will make itself real and produce a content. We will see now in the relation of particular Beings to the Absolute Being how this comes about. For Insight, as the pure insight of universal self-consciousness, transcends diversity and finite reality; that is, it transcends itself as "otherness."

Hegel says, "Finite actualities can, therefore, properly speaking, be taken just in the way people have need of them. Sense facts are thus related now positively to the Absolute *qua* something ultimate—*(an sich),* and sense reality is itself ultimate *per se;* the Absolute makes them, fosters and cherishes them. Then, again, they are related to it as an opposite, that is, to their own non-being; in this case they are not something ultimate, they have being only for another. Whereas in the preceding mode of consciousness the conceptions involved in the opposition took shape as good and bad, in the case of pure insight they pass into the more abstract forms of what is *per se (Ansich)* and what is for another."

"Both ways of dealing with the positive as well as the negative relation of finitude to what is *per se (Ansich),* are, however, equally necessary as a matter of fact, and everything is thus as much something *per se (Ansich)* as it is something for another: in other words everything is "useful." (578)

This is plain to see. Everything exists for others and for other things and likewise, everything exists for itself. In fact the extent to which each looks after his own welfare is the extent to which he acquires the power to be of most service to others. From the smallest to the greatest there is among all things a reciprocity of service. Herein lay the relation (with its aspects of positive and negative) of particular beings to the Absolute Being. In consideration of this, Hegel draws the following observations:

"From this, as a result, man, being the thing conscious of this relation, derives his true nature and place. As he is immediately, man is good, *qua* natural consciousness *per se,* absolute *qua* individual and all else exists for him: and further, since the moments have the significance of universality for him *qua* self-conscious animal, everything exists to please and delight him, and, as he first comes from the hand of God, he walks the earth as in a garden planted for him. He is bound also to have plucked the fruit of the tree of knowledge of good and evil; he claims to have a use for it which distinguishes him from every other being, for, as it happens, his inherently good nature is also so constituted that the superfluity of delight does it harm, or rather his singleness contains as a factor in its constitution a principle that goes beyond it; his singleness can overreach itself and destroy itself. To prevent this, he finds reason a useful means serving himself when he does go beyond the determinate; for such is the force of consciousness." (579)

Everything is useful to man and man is useful in his turn.

Of all the things in the world each has its proper usefulness. In Hegel's words, "All things, however, have this reciprocity of utility by their very nature, by being related to the Absolute in the twofold manner, the one positive, whereby they have a being all their own, the other negative and thereby exist for others. The relation to Absolute Being, or Religion, is therefore of all forms of profitableness the most supremely profitable; for it is profiting pure and simple; it is that by which all things stand—by which they have a being all their own—and that by which all things fall—have an existence for something else. . . . This enlightened insight into absolute Being, that sees nothing in it but just Absolute Being, the *être supreme,* the great Void—this intention to find that everything in its immediate existence is inherently real (*an sich*) or good, and finally to find the relation of the individual conscious entity to the Absolute Being, Religion, exhaustively summed up in the conception of profitableness—all this is for belief utterly and simply revolting. This special and peculiar wisdom of enlightenment necessarily seems at the same time to the believing mind to be sheer insipidity and the confesssion of insipidity; because it consists in knowing nothing of Absolute Being, or, what amounts to the same thing, in knowing this entirely accurate platitude regarding it—that it is merely absolute being, and, again, in knowing nothing but finitude, taking this, moreover, to be the truth, and thinking this knowledge about finitude as the truth to be the highest knowledge attainable." (580)

Now Hegel continues in the explanation that Belief has a certain right to this attitude of opposition to the findings of Enlightenment because Belief has on its side the right of pure thought—which is the divine right of absolute self-identity. Over against this Enlightenment has but the human right of self-consciousness and can put in this claim only. "But" says Hegel, "since the right of enlightenment is the right of self-consciousness, it will not merely retain its own right, too, in such a way that two equally valid rights of spirit would be left standing in opposition to one another without either satisfying the rights of the other; it will maintain the absolute right, because self-consciousness is the negative function of the notion (Begriff), a function which does not merely operate in independence, but also gets control over its opposite. And because belief is a mode of consciousness, it will not be able to balk enlightenment of that right." (581)

"For enlightenment does not operate against the believing mind with special principles of its own, but with those which belief itself implies and contains. Enlightenment merely brings together and presents to belief its own thoughts, the thoughts that lie scattered and apart within belief, all unknown to it. Enlightenment merely reminds belief, when one of its own forms is present, of others it also has but which it is always forgetting when the one is there. Enlightenment shows itself to belief to be pure insight, by the fact that it, in a given determinate moment, sees the whole, brings forward the opposite element standing in direct relation to that moment and, converting the one in the other, brings out the negative principle which is the essence of both thoughts—the notion." (581)

Continuing Hegel develops this phase more fully and says: "At first enlightenment emphasizes the moment that the notion is an act of consciousness; it maintains in the face of belief that the Absolute Being belief accepts is a Being of the believer's consciousness *qua* a self, or that this Absolute Being while it is in itself objective for the believer, is also and at the same time not like a foreign thing standing therein, having come there no one knows how or whence. The trust of belief consists just in finding itself as a particular personal consciousness in Absolute Being, and its obedience and service consist in producing, through its activity, that Being as *its* own Absolute. Enlightenment, strictly speaking, only reminds belief of this, if belief affirms without qualifications the ultimate nature *(Ansich)* of Absolute Being to be something beyond the action of consciousness." (583)

In this manner does enlightenment isolate for belief the

unrealized inwardness as over against the concrete actuality and belief finds this gives a new significance to the moments of its consciousness. It realizes in the pain of its sundered unity of assurance that enlightenment has really brought to pass the abolition of a state of unthinking wherein all of its ideas have been duplicated, the one of an uncomprehending heaven, the other in the world of sense.

"Enlightenment illuminates that world of heaven," says Hegel, "with ideas drawn from the world of sense, pointing out there this element of finitude which belief cannot deny or repudiate, because it is self-consciousness, and in being so is the unity to which both kinds of ideas belong, and in which they do not fall apart from one another; for they belong to the same indivisible simple self into which belief has passed, and which constitutes its life. . . ." (588)

"Belief in this manner has in fact become the same as enlightenment—the conscious attitude of relating a finite that inherently exists to an unknown and unknowable Absolute without predicates; the difference is merely that the one is enlightenment satisfied, while belief is enlightenment unsatisfied." (588)

Enlightenment has encompassed belief—but there is still present the unsatisfied longing of the troubled spirit over the loss of its spiritual world in the heavenly beyond. The contrast that existed formerly between belief and enlightenment becomes a contrast inside of enlightenment itself—one, however, which it will remove.

The Truth of Enlightenment

In coming to this phase of the Unfoldment of the Hegelian Phenomenology of Mind we approach the ultimates of substance and essence as they meet and become unified in an enlightened self-consciousness. This being the crux of philosophical self-knowing there must be no intrusion of alien thought. The subject will be rendered verbatim in its entirety as Hegel has it under the caption "The Truth of Enlightenment," which follows:

"The spirit that sullenly works and weaves without further distinctions within itself has thus passed into itself away beyond consciousness, which, on the other hand, has arrived at clearness as to itself. The first moment of this clearness of mind is determined, in regard to its necessity and condition, by the fact that pure insight, or insight that is implicitly and *per se* notion, actualizes itself; it does so when it gives otherness or determinateness a place in its own nature. In this manner it is negative pure insight, i.e., the negation of the notion; this negation is equally pure; and herewith has arisen the pure and simple 'thing,' the Absolute Being, that has no further determination of any sort. If we define this more precisely, insight in the sense of absolute notion is a distinguishing of distinctions that are not so any longer, of abstractions or pure notions that no longer support themselves but find a fixed hold and a distinction only by means of the whole life of the process. This distinguishing of what is not distinguished consists just in the fact that the absolute notion makes itself its object, and as against that process asserts itself to be the essence. The essence hereby is without the aspect wherein abstractions or distinctions are kept apart, and hence becomes pure thought in the sense of a pure thing. (590)

"This, then, is just the dull, silent, unconscious working and weaving of the spirit at the loom of its own being, to which belief, as we saw, sank back when it lost all distinction in its content. And this is at the same time that movement of pure self-consciousness in regard to which the essence is intended to be the absolutely external beyond. For, because this pure self-consciousness is a movement working in pure notions, in distinctions that are no distinctions, pure self-consciousness collapses in fact into that unconscious working and weaving spirit, i.e., into pure feeling, or pure thinghood. (590)

"The self-alienated notion—for the notion still stands here at the level of such alienation—does not, however, recognize this identical nature constituting both sides,—the movement of self-consciousness and its absolute Reality,—does not recognize the identity of their nature, which, in point of fact, is their very substance and subsistence. Since the notion is not aware of this unity, absolute Reality has significance for it merely in the form of an objective beyond, while the consciousness making these distinctions, and in this way keeping the ultimate reality outside itself, is treated as a finite consciousness. (591)

"Regarding that Absolute Being, enlightenment itself falls out with itself in the same way as it did formerly with belief, and is divided between the views of two parties. One party proves itself to be victorious by the fact that it breaks up into two parties; for in that fact it shows it possesses within it the principle it combats, and consequently shows it has abolished the one-sidedness with which it formerly made its appearance. The interest which was divided between it and the other, now falls entirely within it, and forgets the other, because that interest finds lying in it alone the opposition on which its attention is directed. At the same time, however, the opposition has been lifted into the higher victorious element, where it manifests itself in a clarified form. So that the schism that arises in one party, and seems a misfortune, demonstrates rather its good fortune. (591)

"The pure essence itself has in it no distinction; consequently distinction is reached by two such pure essences being put forward for consciousness to be aware of, or by a twofold consciousness of the pure reality. The pure absolute essence is only in pure thought, or rather it is pure thought itself, and thus absolutely beyond the finite, beyond self-consciousness, and is merely the ultimate essence in a negative sense. But in this way it is just being, the negative of self-consciousness. Being negative of self-consciousness, it is also related to self-consciousness. It is *external being,* which, placed in relation to self-consciousness within which distinctions and determinations fall, acquires within it the distinctions, of being tasted, seen, and so on; and the relationship is that of sense-experience and perception. (591-92)

"Taking the point of departure from this sense-existence, into which that negative beyond necessarily passes, but abstracting from those various ways in which consciousness is related to sense-existence, there is left pure matter as that in which consciousness weaves and moves inarticulately within itself. In dealing with this, the essential point to note is that pure matter is merely what remains over when we abstract from seeing, feeling, tasting, etc., i.e., it is not what is seen, tasted, felt, and so on; it is not matter that is seen felt or tasted but colour, a stone, a salt, and so on. Matter is really pure abstraction; and, being so, we have here the pure essential nature of thought, or pure thought itself, as the Absolute without predicates, undetermined, having no distinctions within it." (592)

As Schopenhauer has said, "The absolute without predicates is just matter."

"The one kind of enlightenment calls absolute Being that predicateless Absolute, which exists in thought beyond the actual consciousness from which this enlightenment started; the other calls it matter. If they were distinguished as Nature and Spirit or God, the unconscious inner working and weaving would have nothing of the wealth of developed life required in order to be nature, while Spirit or God would have no self-distinguishing consciousness. Both, as we saw, are entirely the same notion; the distinction lies not in the objective fact, but purely in the diversity of starting-point adopted by the two developments of thought, and in the fact that each stops at its own special point in the thought-process. If they rose above that, their thoughts would coincide, and they would find what to the one is, as it professes, a horror, and to the other a folly, is one and the same thing. For to the one, absolute Being is in its pure thought, or is immediately *for* pure consciousness—is outside finite consciousness, is the negative beyond of finite mind. If it would reflect that in part that simple immediacy of thought is nothing else than pure being, that in part, again, what is negative judgment the copula "is" connects as well as separates the two factors—it would come to see that this beyond, having the character of an external existence, stands in a relation to consciousness, and that in so doing it means the same as what is called pure matter. The missing moment of presence would then be secured. (592-93)

"The other enlightenment starts from sense-existence; it then abstracts from the sensuous relation of tasting, seeing, etc., and turns sense-existence into purely inherent being *(an sich)* absolute matter, something neither felt nor tasted. This being has in this way become the inner reality of pure consciousness, the ultimately simple without predicates; it is the pure notion, *qua* notion whose being is implicit, or it is pure thought within itself. This insight in its conscious activity does not go through the reverse process of passing from being, which is purely being, to an opposite in thought, which is the same as mere being, or does not go from the pure positive to the opposite pure negative; although after all the positive is really pure simply and solely through negation, while the negative *qua* pure is self-identical and one within itself, and precisely on that account positive. (593)

"Or again, these two have not come to the notion found in Descartes' metaphysics that being and thought are inherently the same; they have not arrived at the thought that being, pure being, is not a concrete actual reality, but pure abstraction, and conversely that pure thought, self-identity or inner essence, is partly the negative of self-consciousness, and consequently is being, and partly, *qua* immediate simple entity, is likewise nothing else than being. Thought is thinghood, or thinghood is thought. (594)

"The real essence is here divided asunder in such a way that, to begin with, it appertains to two specifically distinct modes of thinking. In part, the real must hold distinction in itself; in part, just by so doing, both ways of considering it merge into one; for then the abstract moments, of pure being and the negative, by which their distinction is expressed, are united in the object with which these modes of treatment deal.

"The universal common to both is the abstraction of pure self-thinking, of pure quivering within the self. This simple motion of rotating on its own axis is bound to resolve itself into separate moments, because it is itself only motion by distinguishing its own moments. This distinguishing of the moments leaves the unmoved (unity) behind as the empty shell of pure being, that is no longer actual thought, has no more life within it; for *qua* distinction this process is all the content. The process, which thus puts itself outside that unity thereby constitutes, however, the shifting change—a change that does not return into itself—of the moments of being-in-itself, of being-for-another, and of being-forself: it is actual reality in the way this is object for the concrete consciousness of pure insight-viz. Utility. (594)

"Bad as utility may look to belief or sentimentality, or even to the abstraction that calls itself speculation, and deals with the inherent nature in fixed isolation; yet it is that in which pure insight finds its realization and is itself the object for itself, an object which insight now no longer repudiates, and which, too, it does not consider as the void or the pure beyond. For pure insight, as we saw, is the living notion itself, the self-same pure personality, distinguishing itself within itself in such a way that each of the distinguished elements is itself pure notion, i.e., is *eo ipso* not distinct; it is simple undifferentiated pure self-consciousness, which is for itself as well as in itself within an immediate unity. Its inherent being *(an sich sein)* is therefore not fixed and permanent, but at once ceases, in its distinction, to be something distinctive. A being of that kind, however, which is immediately without support and cannot stand of itself, has no being in itself, no inherent existence, it is essentially for something else, which is the power that consumes and absorbs it. But this second moment, opposed to that first one, disappears just as immediately as the first; or, rather, *qua* being merely for some other, it is the very process of disappearing, and there is thus affirmed being that has turned back into itself, being for itself. This simple being-for-self, however, *qua* self-identity, is rather an objective being, or is thereby for an other." (595)

"This nature of pure insight in thus unfolding and making explicit its moments, in other words insight *qua* object, finds expression in the useful, the profitable. What is useful is a thing, something that subsists in itself; this being in itself is at the same time only a pure moment: it is in consequence absolutely for something else, but is equally for an other merely as it is in itself: these opposite moments have returned into the indivisible unity of being-for-self. While, however, the useful doubtless expresses the notion of pure insight, it is all the same not insight as such, but insight as conscious presentation, or as object for insight. It is merely the restless shifting change of those moments, of which one is indeed Being-returned-into-itself, but merely as being-for-itself, i.e., as abstract moment, appearing on one side over against the others. The useful itself does not consist in the negative fact of having these moments in their opposition at the same time undivided in one and the same respect, of having them as a form of thought *per se* in the way they are *qua* pure insight. The moment of being-for-self is doubtless a phase of usefulness, but not in the sense that it swamps the other moments, being-*per-se* and being-for-another; if so, it would be the whole self. In the useful, pure insight thus possesses as its object its own peculiar notion in the pure moments constituting its nature; it is the consciousness of this metaphysical principle, but not yet its conceptual comprehension, it has not yet itself reached the unity of being and notion. Because the useful still appears before insight in the form of an object, insight has a world, not indeed any longer a world all by itself and self-contained, but still a world all the same, which it distinguishes from itself. Only, since the opposites have appeared at the supreme point of the notion, the next step will be for them to collide and collapse together and for enlightenment to experience the fruits of its deeds. (595-96)

"When we looked at the object reached in relation to this

entire sphere of spiritual life, we found the actual world of culture summed up in the vanity of self-consciousness—in independent self-existence, whose content is drawn from the confusion characteristic of culture, and which is still the individual notion, not yet the self-conscious (*für sich*) universal notion. Returned into itself, however, that (individual) notion is pure insight—pure consciousness qua pure self or negativity, just as belief, too, is pure consciousness, *qua* pure thought or positivity. Belief finds in that self the moment that makes it complete;—but, perishing through being thus completed, it is in pure insight that we now see both moments as absolute Being, which is purely thought-constituted or is a negative entity, and as matter, which is the positive entity. (596)

"This completion still lacks that actual reality of self-consciousness—the world out of which thought raised itself up to itself. What is thus wanting is reached in the fact of utility so far as pure insight secures positive objectivity there; pure insight is thereby a concrete actual consciousness satisfied within itself. This objectivity now constitutes its world, and is become the final and true outcome of the entire previous world, ideal as well as real. The first world of spirit is the expanded realm of spirit's self-dispersing existence and of certainty of self in separate individual shapes and forms: just as nature disperses its life in an endless multiplicity of forms and shapes, without the generic principle of all the forms being present therein. The second world contains the generic principle, and is the realm of the ultimate inherent nature *(an sich sein)* or the essential truth, over against that individual certainty. The third world, however, that of the useful, is the truth which is certainty of self as well. The realm of the truth of belief lacks the principle of concrete actuality, or of certainty of self in the sense of this individual self. But, again, concrete actuality, or certainty of self *qua* this individual, lacks the ultimate inherent nature *(an sich)*. In the object of pure insight both worlds are united. The useful is the object so far as self-consciousness sees through it, and individual certainty of self finds its enjoyment (its self-existence) in it; self-consciousness sees into it in this manner, and this insight contains the true essence of the object (which consists in being something seen through, in other words, in being for an other). This insight is thus itself true knowledge; and self-consciousness directly finds in this attitude universal certainty of itself as well, has its pure consciousness in this attitude, in which truth as well as immediateness and actuality are united. Both worlds are reconciled and heaven is transplanted to the earth below." (598)

The Awakening of Subjectivity as Absolute Freedom

At this point consciousness has found that in the principle of utility is its notion. Yet in this phase it is still not the true immediate and sole actuality. It is still more in the sense of a self-consciousness with something possessed—namely the insight that its notion is the principle of utility. As the outcome of this internal conviction there comes to consciousness a new mode of life—a sense of actual possession—of absolute freedom. This organized world has nothing left for itself; to consciousness it is pure metaphysic, pure notion, pure knowledge of self-consciousness. Hegel says, "If the useful were merely the shifting change of the moments, without returning into its own proper unity, and was still hence an object for knowledge to deal with, then *it* ceases to be that now. For knowing is itself the process and movement of those abstract moments; it is the universal self, the self of itself as well as of the object, and, being universal, is the unity of this process, a unity that returns into self." (600)

"This brings on the scene spirit in the form of absolute freedom. It is the mode of self-consciousness which clearly comprehends that in its certainty of self lies the essence of all the component spiritual spheres of the concrete sensible as well as of the supersensible world, or, conversely, that essential being and concrete actuality consist in the knowledge consciousness has of itself." (600)

"It is conscious of its pure personality and with that of all spiritual reality; and all reality is solely spirituality; the world is for it absolutely its own will, and this will is universal will. And further, this will is not the empty thought of will, which is constituted by giving a silent assent, or an assent through a representative, a mere symbol of willing; it is concretely embodied universal will, the will of all individuals as such. For will is in itself the consciousness of personality, of every single one; and it has to be as this true concrete actual will, as self-conscious essential being of each and every personality, so that each, single and undivided, does everything, and what appears as done by the whole is at once and consciously the deed of every single individual." (601)

Hegel says: "It exists in such a way that each individual consciousness rises out of the sphere assigned to it, finds no longer its inmost nature and function in this isolated area, but grasps itself as the notion of will, grasps all the various spheres as the essential expression of this will, and is in consequence only able to realize itself in a work which is a work of the whole. In this absolute freedom all social ranks or classes, which are the component spiritual factors into which the whole is differentiated, are effaced and annulled; the individual consciousness that belonged to any such group and exercised its will and found its fulfilment there, has removed the barriers confining it; its purpose is the universal purpose, its language universal law, its work universal achievement." (601)

But in this subjectivizing of the universal will it becomes transformed. The individual will had its particular place in the universal law and the universal work. Now its purpose becomes obscure, or even opposed to its true self. Yet consciousness continues equally certain of itself as universal will and in creating its objectivity, it thinks that it is doing nothing individual.—It feels proud to be using its power to be executing laws and functions of the whole. This process is the interaction of consciousness with itself and in this it persists —allowing nothing to be detached from it and to assume a shape of its own. It does not recognize that in this attitude there can be no positive accomplishment of anything. On the other hand, this Universal Freedom could more properly differentiate itself into various parts—thought conditioned factors into which could be apportioned the plurality of individuals serving the different needs of the organic totality. But by so doing this consciousness of Absolute Freedom would have to bear the limitation of a determined personality which it is unwilling to do, because by so doing, it would be cheated out of the role of itself laying down the law and accomplishing the universal task. Yet by its own action Universal Freedom can produce neither a positive achievement nor a deed. What it does becomes merely a negative action—which is the destruction of the order of the organic whole. When this destruction of the organization of the actual world is accomplished, then consciousness finds itself in isolated singleness with no other content than this knowledge of itself as absolutely pure, free, individual self. This is its high reality and it stands over against its absolute freedom. All determined elements disappear in disaster, ruin and death as negation overtakes it.

"At the same time," says Hegel, "this negation in its actual manifestation is not something alien and external. It is neither that universal background of necessity in which the moral world is swamped, nor the particular accident of private possession, the whims and humors of the owner, on which the distraught consciousness finds itself dependent; it is universal will, which in this its last abstraction has nothing positive, and hence can give nothing in return for the sacrifice. But just on that account this will is in unmediated oneness with self-consciousness, it is the pure positive because it is the pure negative, and that meaningless death, the unfilled, vacuous negativity of self, in its inner constitutive principle, turns around into absolute positivity. For consciousness, the immediate unity of itself with universal will, its demand to know itself as this particular determinate centre in the universal will, is changed and converted into the absolutely opposite experience. What it loses there, is abstract being, the immediate existence of that insubstantial centre; and this vanished immediacy is the universal will as such which it now knows itself to be, so far as it is superseded and cancelled immediacy, so far as it is pure knowledge or pure will. By this means it knows that will to be itself, and knows itself to be essential reality; but not as the immediate essence, not will as revolutionary government or anarchy struggling to establish an anarchical constitution, nor itself as a centre of this faction or the opposite; the universal will is its pure knowing and willing, and *it* is universal will *qua* this pure knowledge and volition. It does not lose itself there, for pure knowledge and volition is it far more than that atomic point of consciousness. It is thus the interaction of pure knowledge with itself; pure knowledge *qua* essential reality is universal will, while this essence is simply and solely pure knowledge. Self-consciousness is thus pure knowledge of essential reality in the sense of pure knowledge. Furthermore, *qua* single self it is merely the form of the subject or concrete real action, a form which by it is known as form. In the same way objective reality, "being", is for it absolutely self-less form; for that objective reality would be what is not known: this knowledge, however, knows knowledge to be the essential fact." (610)

"Absolute freedom has thus squared and balanced the self-opposition of universal and single will. The self-alienated type of mind, driven to the acme of its opposition, where pure volition and the purely volitional agent are still kept distinct, reduces that opposition to a transparent form, and therein finds itself." (610)

"Just as the realm of the real and actual world passes over into that of belief and insight, absolute freedom leaves its self-destructive sphere of reality, and passes over into another land of self-conscious spirit, where in this unreality freedom is taken to be and is accepted as the truth. In the thought of this truth spirit refreshes and revives itself (so far as spirit is thought and remains so), and knows this being which self-consciousness involves (viz. thought) to be the complete and entire essence of everything. The new form and mode of experience that now arises is that of the Moral Life of Spirit." (610)

Spirit Certain of Itself: Morality

We now move into the sphere where the content of the self-conscious individual is the substance of the social order. This is the highest stage in the life of finite spiritual experience in the concrete form of the social process. The discord found in the spheres of culture and enlightenment have been overthrown and we have here a completely universal self-determining free will, "its world within itself and itself its own world." Self-consciousness has at last got mastery over all opposition; its object is the certainty of self as pure knowledge—pure knowledge is its substance and truth is this knowledge. It is immediate, it is also absolute mediation. It is the knowledge of itself become transparently visible. Turning to Hegel: "Absolute essential Being is, therefore, not exhausted by the characteristic of being the simple essence of thought; it is all actuality, and this actuality exists merely as knowledge. What consciousness did not know would have no sense and can be no power in its life. Into its self-conscious knowing will, all objectivity, the whole world has withdrawn. It is absolutely free in that it knows its freedom, and just this very knowledge of its freedom is its substance, its purpose, its sole and only content. . ." (614) "Self-consciousness knows and accepts duty as the Absolute." (615)

Letting Hegel speak: "To begin with, then, the moral consciousness in general is presupposed. It takes duty to be the essential reality: itself is actual and active, and in its actuality and action fulfils duty. But this moral consciousness at the same time, finds before it the assumed freedom of nature; it learns by experience that nature is not concerned about giving consciousness a sense of the unity of its reality with that of nature, and hence discovers that nature may let it become happy, but perhaps also may not. The non-moral consciousness on the other hand finds, by chance perhaps, its realization where the moral consciousness sees merely an occasion for acting, but does not see itself obtaining through its action the happiness of performance and of the enjoyment of achievement. It therefore finds reason for bewailing a situation where there is no correspondence between itself and existence, and lamenting the injustice which confines it to having its object merely in the form of pure duty, but refuses to let it see this object and itself actually realized. . ." (616)

"While experience must necessarily bring to light the disharmony between the two aspects, seeing that nature is detached and free, nevertheless duty is alone the essential fact and nature by contrast is devoid of self-hood. That purpose in its entirety which the harmony of the two constitutes, contains within it actuality itself. It is, at the same time, the thought of actuality. The harmony of morality and nature, or—seeing that nature is taken account of merely so far as consciousness finds out nature's unity with it—the harmony of morality and happiness, is thought of as necessarily existing; it is *postulated*. For to postulate or demand means that something is *thought as being* which is not yet actual—a necessity affecting, not the conception *qua* conception, but existence. But necessity is at the same time essentially relation through the conception. The postulated existence thus is not something that concerns the imagination of some chance individual consciousness, but is implied in the very notion of morality itself, whose true content is the unity of pure with individual consciousness. It falls to the individual consciousness to see that this unity is, for it, an actuality:—which means happiness as regards the content of the purpose, and existence in general as regard its form. The existence thus demanded—the unity of both—is therefore not a wish, nor, looked at *qua* purpose, it is of such a kind as to be still uncertain of attainment; the purpose is rather a demand of *reason,* or an immediate certainty and presupposition of reason." (617)

However, there comes into being another factor for consciousness—that of *sensibility*. This sensibility takes the form of impulses and inclinations in a negative volition. We have here two factors in opposition. The final purpose must therefore be the harmonizing of morality and will in its sensuous form. Also the harmony of morality and objective nature. It is the process of concrete action itself which must connect these two. Turning to Hegel for amplification we have the following:

"The first postulate was the harmony of morality and objective nature—the final purpose of the world: the other was the harmony of morality and will in its sensuous form, in the form of impulse, etc.—the final purpose of self-consciousness as such. The former is the harmony in the form of implicit immanent existence; the latter the harmony in the form of explicit self-existence. That however, which connects these two extreme final purposes, which are thought and operates as their mediating ground, is the process of concrete action itself. They are harmonies whose moments have not yet become definitely objective in their abstract distinctiveness from each other: this takes place in concrete actuality, in which the aspects appear in consciousness proper, each as the other of the other. The postulates arising by this means contain harmonies which are now both immanent and self-existent whereas formerly they were postulated merely separately, the one being the immanent harmony, the other self-existent." (620)

"The moral consciousness, *qua* simple knowledge and willing pure duty, is brought, by the process of acting, into relation with an object opposed to that abstract simplicity, into relation with the manifold actuality which various cases present, and thereby assumes a moral attitude varied and manifold in character. Hence arise, on the side of content, the plurality of laws generally, and, on the side of form, the contradictory powers of intelligent knowing consciousness and of a being devoid of consciousness." (621)

At this point Hegel takes up the contradictory phases through which morality passes showing up the condition of self-sophistication as well as self-realization, and he names these contradictory aspects 'dissemblance.'

These contradictory phases, however, are swallowed up and disappear when moral consciousness emerges in its next higher sphere—that of Conscience.

"This self of Conscience, the mode of spirit immediately certain of itself as absolute truth and objective being, is the third type of spiritual self. It is the outcome of the third sphere of the Spiritual world and may be shortly compared with the two former types of self." (644)

"The totality or actuality which is revealed as the truth of the ethical world, the world of the social order, is the self of a Person (the legal self): its existence lies in being recognized and acknowledged. As the person is the self devoid of substance, this its existence is abstract reality too. The person has a definite standing, and that directly and immediately; its self is the point in the sphere of its existence which is immediately at rest. That point is not torn away from its universality; the two (the particular focus and its universality) are therefore not in a relational process with regard to one another: the universal is in it without distinction, and is neither the content of the self, nor is the self filled by itself." (645)

"The second self is the truth and outcome of the world of culture, is spirit that has recovered itself after and through disruption, is absolute freedom. In this self, the former immediate unity of individual existence and universality breaks up into its component elements. The universal, which remains at the same time a purely spiritual entity, the state of recognition or universal will and universal knowledge—the universal is object and content of the self, and its universal actuality. But the universal has not there the form of existence detached from the self: in this mode of self it therefore gets no filling, no positive content, no world." (645)

"Moral self-consciousness, indeed, lets its universal aspect get detached, so that this aspect becomes a nature of its own; and at the same time it retains this universality within itself in a superseded form. But it is merely a game of dissembling; it constantly interchanges these two characteristics. In the form of Conscience, with its certainty of itself, it first finds the content to fill the former emptiness of duty as well as the emptiness of right and the empty universal will. And because this certainty of self is at the same time immediacy, it finds in conscience, definite existence." (645)

"The actual reality of conscience, however, is one which is a self, *i.e.*, an existence conscious of itself, the spiritual element of being recognized. Doing something is, therefore, merely the translation of its individual content into that objective element where it is universal and is recognized, and this very fact, that the content is recognized, makes the deed an actuality. The action is recognized and thereby real, because the actual reality is immediately bound up with conviction or knowledge; or in other words, knowledge of one's purpose is immediately and at once the element of existence, is universal recognition. For the essence of the act, duty, consists in the conviction conscience has of it. This conviction is just the inherent principle itself; it is inherently universal self-consciousness—in other words, is recognition and hence reality." (650)

"Conscience, then, in its majestic sublimity above any specific law and every content of duty, puts whatever content it pleases into its knowledge and willing. It is moral genius and originality, which know the inner voice of its immediate knowledge to be a voice divine; and since in such knowledge it directly knows existence as well, it is divine creative power, which contains living force in its very conception. It is in itself, too, divine worship, "service of God," for its action is the contemplation of this its own proper divinity." (663)

"This solitary worship, this "service of God" in solitude of soul, is at the same time essentially "service of God" on the part of a religious community; and pure inward self-knowledge and perception of self pass to being a moment of consciousness. Contemplation of itself is its objective existence, and this objective element is the utterance of its knowledge and will as a universal. Through such expression the self becomes established and accepted, and the act becomes an effective deed, a deed carrying out a definite result. What gives reality and subsistence to its deed is universal self-consciousness. When, however, conscience finds expression, this puts the certainty of itself in the form of pure self and thereby as universal self. Others let the act hold as valid, owing to the explicit terms in which the self is thus expressed and acknowledged to be the essential reality. The spirit and the substance of their community are, thus, the mutual assurance of their conscientiousness, of their good intentions, the rejoicing over this reciprocal purity of purpose, the quickening and refreshment received from the glorious privilege of knowing and of expressing, of fostering and cherishing, a state so altogether admirable." (664)

"So far as this sphere of conscience still distinguishes its abstract consciousness from its self-consciousness, its life is merely hid in God. God is indeed immediately present to its mind and heart, to its self. But what is revealed, its actual consciousness and the mediating process of this consciousness, is, to it, something other than that hidden inner life and the immediacy of God's presence. But, with the completion of conscience, the distinction between its abstract consciousness and its self-consciousness is done away. It knows that the abstract consciousness is just this self, this individual self-existence which is certain of itself: that the very difference between the terms is abolished in the *immediateness* of the relation of the self to the ultimate Being, which, when placed outside the self, is the abstract essence, and a Being concealed from it. For a relation is mediate when the terms related are not one and the same, but each is a different term for the other, and is one only with the other in some third term: an *immediate* relation, however, means, in fact, nothing else than the unity of the terms. Having risen above the meaningless position of holding these distinctions, which are not distinctions at all, to be still such, consciousness knows the immediateness of the presence of ultimate Being within it to be the unity of that Being and its self: it thus knows itself to be the living inherent reality, and knows its knowledge to be Religion, which, *qua* knowledge viewed as an object or knowledge with an objective existence is the utterance of the religious communion regarding its own spirit." (664)

V

FREE CONCRETE MIND
RELIGION
THE REALITY OF THE SELF
RELIGION. ABSOLUTE KNOWLEDGE

We are about to pass to the consideration of the two final sections of The Phenomenology of Mind which are devoted to the consideration of Religion and Absolute Knowledge.

But before considering these next divisions of the subject Hegel discusses under the present caption *Evil and Forgiveness,* the subjects of *Judgment,* which he says, "cannot oppose the personal aspect of the individuality to the universal aspect of the act;" he discusses the sorrow-laden, or so-called "beautiful soul,"—by which is designated one who, to preserve the purity of its heart, flees from contact with actuality; he also discusses the various phases which lead up to the final consummation of this state of consciousness—that state which opens into the Sphere of Religion proper. When the stage of Religion proper is reached, Hegel begins by taking us through a detailed review of all the states leading up to Religion in order to show that it was an ever present factor. But in all of this there is no more condensed statement of the nature of so called evil and no more masterful exposition of the consummation of Religion per se than is contained in the concluding paragraphs of the present section now quoted.

"Absolute Spirit enters existence merely at the culminating point at which its pure knowledge about itself is the opposition and interchange with itself. Knowing that its pure knowledge is the abstract essential reality, Absolute Spirit is this knowing duty in absolute opposition to the knowledge which knows itself, *qua* absolute singleness of self, to be the essentially real. The former is the pure continuity of the universal, which knows the individuality, that knows itself the real, to be inherently naught, to be evil. The latter, again, is absolute discreteness, which knows itself absolute in its pure oneness, and knows the universal is the unreal which exists only for others. Both aspects are refined and clarified to this degree of purity, where there is no self-less existence left, no negative of consciousness in either of them, where, instead, the one element of "duty" is the self-identical character of its self-knowledge, and the other element of "evil" equally has its purpose in its own inner being and its reality in its own mode of utterance. The content of this utterance is the substance that gives this spirit subsistence; the utterance is the assurance of the certainty of spirit within its own self." (678)

"These spirits, both certain of themselves have each no other purpose than its own pure self, and no other reality and existence than just this pure self. But they are still different, and the difference is absolute, because holding within this element of the pure notion. The difference is absolute, too, not merely for *us* (tracing the experience), but for the notions themselves which stand in this opposition. For while these notions are indeed determinate and specific relatively to one another, they are at the same time in themselves universal so that they fill out the whole range of the self; and this self has no other content than this its own determinate constitution, which neither transcends the self nor is more restricted than it. For the one factor, the absolutely universal, is pure self-knowledge as well as the other, the absolute discreteness of single individuality, and both are merely this pure self-knowledge. Both determinate factors, then, are cognizing pure notions which know *qua* notions, whose very determinateness is immediately knowing, or, in other words, whose relationship and opposition is the Ego. Because of this they are *for one another* these absolute opposites; it is what is completely inner that has in this way come into opposition to itself and entered objective existence; they constitute pure knowledge, which, owing to this opposition, takes the form of consciousness. But as yet it is not *self-consciousness.* It obtains this actualization in the course of the process through which this opposition passes. For this opposition is really itself the indiscrete continuity and identity of ego=ego; and each by itself inherently cancels itself just through the contradiction in its pure universality, which, while implying continuity and identity, at the same time still resists its identity with the other, and separates itself from it. Through this relinquishment of separate selfhood, the knowledge, which in its existence is in a state of diremption, returns into the unity of the self; it is the concrete actual Ego, universal knowledge of self in its absolute opposite, in the knowledge which is internal to and within the self, and which, because of the very purity of its separate subjective existence, is itself completely universal. The reconciling affirmation, the "yes," with which both egos desist from their existence in opposition, is the existence of the ego expanded into a duality, an ego which remains therein one and identical with itself, and possesses the certainty of itself in its complete relinquishment and its opposite: it is God appearing in the midst of those who know themselves in the form of pure knowledge." (679)

Religion in General

Although Religion and its consummation in Absolute Knowledge constitute the efflorescence of the pilgrimage of consciousness which it is the purpose of The Phenomenology of Mind to survey and delineate, yet, when we reach this lofty summit, Hegel desires that we pause, look back and recapitulate. He wishes to point out that throughout all of the journey, and at each of its stages, it was religion that was there. He wants to show us how, as a mere germ in consciousness it was animating the growth toward fulfillment. He shows how its ever present urge exhibited itself in various forms and gave rise to various expressions. Religion is a factor throughout each day of the long journey of The Phenomenology—which is the voyage of the discovery of mind as consummated in Absolute Knowledge. Here absolute Spirit is conscious of itself in its own distinctive existence. And although it is not until the final stage that Absolute Spirit makes its appearance as realized in Self-consciousness, yet Spirit is present as the motivating potency in all of the previous stages;—the stage of consciousness; of self-consciousness; of reason; of Spirit; in all of these it is present as a principle—yet as a principle unrealized. Now in its final stage consciousness may use any of these media. It has made them all its own, and holds them within as ever present. Formerly, and on the way of its development, it was limited according to its stage of progress. In the first level of experience, that of consciousness, the principle of Religion manifested in its first stage and we had Natural Religion. In the second stage, that of self-consciousness, the principle of Religion manifested in its second stage and we had Religion in the Form of Art. In the third stage, that of Reason and Spirit, we had Revealed Religion.

Each of these Religious forms is circumscribed and inadequate to the complete realization that is to come; yet each is necessitated by the nature of the case. Hegel even discerns a law operating which follows the same pattern as that given for Mind in the Phenomenology. For instance, the first level of experience is Consciousness and it has its different stages of development—Sense-certainty, Perception and Understanding. The second level is Self-consciousness with its stages of Independence and Dependence, or Lordship and Bondage; Freedom of Self-consciousness—or Stoicism, Scepticism. The third stage is Free Concrete Mind, or Reason, with its stages of Observation of Nature; Observation of Organic Existence; Observation of Nature as an Organic Whole; and Realization of Rational Self-Consciousness through Itself. Finally there is the highest level,—that of Spirit with its divisions of The

Ethical Order, The Discipline of Culture and Civilization,—Enlightenment, Morality and Conscience. Hegel literally rewrites the processes of advance which are delineated in The Phenomenology to show the factor of Religion expressing itself in each stage and to show how its forms vary according to the stage in which consciousness finds itself. For instance, in the first stage—that of Consciousness, we find Religion expressed at the primitive level—the level of Natural religion. As Consciousness advances to Sense Certainty, to Perception, to Understanding, we find that Religion advances respectively to the Religion of Light, the Religion of Life, and the Religion of the Artificer—whose creations show forth the religious conceptions at the level of Understanding. Hegel goes through the entire course of the journey of consciousness with much interesting analysis of every phase of Religious expression given by humanity on the road to its Spiritual Self-Realization. The section devoted to Religion constitutes a veritable recapitulation of all that has gone before in The Phenomenology of Mind. This time there is a new emphasis—that of Religion. The present review can only indicate the most important of these in outline. The first—that of Natural Religion is introduced by remarks on religion in general.

Religion in General and Natural Religion

"The Shape assumed by religion," says Hegel, "*is* existence contained and preserved in thought as well as a something thought which is consciously existent. It is by the determinate character of this form, in which spirit knows itself, that one religion is distinguished from another. But we have at the same time to note that the systematic exposition of this knowledge about itself, in terms of this individual specific character, does not as a fact exhaust the whole nature of an actual religion. The series of different religions which will come before us, just as much sets forth again merely the different aspects of a single religion, and indeed of every single religion, and the imagery, the conscious ideas, which seem to mark off one concrete religion from another, make their appearance in each. All the same the diversity must also be looked at as a diversity of religion. For while spirit lives in the distinction of its consciousness and its self-consciousness, the process it goes through finds its goal in the transcendence of this fundamental distinction and in giving the form of self-consciousness to the given shape which is object of consciousness." (696)

God As Light

"When the first and immediate cleavage is made within self-knowing Absolute Spirit, its shape assumes that character which belongs to immediate consciousness or to sense-certainty. It beholds itself in the form of *being;* but not being in the sense of what is without spirit, containing only the contingent qualities of sensation—the kind of being that belongs to sense-certainty. Its being is filled with the content of spirit. It also includes within it the form which we found in the case of immediate self-consciousness, the form of lord and master, in regard to the self-consciousness of spirit which retreats from its object." (699)

"This being, having as its content the notion of spirit, is, then, the shape of spirit in relation simply to itself—the form of having no special shape at all. In virtue of this characteristic, this shape is the pure all-containing, all-suffusing Light of the Sunrise, which preserves itself in its formless indeterminate substantiality. Its counterpart, its otherness, is the equally simple negative—Darkness. The processes of its own externalization, its creations in the unresisting element of its counterpart, are bursts of Light. At the same time in their ultimate simplicity they are its way of becoming something for itself, and its return from its objective existence, streams of fire consuming its embodiment. The distinction, which it gives itself, no doubt thrives abundantly on the substance of existence, and shapes itself as the diverse forms of nature. But the essential simplicity of its thought rambles and roves about inconstant and inconsistent, enlarges its bounds to measureless extent, and its beauty heightened to splendour is lost in its sublimity." (700)

"The content, which this state of pure being evolves, its perceptive activity, is, therefore, an unreal by-play on this substance which merely rises, without setting into itself to become subject and secure firmly its distinctions through the self. Its determinations are merely attributes, which do not succeed in attaining independence; they remain merely names of the One, called by many names. This One is clothed with the manifold powers of existence and with the shapes of reality, as with a soulless, selfless ornament; they are merely messengers of its mighty power, claiming no will of their own, visions of its glory, voices of its praise." (700)

"This revel of heaving life must, however, assume the character of distinctive self-existence, and give enduring subsistence to its fleeting shapes. Immediate being, in which it places itself over against its own consciousness, is itself the negative destructive agency which dissolves its distinctions. It is thus in truth the Self; and spirit therefore passes on to know itself in the form of self. Pure Light scatters its simplicity as an infinity of separate forms, and presents itself as an offering to self-existence, that the individual may take sustainment to itself from its substance." (701)

Plants and Animals as Objects of Religion

As self-conscious spirit rises to the level of Self then unity assumes a manifold of self-existing entities—the religion of spiritual sense-perception. This Pantheism contains in its atomic spiritual collection of all sorts and conditions from the innocent flower and plant religions to the guilty animal religions. Also there is a multiple of folk and nature spirits. These all represent the negative independent self-existence.

The Artificer

Spirit now becomes the artificer. In this the form produced has the abstract character of understanding—not yet endued with spirit. As development goes on the work produced approaches ever closer to the self-consciousness performing it. Turning to Hegel:

"Contrasted with this outer self of the form and shape, stands the other form, which indicates that it has in it an inner being. Nature, turning back into its essential being, degrades its multiplicity of life, ever individualizing itself and confounding itself in its own process, to the level of an unessential encasing shell, which is the covering for the inner being. And as yet this inner being is still simple darkness, the unmoved, the black formless stone." (707) (Reference is here made to the Black Stone of Mecca.)

"Both representations contain inwardness and existence—the two moments of spirit: and both kinds of manifestation contain both moments at once in a relation of opposition, the self both as inward and as outward. Both have to be united. The soul of the statue in human form does not yet come out of the inner being, is not yet speech, objective existence of self which is inherently internal,—and the inner being of multiform existence is still without voice or sound, still draws no distinctions within itself, and is still separated from its outer being, to which all distinctions belong. The artificer, therefore, combines both by blending the forms of nature and self-consciousness; and these ambiguous beings, a riddle to themselves—the conscious struggling with what has no consciousness, the simple inner with the multiform outer, the darkness of thought mated with the clearness of expression—these break out into the language of a wisdom that is darkly deep and difficult to understand." (707) (Reference is here made to combinations of human and animal forms as Pan, the Sphinxes, etc.)

"With the production of this work, the instinctive method of working ceases, which, in contrast to self-consciousness, produced a work devoid of consciousness. For here the activity of the artificer, which constitutes self-consciousness, comes face to face with an inner being equally self-conscious and giving itself expression. He has therein raised himself by his work up to the point where his conscious life breaks asunder, where spirit greets spirit. In this unity of self-conscious spirit with itself, so far as it is aware of being embodiment and object of its own consciousness, its blending and mingling with the unconscious state of immediate shapes of nature become purified. These monsters in form and shape, word and deed, are resolved and dissolved into a shape which is spiritual—an outer which has entered into itself, an inner which expresses itself out of itself and in itself,—they pass into thought, which brings forth itself, preserves the shape and form suited to thought, and is transparent existence. Spirit is *Artist*." (708)

Religion in the Form of Art

The stage of the artist is that of the ethical or objective spirit. In its substance is given "as an objective fact for actual consciousness, the form of consciousness, this amounts to saying that the substance, which is individualized, is known by the individuals within it as their proper essence and their own achievement." (709)

"Later on, spirit goes beyond art in order to gain its higher manifestation, viz., that of being not merely the substance born and produced out of the self, but of being, in its manifestation as object, this very self; it seeks at that higher level not merely to bring forth itself out of its own notion, but to have its very notion as its shape, so that the notion and the work of art produced may know each other reciprocally as one and the same." (711)

Thus through the work of art universal spirit becomes individualized and consciously presented.

The Abstract Work of Art

In the abstract work of art the shape assumes its pure form by being raised into the sphere of the notion. Here the animal is no longer mixed with the human but takes its place outside of it as a symbol—for instance the dove or lamb. As Hegel expresses it, "Nature (is) made transparent by thought and united with self-conscious life. The form of the gods retains, therefore, within it its nature element as something transcended, as a shadowy, obscure memory. The utter chaos and confused struggle amongst the elements existing free and detached from each other, the non-ethical disordered realm of the Titans, is vanquished and banished to the outskirts of self-transparent reality, to the cloudy boundaries of the world which finds itself in the sphere of spirit and is there at peace. These ancient gods, first-born children of the union of Light with Darkness, Heaven, Earth, Ocean, Sun, earth's blind typhonic Fire, and so on, are supplanted by shapes, which do but darkly recall those earlier titans and which are no longer things of nature, but clear ethical spirits of self-conscious nations." (714) Thus we see in the abstract work of art a simple shape which holds peace and "the condition of unrest stands contrasted with this form; confronting quiescent individuality, the essential reality, stands self-consciousness, which being its source and origin, has nothing left over for itself except to be pure activity. He (the artist) could only confer completeness on it by relinquishing his particular nature, divesting himself of his own being, and raising it to the abstraction of pure action." (715)

Another means of expression is Language. Hegel calls this the higher element—"a way of existing which is directly self-conscious existence." Of it Hegel says. "When individual self-consciousness exists in that way, it is at the same time directly a form of universal contagion; complete isolation of independent self-existent selves is at once fluent continuity and universally communicated unity of many selves; it is the soul existing as soul." (717)

The means of language gives rise to other modes of abstract worship as for example, the Hymn. "The hymn," says Hegel, "keeps within it the individuality of self-consciousness, and this individual character is at the same time perceived to be there universal. Devotion, kindled in everyone, is a spiritual stream which in all the manifold self-conscious units is conscious of itself as one and the same function in all alike and a simple state of being. Spirit, being this universal self-consciousness of everyone, holds in a single unity its pure inwardness as well as its objective existence for others and the independent self-existence of the individual units." (717)

Another means of abstract communication which served in a religious character was the Oracle. Hegel writes: "The Oracle, both in case of the god of the religion of art as well as of the preceding religions, is the necessary and the first form of divine utterance. For God's very principle implies that God is at once the essence of nature and of spirit, and hence has not merely natural but spiritual existence as well . . ." Further: "As the statue is existence in a state of rest, the other is existence in a state of transience. In the case of the former, objectivity is set free and is without the immediate presence of a self of its own; in the latter, on the other hand, objectivity is too much confined within the self, attains insufficiently to definite embodiment, and is, like time, no longer there just as soon as it is there." (720)

Hegel continues: "The religious Cult constitutes the process of the two sides—a process in which the divine embodiment in motion within the pure feeling element of self-consciousness and its embodiment at rest in the element of thinghood, reciprocally abandon the different characters each possesses, and the unity, which is the underlying principle of their being, becomes an existing fact. Here in the Cult, the self gives itself a consciousness of the Divine Being descending from its remoteness into it, and this Divine Being, which was formerly the unreal and merely objective, thereby receives the proper actuality of self-consciousness." (720) Hegel further elucidates:

"The practice of the religious Cult begins, therefore, with

the pure and simple "offering up" or "surrender" of a possession, which the owner, apparently without any profit whatsoever to himself, pours away or lets rise up in smoke. By so doing he renounces before the absolute Being of his pure consciousness all possession and right of property and enjoyment thereof; renounced personality and the reversion of his action to his self; and instead, reflects the act into the universal, into the Absolute Being rather than into himself. Conversely, however, the objective ultimate Being too is annihilated in that very process. The animal offered up is the symbol of a god; the fruits consumed are the actual living Ceres and Bacchus. In the former die the powers of the upper law the (Olympians) which has blood and actual life, in the latter the powers of the lower law (the Furies) which possesses in bloodless form secret and crafty power." (722)

"The sacrifice of the divine substance, so far as it is active, belongs to the side of self-consciousness. That this concrete act may be possible, the absolute Being must have from the start *implicitly* sacrificed *itself*. This it has done in the fact that it has given itself definite existence, and made itself an individual animal and fruit of the earth. The self actively sacrificing demonstrates in actual existence, and sets before its own consciousness, this already implicitly completed self-renunciation on the part of absolute Being; and replaces that immediate reality, which absolute Being has, by the higher, viz., that of the self making the sacrifice. For the unity which has arisen, and which is the outcome of transcending the singleness and separation of the two sides, is not merely negative destructive fate, but has a positive significance." (722)

The Living Work of Art

The cult has provided the basis for The Living Work of Art which is the next stage in the development of the Religious Consciousness. In this movement man makes the festival to his own honor. We now behold ultimate Being, which the cult revealed, clothed in the form of living man. Although there is the unity of Self-consciousness and Spiritual Being yet Spirit is not revealed owing to the fact that the balance between the two is lacking. Turning to Hegel: "Thus we here get the abstract moment of the living embodiment of ultimate Being, just as formerly we had the unity of both in the state of unconstrained emotional fervency. In the place of the statue man thus puts himself as the figure elaborated and moulded for perfectly free movement, just as the statue is the perfectly free state of quiescence. If every individual knows how to play the part at least of a torch-bearer, one of them comes prominently forward who is the very embodiment of the movement, the smooth elaboration, the fluent energy and force of all the members. He is a lively and living work of art, which matches strength with beauty; and to him is given, as a reward for his force and energy, the adornment, with which the statue was honoured (in the former type of religion), and the honor of being, amongst his own nation, instead of a god in stone, the highest bodily representation of what the essential Being of the nation is." (728)

"From the ceremonial cult, then, self-consciousness that is at peace and satisfied in its ultimate Being turns away, as also does the god that has entered into self-consciousness as into its place of habitation. This place is, by itself, the night of mere "Substance," or its pure individuality; but no longer the strained and striving individuality of the artist, which has not yet reconciled itself with its essential Being that is striving to become objective; it is the night (substance) satisfied, having its "pathos" within it and in want of nothing because it comes back from intuition, from objectivity which is overcome and superseded." (725-26)

"This "pathos" is, by itself, the Being of the Rising Sun, a Being, however, which has now "set" and disappeared within itself, and has its own "setting," self-consciousness, within it, and so contains existence and reality." (726)

"It has here traversed the process of its actualization. Descending from its pure essentiality and becoming an objective force of nature and the expressions of this force, it is an existence relative to an other, an objective existence for the self by which it is consumed. The silent inner being of selfless nature attains in its fruits the stage where nature, duly self-prepared and digested, offers itself as material for the life which has a self. In its being useful for food and drink it reaches its highest perfection. For therein it is the possibility of a higher existence, and comes in touch with spiritual existence. In its metamorphosis the spirit of the earth has developed and become partly a silently energizing substance, partly spiritual ferment; in the first case it is the feminine principle, the nursing mother, in the other the masculine principle, the self-driving force of self-conscious existence." (726)

"In this enjoyment, then, that orient "light" of the world is discovered for what it really is: Enjoyment is the Mystery of its being. For mysticism is not concealment of a secret, or ignorance; it consists in the self knowing itself to be one with Absolute Being, and in this latter, therefore, becoming revealed. Only the self is revealed to itself; or what is manifest is so merely in the immediate certainty of itself. But it is just in such certainty that simple absolute Being has been placed by the cult. As a thing that can be used, it has not only existence which is seen, felt, smelt, tasted; it is also object of desire, and, by actually being enjoyed, it becomes one with the self, and thereby disclosed completely to this self, and made manifest." (726-27)

"Still, however, it is only Absolute Spirit in the sense of this simple abstract Being, not as spirit *per se,* that is discovered to consciousnesss: i.e., it is merely immediate spirit, the spirit of nature. Its self-conscious life is therefore merely the mystery of the Bread and the Wine, of Ceres and Bacchus, not of the other, the strictly higher, gods (of Olympus), whose individuality includes, as an essential moment, self-consciousness as such. Spirit has not yet *qua* self-conscious spirit offered itself up to it, and the mystery of bread and wine is not yet the mystery of flesh and blood." (728)

THE PHENOMENOLOGY OF MIND

The Spiritual Work of Art

"Pure intuition of self in the sense of universal human nature takes, when the national spirit is actualized, this form: the national spirit combines with the others (which with it constitute, through nature and national conditions, one people), in a common undertaking, and for this task builds up a collective nation, and, with that, a collective heaven. This universality, to which spirit attains in its existence, is, neverthelesss, merely this first universality, which, to begin with, starts from the individuality of ethical life, has not yet overcome its immediacy, has not yet built up a single state out of these separate national elements. The ethical life of an actual spirit rests partly on the immediate confiding trust of the individuals in the whole of their nation, partly in the direct share which all, in spite of differences of class, take in the decisions and acts of their government. In the union, not in the first instance to secure a permanent order but merely for a common act, that freedom of participation on the part of each and all is for the nonce set aside. This first community of life is, therefore, an assemblage of individualities rather than the dominion and control of abstract thought, which would rob the individuals of their self-conscious share in the will and act of the whole." (731)

"The assembly of national spirits constitutes a circle of forms and shapes, which now embraces the whole of nature, as well as the whole ethical world. They too are under the supreme command rather than the supreme dominion of the One. By themselves, they are the universal substances embodying what the self-conscious essential reality inherently is and does. This, however, constitutes the moving force, and, in the first instance, at least the centre, with which those universal entities are concerned, and which, to begin with, seems to unite in a merely accidental way all that they variously accomplish. But it is the return of the divine Being to self-consciousness which already contains the reason that self-consciousness forms the centre for those divine forces, and conceals their essential unity in the first instance under the guise of a friendly external relation between both worlds.

"The same universality, which belongs to this content, attaches necessarily also to that form of consciousness in which the content appears. It is no longer the concrete acts of the cult; it is an action which is not indeed raised as yet to the level of the notion, but only to that of ideas, the synthetic connection of self-conscious and external existence. The element in which these presented ideas exist, language, is the earliest language, the *Epic* as such, which contains the universal content, at any rate universal in the sense of completeness of the world presented, though not in the sense of universality of thought. The Minstrel is the individual and actual spirit from whom, as a subject of this world, it is produced, and by whom it is borne. His "pathos" is not the deafening power of nature, but Mnemosyne, Recollection, a gradually evolved inwardness, the memory of an essential mode of being once directly present. He is the organ and instrument whose content is passing away; it is not his own self which is of any account, but his muse, his universal song. What, however, is present in fact, has the form of an inferential process, where the one extreme of universality, the world of gods, is connected with individuality, the minstrel, through the middle term of particularity. The middle term is the nation in its heroes, who are individual men like the minstrel, but only ideally presented, and thereby at the same time universal like the free extreme of universality, the gods."

"In this Epic, then what is inherently established in the cult, the relation of the divine to the human, is set forth and displayed as a whole to consciousness." (732-33)

Along with the Epic the Spiritual Work of Art produces also The Tragedy and The Comedy. Both of these modes of expression are given a detailed exposition by Hegel. Bringing to a close the remarks on Tragedy, Hegel writes: "Because actual self-consciousness is still distinguished from the substance and fate, it is partly the chorus, or rather the crowd looking on, whom this movement of the divine life fills with fear as being something alien and strange, or in whom this movement, as something closely touching themselves, produces merely the emotion of passive pity. Partly again, so far as consciousness co-operates and belongs to the various characters, this alliance is of an external kind, is a hypocrisy—because the true union, that of self, fate, and substance, is not yet present. The hero who appears before the onlookers, breaks up into his mask and actor, into the person of the play and his actual self." (744)

"The self-consciousness of the hero must step forth from its mask and be represented as knowing itself to be the fate both of the gods of the chorus and of the absolute powers themselves, and as being no longer separated from the chorus, the universal consciousness." (745)

Turning to Comedy, Hegel's summary is as follows: "The religion of art is fulfilled and consummated in it, and is come full circle. Through the fact that it is the individual consciousness in its certainty of self which manifests itself as this absolute power, this latter has lost the form of something ideally presented (vorgestellt), separated from and alien to consciousness in general—as were the statue and also the living embodiment of beauty or the content of the Epic and the powers and persons of Tragedy. Nor again is the unity the unconscious unity of the cult and the mysteries; rather the self proper of the actor coincides with the part he impersonates, just as the onlooker is perfectly at home in what is represented before him, and sees himself playing in the drama before him. What this self-consciousness beholds, is that whatever assumes the form of essentiality as against self-consciousnesss, is instead dissolved within it—within its thought, its existence and action—and is quite at its mercy. It is the return of everything universal into certainty of self, a certainty which, in consequence, is this complete loss of fear of everything strange and complete loss of substantial reality on the part of what is alien and external. Such certainty is a state of spiritual good health and self-abandonment thereto, on the part of consciousness, in a way that, outside this kind of comedy, is not to be found anywhere." (749)

VI

FREE CONCRETE MIND
REVEALED RELIGION

Revealed Religion

"Spirit, . . . has in it two sides, which are . . . represented as the two converse propositions: one is this, that substance empties itself of itself, and becomes self-consciousness; the other is the converse, that self-consciousness empties itself of itself and makes itself into the form of "thing," or makes itself universal self. Both sides have in this way met each other, and, in consequence their true union has arisen. The relinquishment or "kenosis" on the part of the substance, its becoming self-consciousness, expresses the transition into the opposite, the unconscious transition of necessity, in other words, that it is *implicitly* self-consciousness. Conversely, the emptying of self-consciousness expresses this, that implicitly it is Universal Being, or—because the self is pure self-existence, which is at home with itself in its opposite—that the substance is self-consciousness explicitly *for the self,* and, just on that account, is spirit. Of this spirit, which has left the form of substance behind, and enters existence in the shape of self-consciousness, we may say, therefore—if we wish to use terms drawn from the process of natural generation—that it has a real mother but a potential or an implicit father. For actual reality, or self-consciousness, and implicit being in the sense of substance are its two moments; and by the reciprocity of their kenosis, each relinquishing or "emptying" itself of itself and becoming the other, spirit thus comes into existence as their unity." (755-756)

"The immediate inherent nature of Spirit, which takes on the concrete *actual world-spirit* has reached this knowledge of itself. It is then too that this knowledge first enters its consciousness, and enters it as truth. How that came about has already been explained." (757)

"That Absolute Spirit has taken on the shape of self-consciousness inherently, and therefore also consciously to itself —this appears now as the belief of the world, the belief that spirit exists *in fact* as a definite self-consciousness, i.e., as an actual human being; that spirit is an object for immediate experience; that the believing mind *sees, feels,* and *hears* this divinity. Taken thus it is not imagination, not a fancy; it is actual in the believer. Consciousness in that case does not set out from its own inner life, does not start from thought, and in itself combine the thought of God with existence; rather it sets out from immediate present existence, and recognizes God in it. . . . (758)

"The self of the existent spirit has in that way the form of complete immediacy. It is neither set up as something thought, or imaginatively represented, nor as something produced, as is the case with the immediate self in natural religion, or again in religion as art. Rather, this concrete God is beheld sensuously and immediately as a self, as a real individual human being; only so is it a self-consciousness." (758)

"This incarnation of the Divine Being, its having essentially and directly the shape of self-consciousness, is the simple content of Absolute Religion. Here the Divine Being is known as Spirit; this religion is the Divine Being's consciousness concerning itself that it is Spirit. For spirit is knowledge of self in a state of alienation of self: spirit is the Being which is the process of retaining identity with itself in its otherness. This, however, is Substance, so far as in its accidents substance at the same time is turned back into itself; and is so, not as being indifferent towards something unessential and, consequently, as finding itself in some alien element, but as being there within itself, i.e., so far as it is subject or self." (758)

"In this form of religion the Divine Being is, on that account, *revealed.* It being revealed obviously consists in this, that what it is, is known. It is, however, known just in its being known as spirit, as a Being which is essentially self-consciousness." (758-59)

"Here, then, we find as a fact consciousness, or the general form in which Being is aware of Being—the shape which Being adopts—to be identical with its self-consciousness. This shape is itself a self-consciousness; it is thus at the same time an existent object; and this existence possesses equally directly the significance of pure thought, of Absolute Being." (760)

"The Absolute Being existing as a concrete actual self-consciousness, seems to have descended from its eternal pure simplicity; but in fact it has, in so doing, attained for the first time its highest nature, its supreme reach of being. For only when the notion of Being has reached its simple purity of nature, is it *both* the absolute abstraction, which is pure thought and hence the pure singleness of self, *and* immediacy or objective being, on account of its simplicity." (760)

"What is called sense-consciousness is just this pure abstraction; it is this kind of thought for which being is the immediate. The lowest is thus at the same time the highest; the revealed which has come forth entirely to the surface is just therein the deepest reality. That the Supreme Being is seen, heard, etc., as an existent self-consciousness, this is, in very truth, the culmination and consummation of its notion. And through this consummation, the Divine Being is given and exists immediately in its character as Divine Being. . . ." (760)

"For this unity of being and thought is self-consciousness and actually exists; in other words, the thought-constituted unity has at the same time this concrete shape and form of what it is. God, then, is here revealed, as He is; He actually exists as He is in Himself; He is real as Spirit. God is attainable in pure speculative knowledge alone, and only *is* in that knowledge, and is merely that knowledge itself, for He is spirit; and this speculative knowledge is the knowledge furnished by revealed religion. That knowledge knows God to be thought, or pure Essence; and knows this thought as actual being and as a real existence, and existence as the negativity of itself, hence as Self, an individual "this" and a universal self. It is just this that revealed religion knows." (761)

"The hopes and expectations of preceding ages pressed forward to, and were solely directed towards this revelation, the vision of what Absolute Being is, and the discovery of themselves therein. This joy, the joy of seeing itself in Absolute Being, becomes realized in self-consciousness, and seizes the whole world. For the Absolute is Spirit, it is the simple movement of those pure abstract moments, which expresses just this—that Ultimate Reality is then, and not till then, known as Spirit when it is seen and beheld as immediate self-consciousness. . . ." (761)

"Looking at this more precisely, spirit, when self-consciousness is immediate, is "this" individual self-consciousness set up in contrast to the universal self-consciousness. It is a one, an excluding unit, which appears to that consciousness, for which it exists, in the as yet impervious form of a sensuous other, an unresolved entity in the sphere of sense. This other does not yet know spirit to be its own; in other words, spirit, in its form as an individual self, does not yet exist as equally universal self, as *all* self. Or again, the shape it assumes has not as yet the form of the notion, i.e., of the universal self, of the self which in its immediate actual reality is at once transcended, is thought, universality, without losing its reality in this universality." (762)

"The preliminary and similarly immediate form of this universality is, however, not at once the form of thought itself, of the notion as notion; it is the universality of actual reality, it is the "allness," the collective totality, of the selves, and is the elevation of existence into the sphere of figurative thought *(Vorstellung)*; just as in general, to take a concrete example, the "this" of sense, when transcended, is first of all the "thing" of "perception," and is not yet the "universal" of "understanding." (762)

"This individual human being, then, which Absolute Being is revealed to be, goes through in its own case as an individual the process found in sense existence. He is the *immediately* present God; in consequence, His being passes over into His *having been*. Consciousness, for which God is thus sensuously present, ceases to see Him, to hear Him: it *has* seen Him, it *has* heard Him. And it is because it only *has* seen and heard Him, that it first becomes itself spiritual consciousness; or, in other words, he has now arisen in Spirit, as He formerly rose before consciousness as an object existing in the sphere of sense. For, a consciousness which sees and hears Him by sense, is one which is itself merely an immediate consciousness, which has not cancelled and transcended the disparateness of objectivity, has not withdrawn it into pure thought, but knows this objectively presented individual, and not itself, as spirit. In the disappearance of the immediate existence of what is known to be Absolute Being, immediacy acquires its negative moment. Spirit remains the immediate self of actual reality, but in the form of the universal self-consciousness of a religious communion, a self-consciousness which rests in its own proper substance, just as in it this subtance is univeral subject: it is not the individual subject by himself, but the individual along with the consciousness of the communion, and what he is for this communion is the complete whole of the individual spirit."

"The conditions "past" and "distance" are, however, merely the imperfect form in which the immediateness gets mediated or made universal; this is merely dipped superficially in the element of thought, is kept there as a sensuous mode of immediacy, and not made one with the nature of thought itself. It is lifted out of sense merely into the region of pictorial presentation, for this is the synthetic (external) connection of sensuous immediacy and its universality or thought . . ." (762)

"Spirit is content of its consciousness to begin with in the form of pure substance, in other words, it is content of its pure consciousness. This element of thought is the process of descending into existence, or individuality. The middle term between these two is their synthetic connection, the consciousness of passing into otherness, the process of imaginative presentation as such. The third stage is the return from this presentation and from that otherness; in other words, it is the element of self-consciousness itself . . ." (765)

"There are thus three moments to be distinguished: Essential Being; explicit Self-existence, which is the express otherness of essential Being, and for which that Being is object; and Self-existence or Self-knowledge *in* that other. The essential Being beholds only itself in its Self-existence, in its objective otherness. In thus emptying itself, in this kenosis, it is merely within itself: the independent Self-existence which excludes itself from essential Being is the knowledge of itself on the part of essential Being. It is the "Word," the Logos, which when spoken empties the speaker of himself, outwardizes him, and leaves him behind emptied, but is as immediately perceived, and only this act of self-perceiving himself is the actual existence of the "Word." Hence, then, the distinctions which are set up are just as immediately resolved as they are made, and are just as directly made as they are resolved, and the truth and the reality consist precisely in this self-closed circular process." (767)

"This movement within itself expresses the Absolute Being *qua* Spirit. Absolute Being, when not grasped as this process is merely an empty word. Since its moments are grasped *purely as* moments, they are notions in restless activity, which *are* merely in being inherently their own opposite, and in finding their rest in the whole. But the pictorial thought of the religious communion is not this notional thinking, it has the content without its necessity; and instead of the form of the notion it brings into the realm of pure consciousness the natural relations of Father and Son. . . ." (767)

"Merely eternal, or *abstract* Spirit, then, becomes an other to itself: it enters existence, and, in the first instance, enters *immediate* existence. It creates a World. This "Creation" is the word which pictorial thought uses to convey the notion itself in its absolute movement; or to express the fact that the simple which has been expressed as absolute, or pure thought, just because it is abstract, is really the negative, and hence opposed to itself, *the other* of itself; or because, to state the same in yet another way, what is put forward as essential Being is simple immediacy, bare existence, but *qua* immediacy or existence, is without Self, and, lacking thus inwardness, is passive, or exists *for* another. This existence for another is at the same time a world. Spirit, in the character of existing for another, is the undisturbed separate subsistence of those moments formerly enclosed within pure thought, is, therefore, the dissolution of their simple universality, and their dispersion into their own particularity." (770)

"The world, however, is not merely Spirit thus thrown out and dispersed into the plenitude of existence and the external order imposed on it; for since Spirit is essentially the simple Self, this self is likewise present therein. The world is objectively existent spirit, which is *individual* self, that has consciousness and distinguishes itself as other, as world, from itself. In the way this individual self is thus immediately established at first, it is not yet conscious of being Spirit; it thus does not exist as Spirit; it may be called "innocent," but not strictly "good." In order that in fact it may be self and Spirit, is has first to become objectively an other to itself, in the same way that the Eternal Being manifests itself as the process of being self-identical in its otherness. Since this spirit is determined as yet only as immediately existing, or dispersed into the diverse multiplicity of its conscious life, its becoming "other" means that knowledge concentrates itself upon itself. Immediate existence turns into thought, or merely sense-consciousness turns round into consciousness of thought; and, moreover, because that thought has come from immediacy or is conditioned thought, it is not pure knowledge, but thought which contains otherness, and is, thus, the self-opposed thought of good and evil. Man is pictorially represented by the religious mind in this way: it happened once as an event, with no necessity about it, that he lost the form of harmonious unity with himself by plucking the fruits of the tree of the knowledge of good and evil, and was driven from the state of innocence, from Paradise, from the garden with all its creatures, and from nature offering its bounties without man's toil." (770-771)

"Since this self-concentration on the part of the existent consciousness has straightway the character of becoming discordant with itself, Evil appears as the first actual expression of the self-concentrated consciousness. And because the thoughts of good and evil are utterly opposed, and this opposition is not yet broken down, this consciousness is essentially and merely evil. At the same time, however, owing to just this very opposition, there is present also the good consciousness opposing the one that is evil, and again their relation to each other. In so far as immediate existence turns round into thought, and self-concentration is partly itself thought, while partly again the transition to otherness on the part of the inner self (Wesen), is thereby more precisely determined—the fact of becoming evil can be removed further backwards away out of the actually existing world and transferred to the very earliest realm of thought. It may thus be said that it was the very first-born Son of Light (Lucifer) who, by becoming self-concentrated, fell, but that in his place another was at once created. Such a form of expression as "fallen," belonging merely to figurative thought, and not to the notion, just like the term "Son," either (we may say) transmutes and lowers the moments of the notion to the level of imaginative thought, or transfers pictures into the realm of thought. . . ." (771)

"Good and Evil were the specific distinctions of thought which we found. Since their opposition is not yet broken down, and they are represented as essential realities of thought, each of them independent by itself, man is the self with no essential reality of his own and the mere ground which couples them together, and on which they exist and war with one another. But these universal powers of good and evil belong all the same to the self, or the self is their actuality. From this point of view it thus comes about that, as evil is nothing else than the self-concentration of the natural existence of spirit, conversely, good enters into actual reality and appears as an (objectively) existing self-consciousness. That which, when Spirit is interpreted in terms of pure thought, is in general merely hinted at as the Divine Being's transition into otherness, here, for figurative thinking, comes nearer its realization: the realization is taken to consist in the Divine Being "humbling" Itself, and renouncing its abstract nature and unreality. The other aspect, that of evil, is taken by imagination as an event extraneous and alien to the Divine Being: to grasp evil in the Divine Being itself as the wrath of God—that is the supreme effort, the severest strain, of which figurative thought, wrestling with its own limitations, is capable; an effort which, since it is devoid of the notion, remains a fruitless struggle." (773)

"The alienation of the Divine Nature is thus set up in its double-sided form: the self of Spirit, and its simple thought, are the two moments whose absolute unity is Spirit itself. Its alienation with itself consists in the two falling apart from each other, and in the one having an unequal value as against the other. This disparateness is, therefore, twofold in character, and two connections arise, which have in common the moments just given. In the one, the Divine Being stands for what is essential, while natural existence and the self are unessential and are to be cancelled. In the other, on the contrary, it is self-existence which passes for what is essential and the simply Divine for unessential. Their mediating, though still empty ground, is existence in general, the bare community of their two moments." (773-774)

"The dissolution of this opposition does not take effect through the struggle between the two elements, which are pictured as separate and independent Beings. Just in virtue of their independence each must inherently, through its own notion, dissolve itself in itself. The struggle only takes place where both cease to be this mixture of thought and independent existence, and confront each other merely as thoughts. For there, being determinate notions, they essentially exist merely in the relation of opposition; *qua* independent, on the other hand, they have their essential nature outside their opposition; their movement is thus free, self-determined, and peculiar to themselves. If, then, we consider the movement of both as it is in themselves—i.e., as it is essentially—their movement starts only in that one of the two which has the character of being inherently essential as contrasted with the other. This is pictured as a spontaneous action; but the necessity for its self-abandonment lies in the notion that what is inherently essential, and gets this specific character merely through opposition, has just on that account no real independent subsistence. Therefore that element which has for its essence, not independent self-existence, but simple being, is what empties and abandons itself, gives itself unto death, and so reconciles Absolute Being with its own self. For in this process it manifests itself as spirit: the abstract Being is estranged from itself, it has natural existence and the reality of an actual self. This its otherness, or its being sensuously present, is taken back again by the second process of becoming "other," and is affirmed as superseded, as universal. Thereby the Divine Being has come to itself in the sphere of the sensuous present; the immediate existence of actual reality has ceased to be something alien or external to the Divine, by being sublated, universal: this death (of immediacy) is therefore its rising anew as spirit. When the self-conscious Being cancels and transcends its immediate present, it is a universal self-consciousness. This notion of the transcended individual self which is Absolute Being, immediately expresses therefore the establishment of a communion which, while hitherto having its abode in the sphere of pictorial thought, now returns into itself as the Self: and Spirit thus passes from the second element constituting it—figurative thought—and goes over to the third—self-consciousness as such." (775)

"If we further consider the kind of procedure that pictorial thinking adopts as it goes along, we find in the first place the expression that the Divine Being "takes on" human nature.

Here it is *eo ipso* asserted that implicitly and inherently the two are not separate: just as in the statement, that the Divine Being from the beginning empties Itself of Itself, that its objective existence becomes concentrated in Itself and becomes evil, it is not asserted but implied that *per se* this evil existence is *not* something alien to the Divine nature. Absolute Being would be merely an empty name if in very truth there were any other being external to it, if there were a "fall" from it. The aspect of self-concentration really constitutes the essential moment of the self of Spirit." (775)

"That this self-centeredness, whence primarily comes its reality, belongs to the Divine Being—while this is for *us* a notion, and so as far as it *is* a notion—appears to pictorial thinking as an inconceivable happening. The inherent and essential nature assumes for figurative thought the form of an indifferent objective fact. The thought, however, that those apparently mutually repugnant moments, absolute Being and self-existent Self, are not inseparable, comes also before this figurative way of thinking (since it does possess the real content), but that thought appears *afterwards,* in the form that the Divine Being empties Itself of Itself and is made flesh. This figurative idea, which in this manner is still immediate and hence not spiritual, i.e., it knows the human form assumed by the Divine as merely a particular form, not yet as a universal form—becomes spiritual for this consciousness in the process whereby God, who has assumed shape and form, surrenders again His immediate existence, and returns to His essential Being. The essential Being is then Spirit only when it is reflected into itself." (775-776)

"The reconciliation of the Divine Being with its other as a whole, and, specifically, with the *thought* of this other—evil—is thus presented here in a figurative way. If this reconciliation is expressed *conceptually,* by saying it consists in the fact that evil is inherently the same as what goodness is, or again that the Divine Being is the same as nature in its entire extent, just as nature separated from God is simply nothingness—then this must be looked at as an unspiritual mode of expression which is bound to give rise to misunderstandings. When evil is the *same* as goodness, then evil is just not evil nor goodness good; on the contrary, both are really done away with—evil in general, self-centered self-existence, and goodness, self-less simplicity. Since in this way they are both expressed in terms of their notion, the unity of the two is at once apparent; for self-centered self-existence is simply knowledge; and what is self-less simplicity is similarly pure self-existence centered within itself. Hence, if it must be said that good and evil in this their conception, i.e., so far as they are *not* good and evil, are the same, just as certainly it must be said that they are not the same, but absolutely different; for simple self-existence, or again pure knowledge, are equally pure negativity or *per se* absolute distinction. It is only these two propositions that make the whole complete; and when the first is asserted and asseverated, it must be met and opposed by insisting on the other with immovable obstinacy. Since both are equally right, they are both equally wrong, and their wrong consists in taking such abstract forms as "the same" and "not the same," "identity" and "non-identity," to be something true, fixed, real, and in resting on them. Neither the one nor the other has truth; their truth is just their movement, the process in which simple sameness is abstraction and thus absolute distinction, while this again, being distinction *per se,* is distinguished from itself and so is self-identity. Precisely this is what we have in sameness of the Divine Being and Nature in general and human nature in particular: the former is Nature so far as it is not essential Being; Nature is Divine in its essential Being. But it is in Spirit that we find both abstract aspects affirmed as they truly are, viz., as cancelled and preserved at once: and this way of affirming them cannot be expressed by the judgment, by the soulless word "is," the copula of the judgment. In the same way Nature is nothing outside its essential Being (God); but this nothing itself *is* all the same; it is absolute abstraction, therefore pure thought or self-centeredness, and with its moment of opposition to spiritual unity it is the principle of Evil. The difficulty people find in these conceptions is due solely to sticking to the term "is," and forgetting the character of thought, where the moments as much *are* as they *are not*—are only the process which is Spirit. It is this spiritual unity—unity where the distinctions are merely in the form of moments, or as transcended—which became known to pictorial thinking in that atoning reconciliation spoken of above. And since this unity is the universality of self-consciousness, self-consciousness has ceased to be figurative or pictorial in its thinking; the process has turned back into it." (776-77)

"Spirit thus takes up its position in the third element, in universal self-consciousness: Spirit is its own community. The movement of this community being that of self-consciousness, which distinguishes itself from its figurative idea, consists in explicitly bringing out what has implicitly become established. The dead Divine Man, or Human God, is implicitly universal self-consciousness; he has to become explicitly so for this self-consciousness. Or, since this self-consciousness constitutes one side of the opposition involved in figurative thought, viz., the side of evil, which takes natural existence and individual self-existence to be the essential reality—this aspect, which is pictured as independent, and not yet as a moment, has, on account of its independence, to raise itself in and for itself to the level of spirit; it has to reveal the process of Spirit in its self." (778)

"This particular self-consciousness is Spirit in natural form, natural spirit: self has to withdraw from this natural existence and enter into itself, become self-centered; that would mean, it has to become evil. But this aspect is already *per se* evil: entering into itself consists, therefore, in persuading itself that natural existence is what is evil. By picture-thinking the world is supposed actually to become evil and be evil as an actual existent phenomenon. By self-consciousness as such, however, this pictured truth, as regards its form, is considered to be merely a moment that is already superseded and transcended; for the self is the negative, and hence knowledge—a knowledge which is a pure act of consciousness within itself. This moment of the negative must in like manner find expression in the content. Since, that is to say, the essential Being is inherently and from the start reconciled with itself and is a spiritual unity, in which what are part of figurative thought receives here the opposite significance to that which it has before. By this means each meaning finds its completion in the other, and the content is then and thereby a spiritual content. Since the specific determinateness of each is just as much its opposite, unity in otherness—spiritual reality—is achieved: just as formerly we saw the opposite meanings combined objectively (*für uns*) or in themselves, and even the abstract forms of "the same" and "not-the-same," "identity" and "non-identity" cancelled one another and were transcended." (779)

"If, then, from the point of view of figurative thought, the becoming self-centered on the part of the natural self-consciousness was actually existing evil, that process of becoming fixed in itself is in the sphere of self-consciousness, the *knowledge of evil* as something that *per se* belongs to existence. This knowledge is certainly a process of becoming evil, but merely of the *thought* of evil, and is therefore recognized as the first moment of reconciliation. For, being a return into self out of the immediacy of nature, which is specifically characterized as evil, it is a forsaking of that immediacy, and a dying to sin. It is not natural existence as such that consciousness forsakes, but natural existence that is at the same time known to be evil. The immediate process of becoming self-centered, is just as much a mediate process: it presupposes itself, i.e., is its own ground and reason: the reason for self-concentrating is because nature has *per se* already done so. Because of evil man must be self-centered (*in sich gehen*); but evil is itself the state of self-concentration. This first movement is just on that account itself merely immediate, is its simple notion, because it is the same as what its ground or reason is. The movement, or the process of passing into otherness, has therefore still to come on the scene in its own more peculiar form." (779)

"Besides this immediacy, then, the mediation of figurative thought is necessary. The knowledge of nature as the untrue existence of spirit, and this universality of self which has arisen within the life of the self—these constitute implicitly the reconciliation of spirit with itself. This implicit state is apprehended by the self-consciousness, that does not comprehend (*begreifen*), in the form of an objective existence, and as something presented to it figuratively. Conceptual comprehension (*Begreifen*), therefore, does not mean for it a grasping (*Ergreifen*) of this conception (*Begriff*) which knows natural existence when cancelled and transcended to be universal and thus reconciled with itself; but rather a grasping of the imaginative idea (*Vorstellung*) that the Divine Being is reconciled with its existence through an event—the event of God's emptying Himself of His Divine Being through His factual Incarnation and His Death. The grasping of this idea now expresses more specifically what was formerly called in figurative thinking spiritual resurrection, or the process by which God's individual self-consciousness becomes the universal, becomes the religious communion. The death of the Divine Man, *qua* death, is abstract negativity, the immediate result of the process which terminates only in the universality belonging to nature. In spiritual self-consciousness death loses this natural significance; it passes into its true conception, the conception just mentioned. Death then ceases to signify what it means directly—the non-existence of *this* individual—and becomes transfigured into the universality of the spirit, which lives in its own communion, dies there daily, and daily rises again." (780)

"That which belongs to the sphere of pictorial thought—viz., that Absolute Spirit presents the nature of spirit in its existence, *qua* individual or rather *qua* particular—is thus here transferred to self-consciousness itself, to the knowledge which maintains itself in its otherness. This self-consciousness does not therefore really die, as the particular person is pictorially imagined to have really died; its particularity expires in its universality, i.e., in its *knowledge,* which is essential Being reconciling itself with itself. That immediately preceding element of figurative thinking is thus here affirmed as transcended, has, in other words, returned into the self, into its notion. What was in the former merely an (objective) existent has come to assume the form of *Subject.* By that very fact the first element too, pure thought and the spirit eternal therein, are no longer away beyond the mind thinking pictorially nor beyond the self; rather the return of the whole into itself consists just in containing all moments within itself. When the death of the mediator is grasped by the self, this means the sublation of his factuality, of his particular independent existence: this particular self-existence has become universal self-consciousness." (781)

VII

ABSOLUTE KNOWLEDGE

"The Spirit manifested in revealed religion has not as yet surmounted its attitude of consciousness as such; or, what is the same thing, its actual self-consciousness is not at this stage the object it is aware of. Spirit as a whole and the moments distinguished in it fall within the sphere of figurative thinking, and within the form of objectivity. The *content* of this figurative thought is Absolute Spirit. All that remains to be done now is to cancel and transcend this bare form; or better, because the form appertains to consciousness as such, its true meaning must have already come out in the shapes or modes consciousness has assumed." (789)

"The surmounting of the object of consciousness in this way is not to be taken one-sidedly as meaning that the object showed itself returning into the self. It has a more definite meaning: it means that the object as such presented itself to the self as a vanishing factor; and, furthermore, that the emptying of self-consciousness itself establishes thinghood, and that this externalization of self-consciousness has not merely negative but positive significance, a significance not merely *for us* or *per se,* but for self-consciousness itself. The negative of the object, its cancelling its own existence, gets, for self-consciousness, a positive significance; or, self-consciousness knows this nothingness of the object because on the one hand self-consciousness itself externalizes itself; for in doing so it establishes itself as object, or, by reason of the indivisible unity characterizing its self-existence, sets up the object as its self. On the other hand, there is also this other moment in the process, that self-consciousness has just as really cancelled, and superseded this self-relinquishment and objectification, and has resumed them into itself, and is thus at home with itself in its otherness as such. This is the movement of consciousness, and in this process consciousness is the totality of its moments." (790)

"Consciousness, at the same time, must have taken up a relation to the object in all its aspects and phases, and have grasped its meaning from the point of view of each of them. This totality of its determinate characteristics makes the object *per se* or inherently a spiritual reality; and it becomes so in truth for consciousness, when the latter apprehends every individual one of them as self, i.e., when it takes up towards them the spiritual relationship just spoken of."

"The object is, then, partly immediate existence, a *thing* in general—corresponding to immediate consciousness; partly an alteration of itself, its relatedness, (or existence-for-another and existence-for-self), *determinateness*—corresponding to perception; partly essential being or in the form of a *universal*—corresponding to understanding. The object as a whole is the mediated result (the syllogism) or the passing of universality into individuality through specification, as also the reverse process from individual to universal through cancelled individuality or specific determination." (790)

"These three specific aspects, then, determine the ways in which consciousness must know the object as itself. . . ." (790)

"Action is the first inherent division of the simple unity of the notion, and the return out of this division. This first movement turns round into the second, since the element of recognition puts itself forward as simple knowledge of duty in contrast to the distinction and diremption that lie in action as such and, in this way, form a rigid reality confronting action. In pardon, however, we saw how this rigid fixity gives way and renounces its claims. Reality has here, *qua immediate existence,* no other significance for self-consciousness than that of being pure knowledge; similarly, *qua determinate existence,* or *qua* relation, what is self-opposed is a knowledge partly of this purely individual self, partly of knowledge *qua* universal. Herein it is established, at the same time, that the third moment, universality, or the essence, means for each of the two opposite factors merely knowledge. Finally they also cancel the empty opposition that still remains, and are the knowledge of ego as identical with ego:—this individual self which is immediately pure knowledge or universal." (793)

"This reconciliation of consciousness with self-consciousness thus proves to be brought about in a double-sided way; in the one case, in the religious mind, in the other case, in consciousness itself as such. They are distinguished *inter se* by the fact that the one is this reconciliation in the form of implicit immanence, the other in the form of explicit self-existence. As we have considered them, they at the beginning fall apart. In the order in which the modes or shapes of consciousness came before us, consciousness has reached the individual moments of that order, and also their unification, long before ever religion gave its object the shape of actual self-consciousness. The unification of both aspects is not yet brought to light; it is this that winds up this series of embodiments of spirit, for in it spirit gets to the point where it knows itself not only as it is inherently in itself, or in terms of its absolute content, nor only as it is (objectively) for itself in terms of its bare form devoid of content, or in terms of self-consciousness, but as it is in its self-completeness, as it is in itself and for itself. . . ." (793-794)

"That is to say, the "beautiful soul" is its own knowledge of itself in its pure transparent unity—self-consciousness, which knows this pure knowledge of pure inwardness to be spirit, is not merely intuition of the divine, but the self-intuition of God Himself." (795)

Since this notion keeps itself fixedly opposed to its realization, it is the one-sided shape which we saw before disappear into thin air, but also positively relinquish itself and advance further. Through this act of realization, this objectless self-consciousness ceases to hold fast by itself, the determinateness of the notion in contrast with its fulfillment is cancelled and done away with. Its self-consciousness attains the form of universality; and what remains is its true notion, the notion i.e., in unity with its externalization. It is knowledge of pure knowledge, not in the sense of an abstract essence which *is this* knowledge, this individual pure self-consciousness which is therefore at the same time a genuine *object;* for this notion is the self-existing self." (795)

"Now what in the first instance takes place implicitly is at once for consciousness, and is duplicated as well—is both for consciousness and is its self-existence or its own proper action. The same thing that is already inherently established, thus repeats itself now as knowledge thereof on the part of consciousness and as conscious action. Each lays aside for the other the independence of character with which each appears confronting the other. This waiving of independence is the same renunciation of the one-sidedness of the notion as constituted implicitly the beginning; but it is now its own act of renunciation, just as the notion renounced is its own notion. That implicit nature of the beginning is in truth as such mediated, because it is negativity; it now establishes itself as it is in its truth; and the negative element exists as a determinate quality which each has for the other, and is essentially self-cancelling, self-transcending. The one of the two parts of the opposition is the disparity between existence within itself, in its individuality, and universality; the other, disparity between its abstract universality and the self. The former dies to its self-existence, and relinquishes itself, makes confession; the latter renounces the rigidity of its abstract universality, and thereby dies to its lifeless self and its inert universality; so that the former is completed through the moment of universality, which is the essence, and the latter through universality, which is self. By this process of action spirit has come to light in the form of pure universality of knowledge, which is self-consciousness as self-consciousness, which is simple unity of knowledge. It is through action that spirit is spirit so as definitely to exist; it raises its existence into the sphere of thought and hence into absolute opposition, and returns out of it through and within this very opposition." (796-97)

"Thus, then, what was in religion content, or a way of imagining (*Vorstellen*) an other, is here the action proper of the self. The notion is the connecting principle securing that the content is the action proper of the self. For this notion is, as we see, the knowledge that the action of the self within itself is all that is essential and all existence, the knowledge of this Subject as Substance and of the Substance as this knowledge of its action. What we have done here, in addition, is simply to gather together the particular moments, each of which in principle exhibits the life of spirit in its entirety, and again to secure the notion in the form of the notion, whose content was disclosed in these moments, and which had already presented itself in the form of a mode or shape of consciousness." (797)

"This last embodiment of spirit—spirit which at once gives its complete and true content the form of self, and thereby realizes its notion, and in doing so remains within its own notion—this is *Absolute Knowledge.* It is spirit in the shape of spirit, it is knowledge which comprehends through notions. Truth is here not merely *in itself* absolutely identical with certainty; it has also the shape, the character of certainty of self; or in its existence—i.e., for spirit knowing it—it is in the *form* of knowledge of itself. Truth is the content, which in religion is not as yet at one with its certainty. This identification, however, is secured when the content has received the shape of self. By this means, what constitutes the very essence, viz., the notion, comes to have the nature of existence, i.e., assumes the form of what is objective to consciousness. Spirit, appearing before consciousness in this element of existence, or what is here the same thing, produced by it in this element, is systematic Science." (798)

"The nature, moments, and process of this knowledge have then shown themselves to be such that this knowledge is pure self-existence of self-consciousness." (798)

"Time is just the notion definitely existent, and presented to consciousness in the form of empty intuition. Hence spirit necessarily appears in time, and it appears in time so long as it does not grasp its pure notion, i.e., so long as it does not annul time. Time is the pure self in external form, apprehended in intuition, and not grasped and understood by the self, it is the notion apprehended only through intuition. When this notion grasps itself, it supersedes its time character, (conceptually) comprehends intuition, and is intuition comprehended and comprehending. Time therefore appears as spirit's destiny and necessity, where spirit is not yet complete within itself; it is the necessity compelling spirit to enrich the share self-consciousness has in consciousness, to put into motion the immediacy of the inherent nature (which is the form in which the substance is present in consciousness); or, conversely to realize and make manifest what is inherent, regarded as inward and immanent, to make manifest that which is at first within—i.e., to vindicate it for spirit's certainty of self." (800)

"For this reason it must be said that nothing is known which does not fall within experience, or (as it is also expressed) which is not *felt* to be true, which is not given as an inwardly revealed eternal verity, as a sacred object of belief, or whatever other expressions we care to employ. For experience just consists in this, that the content—and the content is spirit—in its inherent nature is substance and so object of consciousness. But this substance, which is spirit, is the development of itself explicitly to what it is inherently and implicitly; and only as this process of reflecting itself into itself is it essentially and in truth spirit. It is inherently the movement which is the process of knowledge—the transforming of that inherent nature into explicitness, of Substance into Subject, of the object of consciousness into the object of self-consciousness, i.e., into an object that is at the same time transcended—in other words, into the notion. This transforming process is a cycle that returns into itself, a cycle that presupposes its beginning, and reaches its beginning only at the end. So far as spirit, then, is of necessity this self-distinction, it appears as a single whole, intuitively apprehended, over against its simple self-consciousness. And since that whole is what is distinguished, it is distinguished into the intuitively apprehended pure notion, Time, and the content, the inherent, implicit, nature. Substance, *qua* subject, involves the necessity, at first an *inner* necessity, to set forth in itself what it inherently is, to show itself to be spirit. The completed expression in objective form is—and is only when completed—at the same time the reflexion of substance, the development of it into the self. Consequently, until and unless spirit inherently completes itself, completes itself as a world-spirit, it cannot reach its completion as self-conscious spirit. The content of religion, therefore, expresses earlier in time than (philosophical) science what spirit is; but this science alone is the perfect form in which spirit truly knows itself." (800-801)

"The process of carrying forward this form of knowledge of itself is the task which spirit accomplishes as actual History. The religious communion, in so far as it is at the outset the substance of Absolute Spirit, is the crude form of consciousness, which has an existence all the harsher and more barbaric the deeper is its inner spirit; and its inarticulate self has all the harder task in dealing with its essence, the content of its consciousness alien to itself. Not till it has surrendered the hope of cancelling that foreignness by an external, i.e., alien, method does it turn to itself, to its own peculiar world, in the actual present." (801-802)

"Spirit, however, has shown itself to us to be neither the mere withdrawal of self-consciousness into its pure inwardness, nor the mere absorption of self-consciousness into Substance and the nothingness of its (self-) distinction. Spirit is the movement of the self which empties (externalizes) itself of self and sinks itself within its own substance, and *qua* subject, both has gone out of that substance into itself, making its substance an object and a content, and also supersedes this distinction of objectivity and content. That first reflexion out of immediacy is the subject's process of distinction of itself from its substance, the notion in a process of self-diremption, the going-into-itself and the coming into being of the pure ego. Since this distinction is the pure action of Ego = Ego, the notion is the necessity for and the rising of existence, which has the substance for its essential nature and subsists on its own account. But this subsisting of existence for itself is the notion established in determinate form, and is thereby the notion's own inherent movement—that of descending into the simple substance, which is only subject by being this negativity and going through this process." (804)

"Ego has not to take its stand on the form of self-consciousness in opposition to the form of substantiality and objectivity, as if it were afraid of relinquishing or externalizing itself. The power of spirit lies rather in remaining one with itself when giving up itself, and, because it is self-contained and self-subsistent, in establishing as mere moments its explicit self-existence as well as its implicit inherent nature. Nor again is Ego a *tertium quid* which casts distinctions back into the abyss of the Absolute, and declares them all to mean the same there. On the contrary, true knowledge lies rather in the seeming inactivity which merely watches how what is distinguished is self-moved by its very nature and returns again into its own unity." (804)

"With absolute knowledge, then, Spirit has wound up the process of its embodiment, so far as the assumption of those various shapes or modes is affected with the insurmountable distinction which consciousness implied (i.e., the distinction of consciousness from its object or content). Spirit has attained the pure element of its existence, the notion. The content is, in view of the freedom of its own existence, the self that empties (externalizes) itself; in other words, that content is the *immediate* unity of self-knowledge. The pure process of thus externalizing itself constitutes—when we consider this process in its content—the *necessity* of this content. The diversity of content is, *qua* determinate, due to relation, and is not inherent; and its restless activity consists in cancelling and superseding itself, or is negativity. Thus the necessity or diversity, like its free existence, is the self too; and in this self-form, in which existence is immediately thought, the content is a notion. Seeing, then, that Spirit has attained the notion, it unfolds its existence and develops its processes in this ether of its life and is *(Philosophical) Science*. The moments of its process are set forth therein no longer as determinate modes or shapes of consciousness, but —since the distinction, which consciousness implies, has reverted to and has become a distinction within the self— as determinate notions, and as the organic self-explaining and self-constituted process of these notions. While in the *Phenomenology of Mind* each moment is the distinction of knowledge and truth, and is the process in which that distinction is cancelled and transcended, Absolute Knowledge does not contain this distinction and supersession of distinction. Rather, since each moment has the form of the notion, it unites the objective form of truth and the knowing self in an immediate unity. Each individual moment does not appear as the process of passing back and forward from consciousness of figurative (imaginative) thought to self-consciousness and conversely: on the contrary, the pure shape, liberated from the condition of being an appearance in mere consciousness—the pure notion with its further development—depends solely on its pure characteristic nature. Conversely, again, there corresponds to every abstract moment of Absolute Knowledge a mode in which mind as a whole makes its appearance. As the mind that actually exists is not richer than it, so, too, mind in its actual content is not poorer. To know the pure notions of knowledge is the form in which they are modes or shapes of consciousness—this constitutes the aspect of their reality, according to which their essential element, the notion, appearing there in its simple mediating activity as thinking, breaks up and separates the moments of this mediation and exhibits them to itself in accordance with their immanent opposition." (804-806)

"Absolute Knowledge contains within itself this necessity of relinquishing itself from the form of the pure notion, and necessarily involves the transition of the notion into consciousness. For Spirit that knows itself is, just for the reason that it grasps its own notion, immediate identity with itself and this, in the distinction that it implies, is the certainty of what is immediate or is sense-consciousness—the beginning from which we start. This process of releasing itself from the form of its self is the highest freedom and security of its knowledge of itself." (806)

"All the same, this relinquishment (externalization) of self is still incomplete. This process expresses the relation of the certainty of its self to the object, an object which, just by being in a relation, has not yet attained its full freedom. Knowledge is aware not only of itself, but also of the negative of itself, or its limit. Knowing its limit means knowing how to sacrifice itself. This sacrifice is the self-abandonment, in which Spirit sets forth, in the form of free fortuitous happening, its process of becoming Spirit, intuitively apprehending outside it its pure self as Time, and likewise its existence as Space. This last form into which Spirit passes, *Nature,* is its living immediate process of development. Nature—Spirit divested of self (externalized)—is, in its actual existence, nothing but this eternal process of abandoning its (Nature's) own independent subsistence, and the movement which reinstates Subject." (807)

"The other aspect, however, in which Spirit comes into being, History, is the process of becoming in terms of knowledge, a conscious self-mediating process—Spirit externalized and emptied into Time. But this form of abandonment is, similarly, the emptying of itself by itself; the negative is negative of itself. This way of becoming presents a slow procession and succession of spiritual shapes (*Geister*), a gallery of pictures, each of which is endowed with the entire wealth of its substance. Since its accomplishment consists in Spirit knowing what it is, in fully comprehending its substance, this knowledge means its concentrating itself on itself (*Insichgehen*), a state in which Spirit leaves its external existence behind and gives its embodiment over to Recollection

(*Erinnerung*). In thus concentrating itself on itself, Spirit is engulfed in the night of its own self-consciousness; its vanished existence is, however, conserved therein; and this superseded existence—the previous state, but born anew from the womb of knowledge—is the new stage of existence, a new world, and a new embodiment or mode of Spirit. Here it has to begin all over again at its immediacy, as freshly as before, and thence rise once more to the measure of its stature, as if, for it, all that preceded were lost, and as if it had learned nothing from the experience of the spirits that preceded. But recollection *(Erinnerung)* has conserved that experience, and is the inner being, and, in fact, the higher form of the substance. While, then, this phase of Spirit begins all over again its formative development, apparently starting solely from itself, yet at the same time it commences at a higher level. The realm of spirits developed in this way, and assuming definite shape in existence, constitutes a succession, where one detaches and sets loose the other, and each takes over from its predecessor the empire of the spiritual world. The goal of the process is the revelation of the depth of spiritual life, and this is the Absolute Notion. This revelation consequently means superseding its "depth," is its "extension" or *spatial* embodiment, the negation of this inwardly self-centred (*insichseiend*) ego—a negativity which is its self-relinquishment, its externalization, or its substance: and this revelation is also its temporal embodiment, in that this externalization in its very nature relinquishes (externalizes) itself, and so exists at once in its spatial "extension" as well as in its "depth" or the self. The goal, which is Absolute Knowledge or Spirit knowing itself as Spirit, finds its pathway in the recollection of spiritual forms (Geister) as they are in themselves and as they accomplish the organization of their spiritual kingdom. Their conservation, looked at from the side of their free existence appearing in the form of contingency, is *History*; looked at from the side of their intellectually comprehended organization, it is the *Science* of the ways in which knowledge appears. Both together, or History (intellectually) comprehended (*begriffen*), form at once the recollection and the Golgotha of Absolute Spirit, the reality, the truth, the certainty of its throne, without which it were lifeless, solitary, and alone." (807)

THE SCIENCE OF LOGIC

"Thought is that *Universal*—that *Species* which is immortal, which preserves identity with itself."

Hegel.

Through the voyage to this insight outlined in *The Phenomenology of Mind,* we have gone with the voyager step by step through every phase of consciousness which experience furnishes to man individually or collectively as races. We reach the summit of human attainment when Spirit is consciously identified with Itself. The long process of development is the road from Being as emptiness—in the simple thought of Being—to Being in its fullness of Consciousness as Self-conscious Self. This is the Self Realization which is Absolute Knowledge. It is the Divine Knowing. As Aristotle said of it, here "Knowing and Willing are one." Between Self Consciousness and Self Realization lay all the miles of human history with the attendant rounds of joy and sorrow. They furnish the long travail of this mighty birth. Yet from the beginning of time this efflorescence is held potentially in the fullness of time as a seed carries hidden within it the plant it is to be, its flower and fruit. This long voyage, having been outlined in *The Phenomenology of Mind,* Hegel proceeds in *The Logic* to give it adequate logical testimony. *The Logic* contains the analysis of the unfoldment in a form that meets the demands of reason. In *The Logic* it is "thought" in its highest and purest form with which we have to deal. Thought in its pure form has no element of experience in it. It is abstract thought. But it is by pursuing thought to its initial abstract realm, beyond experience, to the categories of the mind, that the formal, rigid requirements of reason are met in logical form.

This then is the purport of Hegel's Logic. As it unfolds

there is revealed a "logic of ontology"—which is the certain and rigid demonstration of truth.

It begins with the best known phase of experience, the world of sense perception. This is its most evident realm of existence. But, this world of sense perception naturally presupposes a world of time and space. And, time and space, in their turn, presuppose reason as their logical condition. This gives us a true actual as totality, and, a changeable real. This changeable real is partly actual and partly potential. The process of change is partly affirmative—giving the reality of the phenomena—and partly negative— producing the change which negates the present real, actualizing in its place a new phase of potentiality. The totality of conditions, or the true actual moves through its own other—the changeable real—in a process of independent freedom. It is the demonstration of this fact that is accomplished through the natural unfoldment of the forms of pure thought.

These forms move logically according to a rule of three, giving the three great categories: Being, Essence and Idea.

I.

Thought as by itself and independent.

II.

Thought in negative relation to itself as its own other.

III.

Thought in identity with itself in its other.

This third and last consecutive completes the circuit. In its operation it is seen as only the circuit of a spiral. It brings us repeatedly back into a negative unity of all things, or Pure Being. Each cycle involves a certain inadequacy—the dialectical necessity that will lead to a deeper thought containing *explicitly* what the former thought has held only *implicitly*, and has had to show dialectically as its contradiction.

I

BEING

The starting point of Hegel's logic is pure being—the absolute of the infantile thought of mankind. Pure being is the empty absolute. It is the first stage of the mind in childhood. It is the first great principle discovered by the childhood of the race. It is an empty unity in which all difference and diversity are annulled and reabsorbed into its identity.

Hegel begins by refuting this empty absolute. It is the beginning of logic, but not its finality. The logic, which must necessarily begin with this most elementary pure thought, must proceed to the highest and completest pure thought—the creative Reason—whose self-consciousness is the eternal origin of distinction, difference, individuality and independence. Hence the logic which begins with pure being will be seen to end in the highest pure thought.

The meaning held in the term pure thought must be defined and emphasized as thought from which the element of experience is wholly excluded.

The beginning of pure thought will therefore have no predicate whatever that arises in experience. It is the negation of all that can be found in experience. Yet it does not state such negation, since to do so would thereby imply experience. It is the empty self-affirmation of reason before it identifies anything else. The first and simple thought of being, the thought "I am" is the foundation on which all further perception rests. Perception itself is constituted of determinations or particularizations of this general category of being. The Ego, as pure being, is the ground of all its experience. Now it is the ideas that follow in the mind from reflection on the pure thought of being which unfold the logic of being.

Hegel investigates this category of being to see what follows from the thought. Pure being without any further limitations of determinateness is a thought so simple that there is nothing in it. It is seen to be identical with naught. Pure being and pure naught are therefore the same. This outcome seems paradoxical. For, although they are as pure thoughts indistinguishable, they are not the same, but absolutely distinct. The two thoughts are, however, inseparable. Each one has a way of vanishing into the other. This reveals a new phase of the process into which this thought of being has led. It reveals movement or activity—the immediate vanishing, the one in the other. This activity Hegel names "becoming." It contains both being and naught as distinct, but at the same time as losing their distinctness and becoming indistinguishable. The difference affirmed for the thought—"being" and "naught" is the ground for the substitution of the category of becoming. Let us see how this is. To think pure being we apply the predicate of indeterminateness. But to think is to determine. Hence the act of our thinking determines and thus negates the thought of the pure simple. We see, therefore, that we have really a becoming instead of the isolated term which we named being or naught. It is obvious, there, that thought begins with the category of becoming. Here we have our first insight into Hegel's famous dialectic which is described as the self-movement of the notion. In it each and every incomplete idea gets lost, or is subsumed in a more complete one of which it forms one of the characteristics. And this process, found as a psychological necessity is undoubtedly true ontologically. For what thought finds necessary in regard to existence may be taken as the ontological fact as well.

Looking once more at becoming it will be seen that it, in its turn, is an imperfect and dependent thought. It is made up of "beginning" and "ceasing." We may therefore say that we find the categories of being and naught unthinkable except as categories of becoming—i.e., except as ceasing and beginning. Ceasing and beginning are each a transition to its opposite and each opposite is a transition back to the former. This transition through its opposite to itself can not be thought as becoming; it is return, return to itself, or beginning and ceasing in equipoise, which is an abiding rather than a becoming, and, the vanishing of the category of becoming. For "return-to-self" is a movement to self identity. Becoming has therefore passed over into determinate being—i.e., into a unity of being and naught that has the *form of being*. This is the form of self-identity as annulment of the opposite. This self-return is the only possible form of objective reality. But, these categories must not be thought of as having anything objectively valid in themselves. As each one is found inadequate, it is subsumed in the movement as it advances, and in it is utterly annulled as far as all future use, or reference, is concerned. For the dialectic appertains only to what is finite, inadequate, or incomplete. Hence the necessity for annulment.

This return-to-self is not *simple being* but has the *form* of being that is determinateness. Pure being, as we saw before, was one of the termini of becoming—becoming the process of transition from beginning to ceasing, and, from ceasing to beginning. The form of being therefore must correspondingly have two phases. The positive and negative return to self. The positive return Hegel names "reality." The negative return he names "negation." The difference between reality and negation is like the difference between being and naught, only deeper. The identity is also deeper.

Being and determinateness are not related to one another as general to particular. But both are coextensive; determinateness thus isolated as existing determinateness is quality, a quite simple and immediate determinateness. Here we have the ground for defining quality. For quality is that determinateness which is one with the being of the object. If the quality is changed the being is changed.

As quality, reality and negation are identical, yet they

are distinguished just as being and naught. Quality holds the same relation to reality and negation that "becoming" held to being and naught. Reality returning to itself is "somewhat" negation returning to self is "other." Somewhat and other are the two forms of determined being. Somewhat and other express the two sides of the one thought of determined being. The somewhat is limited by the other; it is dependent on the other. Its dependence constitutes its unity with the other. Hence a dependent being is outside its true self. Here we arrive at the idea of finitude. That is finite which is a somewhat over against another and dependent on that other. This finite is not self active and the cause of its attributes but its characteristics are impressed upon it by outside influences. This is the true insight into the category of quality. To think things under the category of quality is to think them under the relation of "somewhat" and "other." The category of somewhat and other has incidental to it the idea of finitude, just as "return-to-self" was incidental in the two species of becoming. Finitude may be said to be the form of their relation. They are also the two phases of the category of quality. Here arises the category of infinite progress. For each somewhat is an other to the other which is its true self. Seeing the essential relativity of the somewhat—its dependence on another—we transfer our attention to the other. But this "other," too, is a somewhat, or limited being, and is again dependent on another. We pass on to another, and another again. This we may do *ad infinitum.*

We never arrive at a final other. Each is a somewhat which depends on something else beyond it. This is the reciprocal determination of the finite and infinite. We have only to get an insight into what this presupposes to see the true infinite itself. Each step forward is the evolution of a new other which has to be reached. We know that a new other will arise because we see the final nature of this somewhat. It must be its own other. Hence we posit the progress only after we have seen the totality of the somewhat. We must have the true infinite before our minds when we say "and so on forever." For the progress is infinite only for the reason that the true infinite makes it possible. Space is an example. Space can only be limited by space, and herein it can only be continued, and is infinite. That the somewhat is, of necessity, its own other is the fundamental truth in regard to quality. The other on which it depends is its true self. Hence in the change of the finite we have only a process of the manifestation of the self of the finite. We have arrived at the category of "being-for-itself."

We ascend from somewhat and other to the unity of their process which is independent being, or being for itself. The first aspect of this independent being is its infinitude. It contains all the being that the finite contains, and also all the being that it does not contain. It is the affirmative being of the "somewhat" and "other"—nor does it omit their distinction or difference. It is change that annuls itself. It finds itself in "another." Space again will illustrate this, or time, or conscious being. The self as subject is also its own object—its own "other," and, it is thus continued instead of limited by that "other," hence it is infinite.

That the "somewhat" is, and must be, its own other constitutes the dialectic movement from the finite to the infinite. And we see the process of change that constituted the finitude of the somewhat is only a process of seeking its true self. It is the activity of realizing the potential. The "being-in-itself" is becoming "being-for-itself."

Looked at from the standpoint of "somewhat" we see the finite as reality, and all is transitory and evanescent. Looked at from the standpoint of independent being we see the infinite to be the true reality and all change to be only development and self realization.

With the sub-category of infinitude, quality has realized its highest point of perfection. There now emerges from it the category of quantity. The infinite is the continued reflection into itself of what, viewed apart, is the finite. This is an activity of self determination. Taken immediately we have oneness opposed to multiplicity which presupposes our new category, or, quantity.

The one is "negative unity" in which the distinctions of somewhat and other all vanish, because they all "posit" the totality as their sole reality. This "being-for-one" is what Hegel called being-for-other when treating it within the category of the somewhat. The "being-for-one" of the dependent moments is the "being-for-itself" of the independent being.

Now we come to a second consideration. The dependence looked at anew from the point of view of the independent being must assume new phases.

From the category of somewhat and other the dependence seemed to render the being finite, or partial and imperfect. Now that it is seen as the product of self-determined being (for independent being must be self-determined) each dependent being becomes a totality also, and hence it becomes a *one*.

Thus, surprising as is the result it is the "dialectic" through which Hegel comes suddenly upon his "one and many", and further on to his "attraction and repulsion".

The being for itself is independent because it is a reflection-into-itself out of its "other". But the "other" of the independent being is also a totality, and independent, just because it is the result of the self-determination of the independent. Hence the "other" is a one. Thus we have almost arrived at quantity. The same feature that discovers to us infinitude underlying finitude, discovers to us "one and many ones" in the place of "somewhat and other". When we see only dependence, isolatedly, we use the category of somewhat and other; when we see somewhat and other in its ground of reflection into-itself, or totality, we see ones or units. The insight needed to see quantity instead of being-for-itself is this; every one is within itself multiple and every multiplicity is also a unit. In other words we see infinite divisibility. Each unit must appear a composite of other units, which again are composites of other units, and so on *ad infinitum*. Then each unit is an aggregate of ones and all units are constituent ones of including units. This idea is quantity. The being-for-itself is still qualitative when we regard it as the self related negative which distinguishes and excludes, which contains somewhats and others in an "ideal" condition (i.e. as moments.) But when the "being-for-itself" imparts its "one-ness" to each "somewhat" and "other", making them ones over against it, or, within it ("repulsion") and at the same time includes them all as "ideal" (moments), or, as emptied of their qualitative distinctions ("repulsion" annulled by "attraction") we have quantity. The repulsion is the annulment of dependence, the attraction is the reassertion of it. Now that we have a one that is many, and many that are one, we have quantity. Quantity is more adequate than immediate quality to express the truth of the Absolute. Yet, since it does not explicity and adequately state self-activity, it is an imperfect category that will cancel itself necessarily when tested in the role of universality.

Just what are these two, quality and quantity in the light of each other? They are this: quality makes determinateness to be immediately one with being and therefore demands dependence on an outside determiner, quantity makes determinateness to be the result of self-activity—it is the difference of the self from the self,—the self opposition of the one. This view looks straight towards genus (or species) and its included individuals in their external aspect. The universal, or generating cause, repeats itself in individuals, ones, totalities—and thus there are quantities.

No material thing could exist if it were not for this self-repetition. For there would be no homogeneity and hence no aggregation. Without continuity of the same with the same there could be no quantity, and without quantity no masses and no molecules. Hence no material being. Quantity is the non-identity of being and its determinateness; quality is their identity.

Hegel, as we have seen, makes the idea of quantity spring out of the idea of qualitative infinite series, infinitely divisible and infinitely continuable. Its limits, being quantitative, are continuations, and not such limits as make what they limit to be finite. Space and Time are given by Hegel as examples of pure quantity. They are such that any limits assumed in them are continuous with what they limit.

The insight into quantity perceives, *not* the side of dependence and ideality, like quality, but the side of independence belonging to determinateness. In quality, being and determinateness were one, in quantity the determinateness has these two phases, quality, or identity with being, and quantity or non-identity with being. The idea of quality leads over into quantity through its "dialectic". Quantity is the exposition of the sheer independence of determinateness, while quality is the exposition of the sheer dependence of it. Under quantity Hegel treats (a) pure quantity, (b) continuous quantity, (c) limitation of quantity, (d) quantum, or number, (e) extensive and intensive quantum and their unity is an infinite progress ("series"), (f) the quantitative infinitude (resting on the idea of ratio of two numbers), (g) direct ratio (h) inverse ratio, (i) the ratio of powers, which means the ratio of number to itself when it is raised to a power by multiplying it by itself.

Let us look at the nature of quantity itself. As units all numbers are alike but as sums they are different. The sums may be called the numerators but the constituent units are the denominators. The sums give extensive quantity—the units give intensive quantity. Here we arrive at the idea of ratio as the real truths of quantity. One simple number must be placed in relation to another, the one as sum, the other as constituent unity in order to fully express quantity. This gives quantitative ratio as the only adequate expression of determinate quantity. This gives an insight into the progress of mathematics. The mathematician gradually comes to see that quantitative ratio expresses the truth of all quantitative being. The important thought is the development of the two categories of extensive quantity and intensive quantity as the two essential moments of quantity in its ideal totality, or complete definition. The intensive quantity presents one necessary phase of every definite quantity, and the extensive quantity presents the other necessary phase of the same.

In the quantitative ratio each side is a limited quantity but the ratio itself has qualitative aspects. This gives us the category of measure. But the sides of this ratio—which produces measure—become themselves measure when considered as factors of measure. Second, the limitation of quantity is measured by an external standard—so much quantity produces such and such a quality. But these quantities which are externally united are each of them measures and hence measure is a ratio of two measures and we have "being for itself" in measure. In "being for itself" of measure we have a ratio of measures, each side of the ratio being a measure. This brings us to the real measure such as constitutes the intimate nature of space and time, as well as the specific gravity of bodies the chemical properties, the musical tones, etc. But each measure, as the side of a ratio, becomes also in itself a ratio of measures; and there develops a series of measures. "This indifferent manifold ratio becomes excluding being-for-itself", says Hegel, "which is the so-called elective affinity."

The measure ratios are a scale of changing ratios which move by degrees through the compass of one quality and suddenly pass over to a new quality at one leap, as, for example, red heat becomes white; water becomes ice. Quantity is possible only where the quality remains the same. But in quantitative ratio and measure quality reasserts itself, and in the ratio of measures the qualities become dependent on each other through the quantitative ratio. Where the quality breaks on account of change of quantity there can be no continuous measure of degrees. Hence the quantitative measure has to begin anew at each point where a new quality begins. Hence the category of measure itself breaks down here and we have the category of the measureless. Thus ends the last sub-category of the Category of Being. We arrive at the "absolute indifference" which is the becoming of, or transition into, the Category of Essence.

II

ESSENCE

Essence as Reflection

Essence is the second of the three great categories of Pure Thought—namely, Being, Essence and Idea. Being is the category of immediateness, Essence that of pure and utter mediation, while Idea is the category of self-mediation or living energy, Absolute Mind or Personality.

Being is the category that includes all thought of things in themselves and as unrelated. In this first stage of thought, each object is conceived as a real independent substance. When the mind rises to the stage where it sees that there is no such object possible—that all is universally relative—we have arrived at the category of Essence. Being in this sphere is only the movement of nothing to nothing—and this is essence.

Here in the category of Essence we have entire relativity, and, to be relative signifies to be negative. A negative relation to itself takes the form of being. Since this relation to itself is the negating of negation we have (in this sphere of Essence) negation existing as negation, in short, as that whose only being is in its being negated. This is the category of appearance.

Appearance

Appearance when examined is found to be reflection. It is only a one-sided phase of the total activity which is essence.

This reflection is of three forms—positing, external, and determining reflection.

Positing Reflection

Identity with itself which constitutes immediateness is not a first immediateness from which we start (as a fixed reality) and from which we pass over to another, namely to its negation; nor is it a substratum of existence which moves from the first to the other and returns (remaining identical under the movement) but the immediate is only this movement itself. Posited being is the relation of the negative to itself; it is immediateness as the annulment of the negation. So, too, a self relation which does go out and relates to another, but which relates to itself as its own other, is an immediate, or results in an immediate. The mind, for example, is a self related negative activity. Reflection is positing in so far as it is immediateness as return. But the negative in relating to itself must negate itself and annul itself. Hence the immediateness is not only posited by this return to relation to self but it is also annulled or canceled. This new phase is pre-supposition.

Positing and pre-supposing reflection are therefore the two acts of reflection. As self relation it is a positing of immediateness; as self-negating it is a presupposing of being as a substrate. The positing phase of reflection produces identity and the pre-supposing phase produces difference. The return of essence is consequently its repulsion from itself.

External Reflection

With the first phase of this discussion Hegel has discovered two phases, positing and presupposing. Each extends into the other and is productive of the other. Within the total activity of reflection, the former, the positing phase, results in the annulment of the return movement, for it is the production of immediateness, which is no return. But as an annulment of the return movement it is the production of difference and this is a contradiction of the return movement, or the presupposing phase of reflection. Taking these two phases as independent of each other we have what Hegel calls "external reflection". External reflection always presupposes a being as a substrate. It negates and determines some already existent immediate being.

Hegel has only to exhibit the step by which this unconscious procedure becomes conscious of the union of these two phases in one activity to elevate us out of this stage of external reflection into "determining reflection".

Determining Reflection

External reflection has all the phases of the absolute, but not synthetically united. It begins with the presupposing reflection and then proceeds to substitute the positing reflection for it, and returns to the presupposing reflection again in the result; first, two independent beings; second, one of them acts as cause on the other; third, the effect is the result, now independent again.

External reflection coming to consider carefully the extremes, finds each to involve the entire movement of reflection. For being, or reflection in itself involves negative relation which differentiates: The pre-supposing activity which is that of differentiation results again in self-identity. This is the determination of reflection.

Here we have the category which "contains within itself its relation to its other." *Cause* contains within its own definition an express relation to *effect;* effect likewise its essential relation to cause. So, too, force contains express reference to manifestation; identity to difference; positive to negative; essence to phenomena.

To sum up this category one may say:

Reflection as negation related to itself produces identity and then immediateness; and positing becomes presupposing, and thus turns identity into difference and annuls immediateness and thus undermines itself as essence and becomes phenomenon again. Thus do identity and difference alternate as the eternal rhythm of self activity.

The Determinations of Reflection

The "determinations" of reflection, or "categories", are three, identity, difference (or distinction) and contradiction.

These categories of reflection give us the ground of formal logic. And this category of ground is taken by Hegel as the general rubric for form distinctions.

There are several phases of the category. One phase contains (a) the formal ground; (b) the real ground; (c) the perfect ground. Another phase of the category is discussed under the head of condition: (a) The relatively unconditioned; (b) the absolutely unconditioned; (c) How a thing comes into existence.

Phenomenon

Phenomenon is taken as the totality of appearance, i.e. as containing the positive action of the essence—and as revealing its entire negative self-relation.

Force

Force contains the idea of original and independent energy and also the contradictory idea of dependence on an external incitement as necessary for its action. The force never acts except when an occasion comes to it from without and "solicits" it to action. This leads to the concept of a total system of forces in which the energy is self-active—not merely original source of force, but also its own incitement.

There are three ideas, or categories, that form the transition to the explicit idea of self activity—namely, substantiality—causality, and reciprocal action. These are categories in which the idea of self-activity is more explicit than in the category of force and law, and yet not explicit enough to answer for the expression of any form of self-activity. These three categories form the third part of essence as the union of "essence as reflection into itself" and "phenomena." This union means a new thought which contains explicitly both of the former ideas. The general rubric of this third part is actuality and it contains reflection-into-itself and is at the same time phenomenal. It is that which manifests, or reveals its entire internality.

Actuality

Actuality contains the three sub-categories of substance, cause and reciprocal-action. It is in the third place absolute. The idea of the absolute is, according to Hegel, the union of the idea of internality with that of externality. The absolute is that whose internal is also external—and substance and cause must be such absolutes.

We saw in "force" that a system of forces radiated from a self-repelling energy which was its own incitement to act. Its internal immediately repelled itself from itself as external and its external immediately attracted its opposite and became internal.

All duality has disappeared in the sense of dependence on some outside incitement to act. Hence we have the absolute, or the independent. If the internal were not also external, there would be an essence which was not manifested, and hence, an essence that was not fully essential. For essence proves itself to be essence in its phenomena.

Now the Absolute is independent existence, or true reality—named here—actuality.

Actuality is discussed under three aspects:
(a) contingency; (b) relative necessity; (c) absolute necessity. Contingency may be called formal actuality. Kant's expression was possibility. Relative necessity may be called real actuality, Kant's expression was existence, while absolute necessity is the union of real and formal actuality, or the union of possibility and existence. That is to say, when all the possible phases are real, or in existence at once, the form assumed is necessary and cannot change any farther because there are no potentialities into which it may change.

The attributes of the substance cannot be unless they are modes of its activity. The true substance must be self active.

This leads us to the idea of Cause—to that which is self-active. But "Cause" does not name adequately the self-active, it is in fact, only the first or immediate form of seizing the thought.

The cause is conceived as active and only as active. Its action produces an effect on something else. It sends a stream of influence to an effect. This involves the idea of self-separation. For the cause separates this influence and transmits it of its own energy, and not because impelled to do this by some alien energy or cause. That alien energy which impelled the transmission would in that case be the true cause. The cause by itself in the act of self-separation, is, and must be, a self-activity—that which determines itself. Hence *causa sui* is the nucleus of each and every causal act. Causality presupposes self-separation; self activity. The defect of the category lies in the fact that it is used without its true implication being seen. Cause is not an explicit category of self-activity, but is rather what presupposes it.

Reciprocal action as a transition from causality to idea explains in another manner the dialectical evolution of self determination from determination through another.

Reciprocal action is therefore the last form of duality by which the thinking of the understanding is able to postpone the adoption of the form of the thinking of the reason. Here self-activity is the ultimate presupposition of all.

The Notion

This brings us to the form of the reason—which Hegel shows to be the syllogism. One here sees the true reality underlying the science of logic.

The form of self activity, being that of self-opposition and of identification in the opposite is essentially that of logical conception which Hegel names true being. This activity of thinking, or concept-making, constitutes the nature of the Ego. It has three phases; namely, universality, particularity, and individuality.

The pure Ego with its negative power of abstracting from all and any special thoughts gives *Universality*.

But the form of self-activity is "negative-self relation" which is determination and Particularity. The identity of particularity and universality gives Individuality.

Accordingly do we have an unfolding of the subjective nature, of thc constitution of the Ego, in the forms of the judgment and syllogism.

From this follows the *Deduction of the Syllogistic Figures; The Syllogism of determinate being or quality;* The *syllogism of reflection;* The *syllogism of necessity*.

The suggestiveness of Hegel's study of formal logic is inexhaustible.

It brings us, with the syllogism and the forms of the reason—which reason is seen to be self active reason, to the Absolute.

The difficulty of all philosophy is the explanation of the derivation of the imperfect from the all-Perfect.

The Hegelian philosophy—whose Principle is a method, or self-activity which develops itself—explains the rise of the finite by the essential action of its principle. The contemplation of the principle is a contemplation of an activity of creation.

The first principle in knowing Himself generates the Logos from all eternity. The Logos, in knowing his derivation, recognizes his origin in the self knowing of the first. But the first also recognizes the recognition of the second, and this mutual recognition is described in religious language as the mutual love which causes the Holy Spirit to proceed eternally. In philosophical language it is mutual recognition, the knowledge of one's self in another. But the Processio is to be distinguished from the perfect being that proceeds, for the Processio is an evolution, or becoming from that which is not, to that which is, and is perfect. Hence it eternally contains all degrees of imperfection in it at all times. The Processio is, in fact, creation, and not God, nor a person of the Trinity. But it has as creation, unique relations to each of the divine persons. To the First, it is the recognition of his own process of generating through goodness or altruistic action; to the Second, it is the recognition of another's goodness and altruism—namely, that of the First; to the Third, it is a recognition of his own double procession through the altruism of First and Second. The Creation in time and space is a process with one sole final purpose, the evolution of rational immortal souls, and their perfection in institutions (whose aggregate is the invisible church). The world is not divine but it has a divine function to perform, because it is the Processio of the Holy Spirit. God is living God, and is absolute Spirit. He is recognized in his deeds.

Objectivity has cancelled its mediation, and reached immediate self-relation. Objectivity must be approached since it is the dialetical outcome of subjectivity as it is exhibited in the exposition of the syllogism. The subject makes itself its own object. The syllogistic constitution of the Ego opposes itself in its completeness and independence to itself as object. This is the nature of mind itself; it is the nature of the divine mind to do this. Objectivity has three forms. The first is objectivity undeveloped and devoid of subjectivity—namely mechanism. The second is objectivity in which subjectivity appears—law and ratio, and measure of differences—chemism. The third is objectivity in which subjectivity manifests as dependence on a purpose or aim,—teleology.

In mechanism each part is indifferent to every other, and this holds good whether the mechanism is material or spiritual. The elements have no inner connection. The thoughts of space and time come under this category. The act of consciousness begins with the antithesis of empty subject to empty object—a point opposed to a point—and proceeds from this—the space concept—to the identification or recognition of the object by the subject—the time concept. For the act of recognition or identification annuls the separation or antithesis, and thus the points all become one, and a real one, The separation becomes unreal. Time has one reality—the now, a single point of time; all separation or extension is cancelled and unreal—a past or future that exists not now. This is the dialectic connection of time and space in the *Processio*.

In mechanism we have independence conjoined with indifference of distinctions. The dialectic begins in the contradiction between the perfect indifference of each part to every other and this perfect identity of properties and qualities. This, according to Hegel, should produce the "mechanical process"—as a unity of mutually excluding objects. (a) The formal process; (b) the real process. Through action and reaction in the formal process a result arises that was not contained in the process at first; the product is some external arrangement or order of the parts. The second step (b) the real process—contains the dynamic side of the process, that of the influence of the stronger on the weaker. (c) There results a center of movement as the product. This brings us to "absolute mechanism" with (a) its center, and (b) its law. To be related to a center is to have an ideal. Gravitation is the ideal that each separate body posseses of the totality of matter. Each body feels ideally all the other bodies, in proportion to their magnitudes and distances. With centrality, or the ideal presence of the mechanical whole in each mechanical part, we have transcended the sphere of mechanism and come to the specification of objectivity—the stage of chemism.

The stage of chemism includes not only the relation of chemical elements but also the meteorological process, the sexual relation of plants and animals, the spiritual relations of love and friendship. Chemism is the ground of these. Teleology, which is conformity to end, or purpose, is a more explicit and fully realized form than this blind affinity. Hegel calls teleology "the truth of mechanism". The three phases of the category are: (a) the subjective aim, (b) the means, (c) the realized aim. A being that moves or acts with a purpose shows that it has ideals, and hence that it is a synthesis of its self and its not self. Hence through the category of teleology, we return out of mere objectivity into subjectivity again, and now have subject-objectivity which is the realm of the idea. We pass out of the category of Essence, which is the second of the great categories of Hegel's Logic, and into the third, namely The Category of The Idea.

III

"IDEA"—OR PERSONALITY

The stage of the idea is that stage where the real objective existence is also subjective—the stage of life, intellect and will.

Life is the first, the immediate and most inadequate form of the stage "idea". Intellect and will are its complements. The true concrete idea is the unity of life, intellect and will.

I. Life has three categories: (a) the living individual; (b) the life process; (c) the generic. Intelligence has (a) the true; (b) the good. Under the true is included 1. Analytic knowing; 2. Synthetic knowing (i, definition; ii, classification; and iii, theorem.)

II. The Absolute Idea comprises (a) method (b) dialectic (c) system. There is plain evidence that Hegel has always a personal first principle as the result of his system.

He treats first of the forms of the idea in the world of nature.

Life has the power of self determination. The living can make the "not self" become self. It can impress its determinations upon its environment.

In feeling, the self-activity commences an ideal reproduction of its environment. Desire is feeling accompanied with the additional sense of self-hood. In the case of desire the self extends ideally beyond its limits. When the self is realized as Ego, we have knowledge. By realizing the self as Ego is meant "self-determining" as opposed to "self-determined." Here is admitted the process of ideal determination that defines the environment and yet can be distinguished from it. A still higher realization of self-determination than is given by feeling arises in memory. From the exercise of the memory comes the birth of general ideas.

The generic Hegel defines as the transition from plant life to the higher realization of the idea in intelligence. The mind in its theoretical activity seeks to know the true, while in its practical activity it seeks to realize the good through action of the will. These two opposite forms of activity constitute the two forms of the same self-realization of the idea. Of the absolute idea, Hegel says: "The absolute Idea, as the reasonable Notion which in its reality coincides only with itself is the return to life by reason of this immediacy of its objective identity; but on the other hand it has equally transcended this form of its immediacy and contains the highest opposition within itself.

"The absolute Idea is the only object and content of philosophy. As it contains every determinateness, and its essence is to return to itself through its self-determination of particularization, it has various phases. It is the business of philosophy to recognize it in them. Nature and Spirit are different manners of presenting its existence; art and religion, different manners in which it comprehends itself and gives itself an adequate existence. Philosophy has the same content and end as art and religion, but it is the highest manner of comprehending the Absolute Idea, because its manner is the highest—the Notion." (Science of Logic, V.2, p.466.)

"According to this method every step forward is a step in further determination and in further removal from the indeterminate beginning; this is also a return—a process of finding the grounds of the thought with which we began." (III 339)

The logic of pure thought as revealed in the Hegelian method has led us through the dialectical process by which man purifies himself of his lower categories and rises to the contemplation of the only true and adequate one—the absolute idea.

The absolute idea is to be comprehended as the highest unity of intellect and will. In it, perfect subject and perfect object are united in a comprehension that gives complete personality.

Thus does the Hegelian philosophy through the method of the dialectic lead us from the first and simplest thought of empty indeterminate being to the one, true, adequate and absolute idea—"the vision of God"—as personality.

THE PHILOSOPHY OF HISTORY

We now come to THE PHILOSOPHY of HISTORY. In order to approach it in its proper setting it is necessary to recall that in THE PHENOMENOLOGY of MIND, Hegel shows how the world spirit moves through states of consciousness from the lowest, simplest category to the highest and most complex. In The Logic he shows these categories in their pure thought forms as a logical genesis. In THE PHILOSOPHY of HISTORY he traces this logic of ontology as it is being actualized in the historic process. Here its consummation is finally realized in the State.

In connection with "The State" Hegel has been misunderstood. Popular conception makes him responsible for the totalitarian spirit of world conquest and the wars that result therefrom. He is quoted as saying that the state is greater than the individual and therefore has the inherent right to use the individual for its own ends. What he did say may be construed to mean this, if subtle perception gives way and does not realize the difference between such an interpretation and his implied meaning. But it would be like saying that the orchestra may usurp the individuality of the violin, instead of that the violin finds the highest fulfillment of expression of itself in the orchestra. The difference is a subtle one, but it is also very real.

To offer one quotation from Hegel concerning The State will suffice at this point.

"We observe an essential union between the objective side —The Idea—and the subjective side—the personality that conceives and wills it. The objective existence of this union is The State—the basis and center of the other elements of life of a whole people—of Art, of Law, of Morality, of Religion, of Science." (49)

Hegel traces this logic of ontology as it unfolds in the

historic process in a cautious, empirical manner. He makes a definite distinction between a principle, or truth, limited to an abstract form and its determined application and actualization in the concrete. In fact on this point rests the understanding of the whole purport of philosophy. On the one hand there is the Abstract Reason—on the other hand it is making itself manifest as thought and becoming actualized in existence. Hegel gives the definition "Reason is Thought conditioning itself with perfect freedom." In Religion the term used for this Absolute Reason is Divine Providence. Philosophy states the same truth as is held by Religion when it says that Reason is the sovereign of the world. Here it is necessary to use the caution stated above regarding the distinction which must be made between that which is as yet abstract and its concrete realization. And philosophy claims to have proved by speculative cognition that, in Hegel's words, [Reason] "is *Substance* as well as *Infinite Power;* its own *Infinite Material* underlying all the natural and spiritual life which it originates, as also the *Infinite Form*—that which sets this material in motion. On the one hand, Reason is the *substance* of the Universe; viz., that by which and in which all reality has its being and subsistence. On the other hand it is the *Infinite Energy* of the Universe; since Reason is not so powerless as to be a mere intention—having its place outside reality, nobody knows where; something separate and abstract, in the heads of certain human beings. It is *the infinite complex of things,* their entire Essence and Truth. It is its own material which it commits to its own Active Energy to work up; not needing as finite action does, the conditions of an external material of given means from which it may obtain its support, and the objects of its activity. It supplies its own nourishment, and is the object of its own operations. While it is exclusively its own basis of existence, and absolute final aim, it is also the energizing power realizing this aim; developing it not only in the phenomena of the Natural, but also of the Spiritual Universe—the History of the World. That this

"Idea" or "Reason" is the *True,* the *Eternal,* the absolutely *powerful* essence; that it reveals itself in The World, and that in that World nothing else is revealed but this and its honor and glory—is the thesis which, as we have said, has been proved in Philosophy, and is here regarded as demonstrated . . ." (9)

"It is only an inference from the history of the World, that its development has been a rational process; that the history in question has constituted the rational necessary course of the World-Spirit—that Spirit whose nature is always one and the same, but which unfolds this its one nature in the phenomena of the World's existence." (10)

The term world must be understood as including both physical and psychical Nature. The task that is presented is the comprehension of the mode by which the Absolute Reason, on the one hand, and the phenomena of existence, on the other, are to be distinguished as antithetical and at the same time to be known in an eternal interplay by which Reason of abstract totality, makes itself actual in specialized, concrete existence. It finally gives itself embodiment in the State—its most perfect realization. It is, therefore, necessary to know the nature of Spirit, its mode of operation and its final form in the State. "The nature of Spirit," Hegel says, "may be understood by a glance at its direct opposite—*Matter.* As the essence of Matter is Gravity, so, on the other hand, we may affirm that the substance, the essence of Spirit is Freedom. All will readily assent to the doctrine that Spirit, among other properties, is also endowed with Freedom; but philosophy teaches that all the qualities of Spirit exist only through Freedom; that all are but means for attaining Freedom; that all seek and produce this and this alone. It is a result of speculative Philosophy that Freedom is the sole truth of Spirit. Matter possesses gravity in virtue of its tendency toward a central point. It is essentially composite; consisting of parts that *exclude* each other. It seeks its Unity; and therefore exhibits itself as self-destructive, as verging toward its opposite (an indivisible point). If it could attain this, it would be

Matter no longer, it would have perished. It strives after the realization of its Idea; for in Unity it exists *ideally*. Spirit, on the contrary, may be defined as that which has its centre in itself. It has not a unity outside itself, but has already found it; it exists *in* and *with itself*. Matter has its essence out of itself; Spirit is *self-contained existence* (Bei-sich-selbst-sein). Now this is Freedom, exactly. For if I am dependent, my being is referred to something else which I am not; I cannot exist independently of something external. I am free, on the contrary, when my existence depends upon myself. This self-contained existence of Spirit is none other than self-consciousness—consciousness of one's own being. Two things must be distinguished in consciousness; first, the fact *that I know;* secondly, *what I know*. In self-consciousness these are merged in one; for Spirit *knows itself*. It involves an appreciation of its own nature, as also as energy enabling it to realize itself; to make itself *actually* that which it is *potentially*. According to this abstract definition it may be said of Universal History, that it is the exhibition of Spirit in the process of working out the knowledge of that which it is potentially. And as the germ bears in itself the whole nature of the tree, and the taste and form of its fruits, so do the first traces of Spirit virtually contain the whole of that History." (17)

"The question of the *means* by which Freedom develops itself to a World, conducts us to the phenomenon of History itself. Although Freedom is, primarily, an undeveloped idea, the means it uses are external and phenomenal; presenting themselves in History to our sensuous vision. The first glance at History convinces us that the actions of men proceed from their needs, their passions, their characters and talents; and impresses us with the belief that such needs, passions and interests are the sole springs of action—the efficient agents in this scene of activity" . . . (20) "The first remark we have to make, and which—though already presented more than once—cannot be too often repeated when the occasion seems to call for it—is that what we call *principle, aim, destiny,* or the nature and idea of Spirit, is something merely general and abstract. Principle—Plan of Existence—Law—is a hidden, undeveloped essence, which *as such*—however true in itself—is not completely real. Aims, principles, etc., have a place in our thoughts, in our subjective design only; but not yet in the sphere of reality. That which exists for itself only, is a possibility, a potentiality; but has not yet emerged into Existence. A *second* element must be introduced in order to produce actuality—viz., actuation, realization; and whose motive power is the Will—the activity of man in the widest sense. It is only by this activity that the Idea as well as abstract characteristics generally, are realized, actualized; for of themselves they are powerless. The motive power that puts them in operation, and gives them determinate existence, is the need, instinct, inclination, and passion of man" (22) . . . "We assert then that nothing has been accomplished without interest on the part of the actors; and—if interest be called passion, inasmuch as the whole individuality, to the neglect of all other actual or possible interests and claims, is devoted to an object with every fibre of volition, concentrating all its desires and powers upon it—we may affirm absolutely that *nothing great in the World* has been accomplished without *passion.* Two elements, therefore, enter into the object of our investigation; the first the Idea, the second the complex of human passions; the one the warp, the other the woof of the vast arras-web of Universal History. The concrete mean and union of the two is Liberty, under the conditions of morality in a State" . . . (23) "From this comment on the second essential element in the historical embodiment of an aim, we infer—glancing at the institution of the State in passing—that a State is then well constituted and internally powerful, when the private interest of its citizens is one with the common interest of the State; when the one finds its gratification and realization in the other—a proposition in itself very important. But in a State many institutions must be adopted, much political machinery invented, accompanied by appropriate political arrangements—necessitating long struggles of the understanding before what is really appropriate can be discovered—involving, moreover, contentions with private interest and passions, and a tedious discipline of these latter, in order to bring about the desired harmony." (24)

At this point let there be a pause for the consideration of the meaning of these various stipulations given by Hegel concerning the requirements of a State and the growth of the perfect state. For they bear on the world as we know it today. They will interpret the phases of history now being enacted—the *raison d'être* of the world wars and the significance of its post war problems. Notice that Hegel designates the perfect state in terms which include all the phases of development along the road of progress to that end. He makes it clear that this goal is reached only after a long and varied journey. He enumerates many of the problems that will arise. As we look at the struggles of present day humanity, in the frame of reference which Hegel presents, it becomes clear that the races of mankind are on the march towards an ideal. This ideal is the perfect state, as yet not with us, but it has been conceived. An image of freedom and liberty has come into the minds of men. In this new image mankind beholds the individual as something of dignity and worth—possessing unmeasured potential power for creative achievement. This advance in understanding is at work throughout the world urging men on in order that liberty and freedom become an actuality, a reality.

This new global consciousness is a far cry from the early dawn of existence. Of this Hegel says: "But the history of mankind does not begin with a *conscious* aim of any kind, as it is the case with the particular circles into which men form themselves of set purpose. The mere social instinct implies a conscious purpose of security for life and property; and when society has been constituted, this purpose becomes more comprehensive. The History of the World begins with its general aim—the realization of the Idea of Spirit—only in an *implicit* form (*an sich*) that is, as Nature; a hidden, most profoundly hidden, unconscious instinct; and the whole process of History (as already observed), is directed to rendering this unconscious impulse a conscious one. Thus appearing in the form of merely natural existence, natural will—that which has been called the subjective side—physical craving, instinct, passion, private interest, as also opinion and subjective conception—spontaneously present themselves at the very commencement. This vast congeries of volitions, interests and activities, constitutes the instruments and means of the World-spirit for attaining its object; bringing it to consciousness, and realizing it. And this aim is none other than finding itself —coming to itself—and contemplating itself in concrete actuality . . . (25) The Union of Universal Abstract Existence generally with the Individual—the Subjective—that this alone is Truth, belongs to the department of speculation, and is treated in this general form in Logic. But in the process of the World's History itself—as still incomplete—the abstract final aim of history is not yet made the distinct object of desire and interest. While these limited sentiments are still unconscious of the purpose they are fulfilling, the universal principle is implicit in them, and is realizing itself through them. The question also assumes the form of the union of *Freedom* and *Necessity;* the latent abstract process of Spirit being regarded as *Necessity,* while that which exhibits itself in the conscious will of men, as their interest, belongs to the domain of Freedom." . . . (26) "The Universal Idea exists thus as the substantial totality of things on the one side, and as the abstract essence of free volition on the other side. This reflection of the mind on itself is individual self-consciousness—the polar opposite of the Idea in its general form, and therefore existing in absolute Limitation. This polar opposite is consequently limitation, particularization, for the universal absolute being; it is the side of its *definite existence;* the sphere of its formal reality, the sphere of the reverence paid to God. To comprehend the absolute connection of this antithesis, is the profound task of metaphysics. This Limitation originates all forms of particularity of whatever kind. The formal volition (of which we have spoken) wills itself; desires to make its own personality valid in all that it purposes and does; even the pious individual wishes to be saved and happy. This pole of the antithesis, existing for itself, is—in contrast with the Absolute Universal Being—a special separate existence, taking cognizance of specialty only, and willing that alone. In short it plays its part in the region of mere phenomena. This is the sphere of particular purposes, in effecting which individuals exert themselves on behalf of their individuality—give it full play and objective realization . . . (26) Reflection on self—the Freedom above described—is abstractly defined as the formal element of the activity of the absolute Idea. The realizing *activity* of which we have spoken is the middle term of the Syllogism, one of whose extremes is the Universal essence, the *Idea,* which reposes in the penetralia of Spirit; and the other, the complex of external things—objective matter. That activity is the medium by which the universal latent principle is translated into the domain of objectivity." (27)

This abstract essence of free volition which stands over against the universal idea—the totality of things—this reflection of the mind is self-consciousness. It must be noted that it is what Hegel well names the *realizing activity*. It is the activity where the past and present merge in a fluidic moment of determination. It is truly the medium by which the latent principle of the universal is brought into objective manifestation. We behold it as that ever vanishing instant, or as the eternally present now. But through its slender portals the pageant of history marches its universal course. As Hegel says, "The State is an *abstraction* having even its generic existence in its citizens; but it is an actuality, and its simple generic existence must embody itself in individual will and activity." "Thus the question would arise: What is the material in which the Ideal of Reason is wrought out? The primary answer would be—Personality itself—human desires—Subjectivity generally. In human knowledge and volition, as its material element, Reason attains positive existence. We have considered subjective volition where it has an object which is the truth and essence of a reality, viz., where it constitutes a great world-historical passion. As a subjective will, occupied with limited passions, it is dependent, and can gratify its desires only within the limits of this dependence. But the subjective will has also a substantial life—a reality—in which it moves in the region of *essential* being, and has the essential itself as the object of its existence. This essential being is the union of the subjective with the *rational* will: it is the moral Whole, the *State,* which is that form of reality in which the individual has and enjoys his freedom; but on the condition of his recognizing, believing in, and willing that which is common to the Whole. And this must not be understood as if the subjective will of the social unit attained its gratification and enjoyment through that common Will: as if this were a means provided for its benefit; as if the individual, in his relations to other individuals, thus limited freedom, in order that this universal limitation—the mutual constraint of all—might secure a small space of liberty for each. Rather, we affirm, are Law, Morality, Government, and they alone, the positive reality and completion of Freedom. Freedom of a low and limited order is mere caprice; which finds its exercise in the sphere of particular and limited desires." (38)

"Subjective volition—Passion—is that which sets men in activity, that which effects "practical" realization. The Idea is the inner spring of action; the State is the actually existing, realized moral life. For it is the Unity of the universal, essential Will, with that of the individual; and this is "Morality." The Individual living in this unity has a moral life; possesses a value that consists in this substantiality alone. Sophocles in his Antigone, says, "The divine commands are not of yesterday, nor of today; no, they have an infinite existence, and no one could say whence they came." The laws of morality are not accidental, but are the essentially Rational. It is the very object of the State that what is essential in the practical activity of men, and in their dispositions, should be duly recognized; that is should have a manifest existence, and maintain its position. It is the absolute interest of Reason that this moral Whole should exist; and herein lie the justification and merit of heroes who have founded states—however rude these may have been. In the history of the World, only those peoples can come under our notice which form a state. For it must be understood that this latter is the realization of Freedom, *i.e.* of the absolute final aim, and that it exists for its own sake. It must further be understood that all the worth which the human being possesses—all spiritual reality consists in this, that his own essence—Reason—is objectively present to him, that is possesses objective immediate existence for him. Thus only is he fully conscious; thus only is he a partaker of morality—of a just and moral social and political life. For Truth is the Unity of the universal and subjective Will; and the Universal is to be found in the State, in its laws, its universal and rational arrangements. The state is the Divine Idea as it exists on Earth. We have in it, therefore, the object of History in a more definite shape than before; that in which Freedom obtains objectivity, and lives in the enjoyment of the objectivity. For law is the objectivity of Spirit; volition in its true form. Only that will which obeys law, is free, for it obeys itself—it is independent and so free. When the State or our country constitutes a community of existence; when the subjective will of man submits to laws—the contradiction between Liberty and Necessity vanishes. The Rational has necessary existence, as being the reality and substance of things, and we are free in recognizing it as law, and following it as the substance of our own being. The objective and the subjective will are then reconciled, and present one identical homogeneous whole." (39)

After Hegel has established the nature of The State as the Idea of Spirit in the external manifestation of human Will and its Freedom, he then shows how the successive phases of the idea manifest as distinct political principles. Each World Historical people has a political principle peculiar to it and directly conditioned on its phase of development in the long process from dependence to Spiritual liberation. In these distinct political principles there is not a development from one people to the other as is the case with art, architecture, music and the sciences. In these the patterns continue to develop and expand in countries other than that in which they originate, whereas the political principle remains distinct for each people. It is the outward manifestation of their inner stage of development—the externalization of their inner being. That which China, India, Egypt or Persia framed as their laws, beliefs, and customs is of little value to us today. This thought makes clear the distinction that exists here. Hegel then shows that such political principles are closely associated with religion; in fact, take their rise from religion. For religion is the expression which a people gives in its relation, as particular thinking entities, to the Universal. It is ever a people's most essential expression. It is in the religion of a people that the political principle is grounded. The national religion and the national political genius are component parts of the same force, they present the stages of growth through which World History evolves.

Although this individual national Spirit is very distinct, and although all things of the national life are of its stamp and are exercised within its limitations, yet it is not a static thing. It has a process of transcending itself. It goes through a series of expressions which result from its Idea. Each one of these is increasingly adequate to the manifestation of Freedom. In order to distinguish these according to the categories of Reason it must be understood that the essential aim of the whole History of the World is to attain to the Consciousness of freedom. History develops the phases which this consciousness assumes on its journey through the nonessentials to the truly essential—the Consciousness of Freedom. For man is a thinking being. Unlike the brute he has thought. Because of his power of thought he has Freedom. He, as a single particular person, is capable of abstracting from all particularity into the universal—realizing himself as inherently infinite. "For thought is that *Universal*—that *Species* which is immortal, which preserves identity with itself." The particular form of Spirit does not merely pass away in the world by natural causes in Time, but is annulled in the automatic self-mirroring activity of consciousness. Because this annulling is an activity of Thought it is at the same time conservative and elevating in its operation. While then, on the one side, Spirit annuls the reality, the permanence of that which it is, it gains on the other side, the essence, the Thought, the Universal element of that which *it only was* (its transient conditions). Its principle is no longer that immediate import and aim which it was previously, but the *essence* of that import and aim." (78)

"The result of this process is then that Spirit, in rendering itself objective and making this its being an object of thought, on the one hand destroys the determinate form of its being, on the other hand gains a comprehension of the universal element which it involves, and thereby gives a new form to its inherent principle. In virtue of this, the substantial character of the National Spirit has been altered—that is, its principle has risen into another, and in fact a higher principle." (78)

"It is of the highest importance in apprehending and comprehending History to have and to understand the thought involved in this transition. The individual traverses as a unity various grades of development, and remains the same individual; in like manner also does a people, till the Spirit which it embodies reaches the grade of universality. In this point lies the fundamental, the Ideal necessity of transition. This is the soul—the essential consideration—of the philosophical comprehension of History" . . . (78)

"While we are thus concerned exclusively with the Idea of Spirit, and in the History of the World regard everything as only its manifestation, we have, in traversing the past—however extensive its periods—only to do with what is *present;* for philosophy, as occupying itself with the True, has to do with the *eternally present.* Nothing in the past is lost for it, for the Idea is ever present; Spirit is immortal; with it there is no past, no future, but an essential *now.* This necessarily implies that the present form of Spirit comprehends within it all earlier steps. These have indeed unfolded themselves in succession independently; but what Spirit is it has always been essentially; distinctions are only the development of this essential nature. The life of the ever present Spirit is a circle of progressive embodiments, which looked at in one aspect still exist beside each other, and only as looked at from another point of view appear as past. The grades which Spirit seems to have left behind it, it still possesses in the depths of its present." (79)

In connection with the natural existence of each World Historical people Hegel brings out certain pertinent considerations, among them the geographical characteristics. He says, "Contrasted with the universality of the moral Whole and with the unity of that individuality which is its active principle, the *natural* connection that helps to produce the Spirit of a People, appears an extrinsic element; but inasmuch as we must regard it as the ground on which that Spirit plays its part, it is an *essential* and *necessary* basis. We began with the assertion that, in the History of the World; the Idea of Spirit appears in its actual embodiment as a series of external forms, each one of which declares itself as an actually existing people. This existence falls under the category of Time as well as Space, in the way of natural existence; and the special principle, which every world-historical people embodies, has this principle at the same time as a *natural* characteristic. Spirit, clothing itself in this form of nature, suffers its particular phases to assume separate existence; for mutual exclusion is the mode of existence proper to mere nature. These natural distinctions must be first of all regarded as special possibilities, from which the Spirit of the people in question germinates, and among them is the Geographical Basis . . . (79) Nature, as contrasted with Spirit, is a quantitative mass, whose power must not be so great as to make its single force omnipotent. In the extreme zones man cannot come to free movement; cold and heat are here too powerful to allow Spirit to build up a world for *itself*. Aristotle said long ago, "When pressing needs are satisfied, man turns to the general and more elevated." But in the extreme zones such pressure may be said never to cease, never to be warded off; men are constantly impelled to direct attention to nature, to the glowing rays of the sun, and the icy frost. The true theatre of History is therefore the temperate zone; or, rather, its northern half, because the earth there presents itself in a continental form, and has a broad breast, as the Greeks say. In the south, on the contrary, it divides itself, and runs out into many points." (80)

On this subject of the geographical basis of World History, Hegel goes into a lengthy discussion. He takes up the continents in turn and the countries within them; also the oceans and seas that separate and unite. He even touches upon the plant and animal life, along with the rivers, the mountains, and the valleys of each country in an elaborate review. One illustration of this part of the work will be sufficient. "America is divided into two parts, which are indeed connected by an Isthmus, but which forms only an external, material bond of union. The Old World, on the contrary, which lies opposite America, and is separated from it by the Atlantic Ocean, has its continuity interrupted by a deep inlet—the Mediterranean Sea. The three Continents that compose it have an essential relation to each other, and constitute a totality. Their peculiar feature is that they lie round this Sea, and therefore have an easy means of communication; for rivers and seas are not to be regarded as disjoining, but as uniting. England and Brittany, Norway and Denmark, Sweden and Livonia, have been united. For the three quarters of the globe the Mediterranean Sea is similarly the uniting element, and the centre of World-History. Greece lies here, the focus of light in History. Then in Syria we have Jerusalem, the centre of Judaism and of Christianity; southeast of it lie Mecca and Medina, the cradle of the Mussulman faith; towards the west Delphi and Athens; farther west still, Rome: on the Mediterranean Sea we have also Alexandria and Carthage. The Mediterranean is thus the heart of the Old World, for it is that which conditioned and vitalized it. Without it the

History of the World could not be conceived: it would be like ancient Rome or Athens without the forum, where the life of the city came together." (87)

Finally there comes the review of the continent of Africa, and of the African race as known prior to Hegel's time nearly two hundred years ago. Of these primitive African races Hegel says: "They have moreover no knowledge of the immortality of the soul, although spectres are supposed to appear. The undervaluing of humanity among them reaches an incredible degree of intensity. Tyranny is regarded as no wrong, and cannibalism is looked upon as quite customary and proper. Among us instinct deters from it, if we can speak of instinct at all as appertaining to man. But with the Negro this is not the case, and the devouring of human flesh is altogether consonant with the general principles of the African race; to the sensual Negro, human flesh is but an object of sense—mere flesh. At the death of a King hundreds are killed and eaten; prisoners are butchered and their flesh sold in the markets; the victor is accustomed to eat the heart of his slain foe. When magical rites are performed, it frequently happens that the sorcerer kills thc first that comes in his way and divides his body among the bystanders. Another characteristic fact in reference to the Negroes is Slavery. Negroes are enslaved by Europeans and sold to America. Bad as this may be, their lot in their own land is even worse, since there a slavery quite as absolute exists; for it is the essential principle of slavery, that man has not yet attained a consciousness of his freedom, and consequently sinks down to a mere Thing—an object of no value. Among the Negroes moral sentiments are quite weak or more strictly speaking, non-existent. Parents sell their children and conversely children their parents, as either has the opportunity." (95)

Hegel concludes this review of Africa—which recounts a number of revolting savage customs—by eliminating Africa, except Egypt, from further consideration—it having exhibited no development worthy of a place in the Historical process of the World. In like manner all other countries not having a recorded history are eliminated. There remains among the most important, China, India, Persia, Greece, Egypt, Rome and the Roman Empire—or Europe after the Reformation—centered in the German people as its moving Spirit. In this vast arena Hegel proceeds to show the unfoldment of the World Spirit after the same law as he has outlined in The Phenomenology of Mind and demonstrated in The Logic. In this case Germany, in the German Reformation, becomes the fulfillment of the world Historical process as far as Hegel was able to delineate it up to 1831. The fact that he carried it no further need not call forth a judgment of inadequacy. For the cycle culminating in freedom of individual consciousness was accomplished. Man as man had come into the consciousness of his subjective freedom—the recognition of the individual in his relation to the universal. There had been certain degrees of freedom before this, but none of them were of the nature of the subjective freedom bestowed by the Reformation. There happens here the same thing as was formerly the case with the emergence by man into the stage of Self-Consciousness, when Lordship and Bondage took their rise, and Self-consciousness must prove itself in a life and death struggle. This process is now repeated at a deeper level. Subjective freedom goes through a life and death struggle in which its life consists *in death to all but the Universal Law*. To exercise this Universal Law is the only freedom for its life. It must be exercised by a will made perfect through enlightenment. On the way to this insight, and before it is understood in its application to living, there is a long process of adjustment. It is the time of humanity's coming of age, or the birth into spiritual maturity. These birth pangs are now being suffered throughout the world. Each country in turn goes through the experience of this development. Finally there will be complete fulfillment, in humanity, of the realization that all men possess the right to freedom from an inherent law of their being. Although one people, namely the Germans, came into their realization first, and led by Martin Luther actualized it in the German

Reformation, they furnished but the vanguard of a movement—of an enlightenment—destined to spread to every people of the earth. The fact that Germany later on demonstrated the antithesis of this freedom does not destroy its truth. In so doing Germany did but fulfill the law of opposites—the eternal swing of the pendulum to its alternating poles. Perhaps the interpreting of the freedom in this negative way, and the endeavor to actualize the negative aspect, were the sole means of demonstrating their lack of truth and of proving their futility. It constituted in fact the establishment of the truth on a firmer basis. The up hill travel to the goal of full accomplishment in subjective freedom is long. The stages of elevation for the consciousness of humanity are gradual and the travail is full of anguish. There are also different grades being experienced by different people at the same time. This can be observed in the world. Yet the various races that exerted their force in the great cycle of life, development, and exploration, which finally completed the settlement and knowledge of the earth, constituted an initial group of nations and races whose influences began in the East and moved westward. It is these races that Hegel reviews in the Philosophy of History now under consideration. He reviews them with the purpose of showing that there is a force at work in them—as a whole—which is analogous to the force in the germ of a seed causing it to develop according to its kind. In *The Philosophy of History* the germ at work is the consciousness of subjective freedom—which will have blossom and then fruitage—in the nature of man's spiritual being. It is this hidden aspect of historical development of which Hegel treats. He shows the role played by each race as it came into the theatre of life onto the stage of the world. It will facilitate our understanding of this unique treatise on history if we hold this fact in mind. We will see with Hegel how the sun of consciousness rises in the East, as does the physical light, and how it travels from East to West. We will also see that in the dawn of this great day of "the light that never was on land nor sea—yet is the whole world's light"—how this light, too, had a gray dawn —turning to crimson and more brilliant light as consciousness progressed on its journey westward and to the circling of the globe. We who are reviewing this process, with a view to understanding ourselves and our world, will observe that for the first time the light of consciousness has made its first round, or day. It has risen in the East; it has traveled west. The first encircling of the globe is accomplished. We witness the evening and the night of the first day. But on the morrow it will shine again, revealing a deeper phase of being. It will bring new things to the light of mind—which are now hidden—asleep in the night—or the darkness of our ignorance of them. We can recall, with a smile, how the continent of America, and other commonplaces were once there. So with Hegel we shall go back to this theatre of life to view consciousness at work in the races of men—a consciousness that holds the latent force of spirit—which is freedom. Hegel will look with the eyes of a philosopher and let us perceive what he discerns. We will go back in time to these early hours as the sun is rising.

"The *Sun*—the Light—rises in the East," says Hegel. "Light is a simple self-involved existence; but though possessing thus in itself universality, it exists at the same time as an individuality in the Sun. Imagination has often pictured to itself the emotions of a blind man suddenly becoming possessed of sight, beholding the bright glimmering of the dawn, the growing light, and the flaming glory of the ascending Sun. The boundless forgetfulness of his individuality in this pure splendor, in his first feeling—is utter astonishment. But when the sun is risen this astonishment is diminished; objects around are perceived, and from them the individual proceeds to the contemplation of his own inner being, and thereby the advance is made to the perception of the relation between the two. Then inactive contemplation is quitted for activity; by the close of day man has erected a building constructed from his own inner Sun; and when in the evening he contemplates this, he esteems it more highly than the original external Sun. For now he stands in a conscious relation to his Spirit, and therefore a *free* relation. If we hold this image fast in mind, we shall find it symbolizing the course of History, the great Day's work of Spirit." (103)

This then is that inner reckoning of the Philosophy of History. The first general deduction that Hegel makes regards consciousness. The East, the Orient, he tells us knows only that One is *Free*. In that mighty One all would merge their being. Next come the Greek and Roman worlds and there is a transition to something higher. These knew that *some* are free. Lastly in the German Reformation we have the German world declaring that *All* are free. Subjective freedom is now realized. The German Reformation is the first development of the consciousnes of the inner individual freedom in the History of the World. This is a great accomplishment. We are to watch the genesis of this consciousness active in the historic process. The pictures that Hegel paints of the races and nations are to show the stages of its advance. The fact that Hegel wrote over one hundred years ago, during which time changes have occurred, does not vitiate the truth of the principle at work. Nor does it seriously affect the assertion made by Hegel that except for one country, Egypt, the theatres of the world's history were the continents of Europe and Asia. The Americas were to be the scene of the New Order of the Ages. If we think in terms of philosophy, without reference to the complex externals, it can be shown that these two continents Asia and Europe do in very truth, furnish the norm for the whole historic process. Its cycle was completed in them. The races designated by Hegel, namely China, India, Persia, Greece, Rome and Germany carry the life cycle to its completion in the German Reformation. It is here that subjective freedom comes to birth. From this time onward the scene of action shifts to the subjective nature for the people of the whole globe. Regardless of the conflicts in the external world it will be the inner nature of man that assumes importance. Indeed, all external acts and conflicts will center around the one supreme fact of the inner man and his values. The whole theatre of life, all the aims and efforts thereof, are but the exhibition of humanity at the different levels of the expanding realization of man's subjective freedom. Nor can anything bring to us a keener realization of subjective freedom than to witness the state of being where it does not yet exist as in the countries reviewed by Hegel, namely China and India, of a couple of hundred years ago.

It is fortunate for us that Hegel contemplated these countries at the time he did. Much has happened later to throw them into confused disorder where it would be more difficult for us to discern the principle operating in them. As a matter of fact there has come into these countries during more recent years a shifting of consciousness to the inner values. So much is this the case that to view them with the eyes of Hegel's time will bring astonishment. Yet, because the process of the unfoldment of the World Spirit has been gradual, we can expect to find more primitive ideas in these earlier periods.

Hegel says that the sun of consciousness rises in the East and moves westward. In its course the uncontrolled natural will is brought into obedience to a universal principle and the full light of Self-realization finally shines forth. China, India, Persia, Greece, Rome and Germany furnish the stations along the way from substantial freedom, [which is] the freedom of substance only, to subjective freedom—the freedom of essential essence; from the substantial objective freedom, which is abstract undeveloped reason, to subjective freedom in which the personal will and insight, as conscience are developed in the individual. These countries, as has been stated before are spoken of in this way: The East, or China and India knew that *One* is Free; the Greek and Roman world knew that *some* are free; the German world knew that *All* are free.

Hegel next proceeds to demonstrate this by a searching investigation of the life, beliefs, laws and customs of these civilizations; in short, he gives a survey of the external and internal status of each. The policy will be to treat these findings of Hegel's with the original quest only in mind—namely to discover the germ of man's inherent spirit and then trace its processes through the national cycle of development.

CHINA

"History begins with the Chinese," says Hegel, writing in the first half of the nineteenth century. "It is the oldest country and has been the most substantial. No other people has so continuous a series of historic records as have the Chinese. These extend to 3000 years before Christ. Until the 18th Century, China resisted all intercourse with the outside world. The constitution was formulated at an early date and up to recent times had remained the same. The Spirit of the Chinese operated through the Emperor, as the father of the nation, and from him through the family—where the father was supreme. In this political totality the individual subjective element is entirely wanting. It is understood that the "Universal Will" immediately commands what the individual is to do and the Emperor is the exclusive embodiment of this will, in the empire, as the father is in the home." "Here we have," says Hegel, "the One Being of the State supremely dominant—the Substance, which, still hard and inflexible resembles nothing but itself—includes no other element." (120)

This is the form of the Chinese state as of Hegel's time. It rested on family piety. The individuals were children of the State under the Emperor. All was operated on this basis. The five supreme duties were, the relation of the Emperor and the people; the relation of the father and the children; of elder brother and younger brother; of husband and wife; of friend and friend. The duties of each were established by law and were absolutely binding. Among the innumerable list may be recounted a few by way of example. The son may not speak first to his father; he may not seat himself in the presence of his father; he may not marry without his father's consent nor may he marry during the three years of mourning for the death of the father. All of the son's merit must be ascribed to the father. Also the father is held responsible for the son's transgressions. The graves of parents must be duly visited and the deaths in the family lamented. These lamentations often extend for long periods. The relations that exist between parents and children, hold good in varying degrees to the other family relationships. The Emperor claims the deepest reverence of all. He is obliged, because of his austere position, to manage the government; but there is little room for the exercise of his will. This is because everything is prescribed by ancient maxims, including the obligations of the princes and numerous imperial officials. These are especially educated for their duties according to state regulations and they serve in a spirit of reverent dignity as well as fear. In China we find a nobility of learning rather than rank by reason of birth. One of the important bodies of officials were those known as mandarins. They were of two classes, the civil and the military. In Hegel's time there were 15,000 civil and 20,000 military mandarins. For their promotions they must needs undergo numerous examinations. In the administration of government great publicity prevailed. The subordinate officers report to the Council of the Empire; the latter lays the matter before the Emperor; the Emperor makes his decision; the decision must be published at once in the court Journal. There are also numerous Censors throughout the empire whose duty it is to give an account of everything that goes on to the Emperor. These censors hold office for life, exercise strict surveillance and are much feared. The whole government is covered by a net work of officials and everything is arranged with great minuteness. These numerous officials are each required to make a confession of the faults he has committed. In case of any neglect of this rule the mandarin and his entire family must suffer severe punishment. The jurisprudence of the empire revolves around the person of the Emperor who regulates according to definite rules. There is legal externality of family relations. Every

Chinaman may sell himself and his children. He also buys his wives. Except for the first wife, all of his wives are slaves, and like the children, may be seized upon in case of confiscation.

Most of the chastisements in the Chinese state are corporal in character. The officials, the ministers, the viceroys and even those close to the Emperor himself must submit, when guilty, to such punishment as one hundred blows with a bamboo rod, or torture with red hot pincers. The friendship of the Emperor is not withdrawn on account of the necessity for this chastisement. It is accepted as a matter of course. Nor does the intention of the act alter it in any degree. This subjective element does not enter into Chinese life. It is entirely nonexistent.

In regard to the religious side of Chinese Polity, Hegel says. "In the patriarchal condition the religious exaltation of man has merely a human reference—simple morality and right-doing. The Absolute itself, is regarded partly as the abstract, simple rule of this right-doing—eternal rectitude; partly as the power which is its sanction. Except in these simple aspects, all the relations of the natural world, the postulates of subjectivity—of heart and soul—are entirely ignored. The Chinese in their patriarchal despotism need no such connection or mediation with the Highest Being; for education, the laws of morality and courtesy, and the commands and government of the Emperor embody all such connection and mediation as far as they feel the need of it. The Emperor, as he is the Supreme Head of the State, is also the Chief of its religion. Consequently, religion is in China essentially State-Religion. The distinction between it and Lamaism must be observed, since the latter is not developed to a State, but contains religion as a free, spiritual, disinterested consciousness. The Chinese religion, therefore, cannot be what we call religion. For to us religion means the retirement of the Spirit within itself, in contemplating its essential nature, its inmost Being. In these spheres, then, man is withdrawn from his relation to the State, and betaking himself to this retirement, is able to release himself from the power of secular government. But in China religion has not risen to this grade, for true faith is possible only where individuals can seclude themselves—can exist for themselves independently of any external compulsory power. In China the individual has no such life;—does not enjoy this independence: in any direction he is therefore dependent; in religion as well as in other things; that is, dependent on objects of nature, of which the most exalted is the material heaven. On this depend harvest, the seasons of the year, the abundance and sterility of crops. The Emperor, as crown of all—the embodiment of power—alone approaches heaven; individuals, as such, enjoy no such privilege. He it is, who presents the offerings at the four feasts; gives thanks at the head of his court, for the harvest, and invokes blessings on the sowing of the seed. This "heaven" might be taken in the sense of our term "God," as the Lord of Nature (we say, for example, "Heaven protect us!"); but such a relation is beyond the scope of Chinese thought, for here the one isolated self-consciousness is substantial being, the Emperor himself, the Supreme Power. Heaven has therefore no higher meaning, than Nature. . ."

"The Chinese religion involves that primitive element of magical influence over nature, inasmuch as human conduct absolutely determines the course of events. If the Emperor behaves well, prosperity cannot but ensue; Heaven must ordain prosperity. A second side of this religion is, that as the general aspect of the relation to Heaven is bound up with the person of the Emperor, he has also its more special bearings in his hands; viz. the particular wellbeing of individuals and provinces. These have each an appropriate Genius (Chen), which is subject to the Emperor, who pays adoration only to the general Power of Heaven, while the several Spirits of the natural world follow his laws. He is thus made the proper legislator for Heaven as well as for earth." (132)

In matters of science there is in China the same deficiency of any genuine subjectivity. The sciences appear to receive honored esteem but their study lacks true scientific interest and the free play of mind to follow truth wherever it may lead. Medicine also is studied only empirically and great superstition prevails in the practice of it. In Art there is remarkable skill as imitators of nature, also as the creators of beautiful design but not the revelation of inner vision. One of the particular distinctions of the Chinese is their Language. It may be said to indicate, in a special way, the unique characteristic that possesses them as a race—that of being devoid of a subjective nature. To quote Hegel. "They have, as is well known, beside a Spoken Language, a Written Language; which does not express, as ours does, individual sounds—does not present the spoken words to the eye, but represents the ideas themselves by signs. . . Their Spoken Language consists of an inconsiderable number of monosyllabic words, which are used with more than one signification. The sole methods of denoting distinctions of meaning are the connection, the accent, and the pronunciation—quicker or slower, softer or louder. . . As to their Written Language, I will specify only the obstacles which it presents to the advance of the sciences. Our Written Language is very simple for a learner, as we analyze our Spoken Language into about twenty-five articulations, by which analysis, speech is rendered definite, the multitude of possible sounds is limited, and obscure intermediate sounds are banished: we have to learn only these signs and their combinations. Instead of twenty-five signs of this sort, the Chinese have many thousands to learn. The number necessary for use is reckoned at 9,353, or even 10,516, if we add those recently introduced; and the number of characters generally, for ideas and their combinations as they are presented in books, amounts to from 80,000 to 90,000. As to the sciences themselves, *History* among the Chinese comprehends the bare and definite facts, without any opinion or reasoning upon them. In the same way their Jurisprudence gives only fixed laws, and their Ethics only determinate duties, without raising the question of a subjective foundation for them. The Chinese have, however, in addition to other sciences, a Philosophy, whose elementary principles are of great antiquity, since the Y-King—the Book of Fates—treats of Origination and Destruction. In this book are found the purely abstract ideas of Unity and Duality; the Philosophy of the Chinese appears therefore to proceed from the same fundamental ideas as that of Pythagoras. The fundamental principle recognized is Reason—Tao; that essence lying at the basis of the whole, which effects everything. To become acquainted with its forms is regarded among the Chinese also as the highest science; yet this has no connection with the educational pursuits which more nearly concern the State. The works of Lao-tse, and especially his work "Tao-te-King," are celebrated. Confucius visited this philosopher in the sixth century before Christ, to testify his reverence for him. Although every Chinaman is at liberty to study these philosophical works, a particular sect, calling itself Tao-tse, "Honorers of Reason," makes this study its special business. Those who compose it are isolated from civil life; and there is much that is enthusiastic and mystic intermingled with their views. They believe, for instance, that he who is acquainted with Reason, possesses an instrument of universal power, which may be regarded as all-powerful, and which communicates a supernatural might; so that the possessor is enabled by it to exalt himself to Heaven, and is not subject to death (much the same as the universal Elixir of Life once talked of among us). With the works of Confucius we have become more intimately acquainted. To him, China owes the publication of the *Kings,* and many original works on Morality besides, which form the basis of the customs and conduct of the Chinese. In the principal work of Confucius, which has been translated into English, are found correct moral apophthegms; but there is a circumlocution, a reflex character, and circuitousness in the thought, which prevents it from rising above mediocrity. As to the other sciences, they are not regarded as such, but rather as branches of knowledge for the behoof of practical ends. The Chinese are far behind in Mathematics, Physics, and Astronomy, notwithstanding their quondam reputation in regard to them. They knew many things when Europeans had not discovered them, but they have not understood how to apply their knowledge; as e.g., the magnet, and the art of Printing. But they have made no advance in the application of these discoveries." (136)

"This is the character of the Chinese people in its various aspects. Its distinguishing feature is, that everything which belongs to Spirit—unconstrained morality, in practice and theory, Heart, inward Religion, Science and Art properly so-called—is alien to it. The Emperor always speaks with majesty and paternal kindness and tenderness to the people; who, however, cherish the meanest opinion of themselves, and believe that they are born only to drag the car of Imperial Power. The burden which presses them to the ground seems to them to be their inevitable destiny; and it appears nothing terrible to them to sell themselves as slaves, and to eat the bitter bread of slavery. Suicide, the result of revenge, and the exposure of children, as a common, even daily occurrence, show the little respect in which they hold themselves individually, and humanity in general. And though there is no distinction conferred by birth, and everyone can attain the highest dignity, this very equality testifies to no triumphant assertion of the worth of the inner man, but a servile consciousness—one which has not yet matured itself so far as to recognize distinctions." (138)

INDIA

We come next to India, the second of the countries of the Orient to be studied. It is found to be, as was China, a country devoid of subjective freedom. India's role in the pageant of nations was partly played in prehistoric times. We are reminded of this fact by the remains we find of gigantic palaces and monuments long since in ruins. In the India of today we behold the interesting spectacle of a country carrying its antiquity and modernity on its shoulders at the same time. There is no other land on earth which presents the strange contrasts to be met here. The progress that has been made in India since Hegel wrote of her will but serve to give his statements more significance. They show the working of the spirit in the consciousness of man—which is the subject of our study. Turning to Hegel to present these people and his analysis of them, made over one hundred years ago, we find the following:

"India, like China, is a phenomenon antique as well as modern; one which has remained stationary and fixed, and has received a most perfect home-sprung development. It has always been the land of imaginative aspiration, and appeared to others as a mystical region, an enchanted World. In contrast with the Chinese State, which presents only the most prosaic Understanding, India is the region of phantasy and sensibility. The point of advance in principle which it exhibits to us may be generally stated as follows:—In China the patriarchal principle rules a people in a condition of nonage, the part of whose moral resolution is occupied by the regulating law, and the moral oversight of the Emperor. Now it is the interest of Spirit that external conditions should become internal ones; that the natural and the spiriutal world should be recognized in the subjective aspect belonging to intelligence; by which process the unity of subjectivity and (positive) Being generally—or the Idealism of Existence—is established. This Idealism, then, is found in India, but only as an Idealism of imagination, without distinct conceptions;—one which does indeed free existence from Beginning and Matter (liberates it from temporal limitations and gross materiality), but changes everything into the merely Imaginative; for although the latter appears interwoven with definite conceptions and Thought presents itself as an occasional concomitant, this happens only through accidental combination. Since, however, it is the abstract and absolute Thought itself that enters into these dreams as their material, we may say that Absolute Being is presented here as in the ecstatic state of a dreaming condition. For we have not the dreaming of an actual Individual, possessing distinct personality, and simply unfettering the latter from limitation, but we have the dreaming of the unlimited absolute Spirit." (139)

"The character of Spirit in a state of Dream, as the generic principle of the Hindoo Nature, must be further defined. In a dream, the individual ceases to be conscious of self as such, in contradistinction from objective existences. When awake, I exist for myself, and the rest of creation is an external, fixed objectivity, as I myself am for it. As external, the rest of existence expands itself to a rationally connected whole; a system of relations, in which my individual being is itself a member—an individual being united with that totality. This is the sphere of Understanding. In the state of dreaming, on the contrary, this separation is suspended. Spirit has ceased to exist for itself in contrast with alien existence, and thus the separation of the external and individual dissolves before its universality—its essence. The dreaming Indian is therefore all that we call finite and individual; and, at the same time—as infinitely universal and unlimited—a something intrinsically divine. The Indian view of things is a Universal Pantheism, a Pantheism, however, of Imagination, not of Thought. One substance pervades the Whole of things, and all individualizations are directly vitalized and animated into particular Powers. The sensuous matter and content are in each case simply and in the rough taken up, and carried over into the sphere of the Universal and Immeasurable. It is not liberated by the free power of Spirit into a beautiful form, and idealized in the Spirit, so that the sensuous might be a merely subservient and compliant expression of the spiritual; but (the sensuous object itself) is expanded into the immeasurable and undefined, and the Divine is thereby made bizarre, confused, and ridiculous. These dreams are not mere fables—a play of the imagination, in which the soul only revelled in fantastic gambols: it is lost in them; hurried to and fro by these reveries, as by something that exists really and seriously for it. It is delivered over to these limited objects as to its Lords and Gods. Everything therefore—Sun, Moon, Stars, the Ganges, the Indus, Beasts, Flowers—everything is a God to it. And while, in this deification, the finite loses its consistency and substantiality, intelligent conception of it is impossible. Conversely the Divine, regarded as essentially changeable and unfixed, is also by the base form which it assumes, defiled and made absurd. In this universal deification of all finite existence, and consequent degradation of the Divine, the idea of Theanthropy, the incarnation of God, is not a particularly important conception. The parrot, the cow, the ape, etc., are likewise incarnations of God, yet are not therefore elevated above their nature. The Divine is not individualized to a subject, to concrete Spirit, but degraded to vulgarity and senselessness. This gives us a general idea of the Indian view of the Universe. Things are as much stripped of rationality, of finite consistent stability of cause and effect, as man is of the steadfastness of free individuality, of personality, and freedom." (141)

"There is a beauty of a peculiar kind in women, in which their countenance presents a transparency of skin, a light and lovely roseate hue, which is unlike the complexion of mere health and vital vigor—a more refined bloom, breathed, as it were, by the soul within—and in which the features, the light of the eye, the position of the mouth, appear soft, yielding, and relaxed." . . .

"Such a beauty we find in its loveliest form in the Indian World; a beauty of enervation in which all that is rough, rigid, and contradictory is dissolved, and we have only the soul in a state of emotion—a soul, however, in which the death of free self-reliant Spirit is perceptible." . . . (140)

India's principal part in general history stems from the fact that she has been a Land of Desire to all the nations of the West. Undisturbed herself by any thought of expanding her possessions, or of conquest; satisfied to live life in her accustomed way on her own homeland, she has yet been a magnet for the allurement of all the nations of the world. But she gives occasion for this not only because of her reputation for the mysterious hidden wisdom she is alleged to possess, but on account of her vast physical riches as well. For India is a veritable treasure store. She has pearls, diamonds, emeralds, gold, sapphires, ivory, teakwood, perfumes, spices, cotton, rice, opium, flax, rose-essences, sandlewood and alabaster along with her coal and iron to mention but a portion. The passage of these treasures into the hands of other nations has been a matter of historical importance and the occasion of historical incidents. Hegel at this point goes into a thorough review of the part that each nation played in India giving historical facts, also an enumeration of the Indian rulers and descriptions of the different geographical sections constituting this vast subcontinent with its three hundred million souls. From this we turn to the political life with an analysis relevant to the study in hand.

"With regard to the *political* life of the Indians," says Hegel, "we must first consider the advance it presents in contrast with China. In China there prevailed an equality among all the individuals composing the empire; consequently all government was absorbed in its centre, the Emperor, so that individual members could not attain to independence and subjective freedom. The next degree in advance of this Unity is Difference, maintaining its independence against the allsubduing power of Unity. An organic life requires in the first place One Soul, and in the second place, a divergence into differences, which become organic members, and in their several offices develop themselves to a complete system; in such a way, however, that their activity reconstitutes that one soul. This freedom of separation is wanting in China. The deficiency is that diversities cannot attain to independent existence. In this respect, the essential advance is made in India, viz.: that independent members ramify from the unity of despotic power. Yet the distinctions which these imply are referred to Nature. Instead of stimulating the activity of a soul as their centre of union, and spontaneously realizing that soul—as is the case in organic life—they petrify and become rigid, and by their stereotyped character condemn the Indian people to the most degrading spiritual serfdom. The distinctions in question are the *Castes*. In every rational State there are distinctions which must manifest themselves. Individuals must arrive at subjective freedom, and in doing so, give an objective form to these diversities. But Indian culture has not attained to a recognition of freedom and inward morality; the distinctions which prevail are only those of occupations, and civil conditions. In a free state also, such diversities give rise to particular classes, so combined, however, that their members can maintain their individuality. In India we have only a division in masses—a division, however, that influences the whole political life and the religious consciousness. The distinctions of class, like that (rigid) Unity in China, remain consequently on the same original grade of *substantiality*, i.e., they are not the result of the free subjectivity of individuals. Examining the idea of a State and its various functions, we recognize the first essential function as that whose scope is the absolutely Universal; of which man becomes conscious first in Religion, then in Science. God, the Divine is the absolutely Universal. The highest class therefore will be the one by which the Divine is presented and brought to bear on the community—the class of Brahmins. The second element or class, will represent subjective power and valor. Such power must assert itself, in order that the whole may stand its ground, and retain its integrity against other such totalities or states. This class is that of the Warriors and Governors—the *Cshatriyas*; although Brahmins often become governors. The Third order of occupation recognized is that which is concerned with the specialities of life—the satisfying of its necessities—and comprehends agriculture, crafts and trade; the class of the *Vaisyas*. Lastly, the fourth element is the class of service, the mere instrument for the comfort of others, whose business it is to work for others for wages affording a scanty subsistence—the caste of *Sudras*. This servile class—properly speaking—constitutes no special organic class in the state, because its members only serve individuals: their occupations are therefore dispersed among them and are consequently attached to that of the previously mentioned castes.—Against the existence of "classes" generally, an objection has been brought—especially in modern times—drawn from the consideration of the State in its "aspect" of abstract equity. But equality in civil life is something absolutely impossible, for individual distinctions of sex and age will always assert themselves. The distinction between poverty and riches, the influence of skill and talent, can be as little ignored—utterly refuting those abstract assertions. But while this principle leads us to put up with variety of occupations, and distinction of the classes to which they are intrusted, we are met here in India by the peculiar circumstance that the individual belongs to such a class essentially by *birth,* and is bound to it for life. All the concrete vitality that makes its appearance sinks back into death. A chain binds down the life that was just upon the point of breaking forth. The promise of freedom which these distinctions hold out is herewith completely nullified. What birth has separated mere arbitrary choice has no right to join together again: therefore, the castes preserving distinctness from their very origin, are presumed not to be mixed or united by marriage." (146)

Hegel next goes into a lengthy description of the four

castes discussing the history of each and the customs, laws and duties pertaining to each. For instance, to quote: "We must next consider the relative position of these castes. Their origin is referred to a myth, which tells us that the Brahmin caste proceeded from Brahma's mouth; the warrior caste from his arms; the industrial classes from his loins; the servile caste from his foot." (146) Hegel also gives other supposed origins and the hypothesis offered by historians. He ends the resume with the following: "Classes cannot be brought together from without; they are developed only from within. They come forth from the interior of the national life, and not conversely. But that these distinctions are here attributed to nature, is a necessary result of the Idea which the East embodies. For while the individual ought properly to be empowered to choose his occupation, in the East, on the contrary, internal subjectivity is not yet recognized as independent; and if distinctions obtrude themselves their recognition is accompanied by the belief that the individual does not choose his particular position for himself, but receives it from Nature." (147)

We have here in India the fact of Nature as the governing power entirely usurping the subjective freedom of man. Speaking of this Hegel says: "But this natural destiny need not have led to that degree of degradation which we observe here, if the distinctions had been limited to occupation with what is earthly—to forms of objective Spirit. In the feudalism of mediaeval times, individuals were also confined to a certain station in life; but for all there was a Higher Being, superior to the most exalted earthly dignity, and admission to holy orders was open to all. This is the grand distinction, that here Religion holds the same position towards *all*; that, although the son of a mechanic becomes a mechanic, the son of a peasant a peasant and free choice is often limited by many restrictive circumstances, the *religious element* stands in the same relation to all, and all are invested with an absolute value by religion. In India the direct contrary is the case. Another distinction between the classes of society as they exist in the Christian world and those in Hindostan is the moral dignity which exists among us in every class, constituting that which man must possess in and through himself. In this respect the higher classes are equal to the lower; and while religion is the higher sphere in which all sun themselves, equality before the law—rights of person and of property—are gained for every class. But by the fact that in India, as already observed, differences extend not only to the objectivity of Spirit, but also to its absolute subjectivity, and thus exhaust all its relations—neither morality, nor justice, nor religiosity is to be found." (147)

In Hegel's words: "For this abstraction, this pure unity, is that which lies at the foundation of All—the root of all definite existence. In the intellection of this unity, all objectivity falls away; for the purely Abstract is intellection itself in its greatest vacuity. To attain this Death of Life during life itself —to constitute this abstraction—requires the disappearance of all moral activity and volition, and of all intellection too, as in the Religion of Fo; and this is the object of the penances spoken of." (156)

"The complement to the abstraction Brahm must then be looked for in the concrete complex of things; for the principle of the Hindoo religion is the Manifestation of Diversity (in "Avatars"). These then, fall outside that abstract Unity of Thought, and as that which deviates from it, constitute the variety found in the world of sense, the variety of intellectual conceptions in an unreflected sensuous form. In this way the concrete complex of material things is isolated from Spirit, and presented in wild distraction, except as re-absorbed in the pure ideality of Brahm. The other deities are therefore things of sense: Mountains, Streams, Beasts, the Sun, the Moon, the Ganges. The next stage is the concentration of this wild variety into substantial distinctions, and the comprehension of them as a series of divine persons. Vishnu, Siva, Mahadeva are thus distinguished from Brahma. In the embodiment Vishnu are presented those incarnations in which God has appeared as man, and which are always historical personages, who effected important changes and new epochs. The power of Procreation is likewise a substantial embodiment; and in the excavations, grottos and pagodas of the Hindoos, the Lingam is always found as symbolizing the male, and the Lotus the female *vis procreandi*." (157)

"With this Duality—abstract unity on the one side and the abstract isolation of the world of sense on the other side—exactly corresponds the double form of Worship, in the relation of the human subjectivity of God. The one side of this duality of worship consists in the abstraction of pure self-elevation—the abrogation of real self-consciousness; a negativity which is consequently manifested, on the one hand, in the attainment of torpid unconsciousness—on the other hand in suicide and the extinction of all that is worth calling life, by self-inflicted tortures. The other side of worship consists in a wild tumult of excess; when all sense of individuality has vanished from consciousness by immersion in the merely natural; with which individuality thus makes itself identical—destroying its consciousness of distinction from Nature." (157)

Turning from this to the Christian World we find that in Christianity, religion is the knowledge of that being of whose life we partake and who is therefore the substance of our knowledge. It therefore becomes the office of the Christian to mirror forth this substance in its purity and truth. "But," says Hegel, "that requires this (Highest) Being to be *in se* a personality, pursuing divine aims, such as can become the purport of human action. Such an idea of the relation of the Being of God as constituting the universal basis or substance of human action—such a morality cannot be found among the Hindoos; for they have not the spiritual as the import of their consciousness. On the one hand their virtue consists in the abstraction from all activity—the condition they call "Brahm." On the other hand every action with them is a prescribed external usage; not free activity, the result of inward personality. Thus the moral nature of the Hindoos (as already observed) shows itself most abandoned." (158)

The next subjects that Hegel takes up are the Hindoo Arts and Sciences. He enumerates the various Hindoo ancient and canonical books, the history of their coming to light and gives accounts of how written, of their translators and contents. He reviews the Vedas—which date from a remote antiquity and are found to be in a language much older than the Sanscrit. He gives an account of the two great epic poems, the Ramayana and the Mahabharata, besides the *Puranaś* and the code of *Manu*. "The traditions of the last named," he says, "reach beyond twenty-three centuries before the birth of Christ; a dynasty of the Children of the Sun is mentioned on which followed one of the Children of the Moon." (160) Concerning these it is possible that such citations may be allusions of astrological significance. In this subject the Hindoos are considered well versed. In the same category may also be the claim that Brahma is the first figure in the Cosmogony—self-produced and the claim that Vishnu has had innumerable incarnations. The Hindoo literature abounds with characters of a fabulous and mythological nature, many of which are symbolical. In consonance with this it is found that with the Hindoos, History as such, does not exist. Says Hegel "Though the recent discoveries of the treasures of Indian Literature have shown us what a reputation the Hindoos have acquired in Geometry, Astronomy, and Algebra—that they have made great advances in Philosophy, and that among them, Grammar has been so far cultivated that no language can be regarded as more fully developed than the Sanscrit—we find the department of *History* altogether neglected, or rather—non-existent." (162) Hegel then explains that history requires Understanding, i.e., looking at events and circumstances in an objective light. This mode of mentality is foreign to the Hindoo temperament which finds it more natural to dream and yield to destiny by which means its Spirit is kept in an exalted imaginary realm. Thus historical events, as such, their comprehension and a fidelity in recording them, does not hold the attention of the Hindoo mind. Hegel delivers the following appraisal of History: "But

History is always of great importance for a people; since by means of that it becomes conscious of the path of development of its own Spirit, which expresses itself in laws, manners, Customs, and Deeds. Laws, comprising morals and judicial institutions, are by nature the permanent elements in a people's existence. But History presents a people with their own image in a condition which thereby becomes objective to them. Without History their existence in time is blindly self-involved—the recurring play of arbitrary volition in manifold forms. History fixes and imparts consistency to this fortuitous current—gives it the form of Universality, and by so doing posits a directive and restrictive rule for it. It is an essential instrument in developing and determining the Constitution—that is a rational political condition; for it is the empirical method of producing the Universal, in as much as it sets up a permanent object for the conceptive powers.—It is because the Hindoos have no History in the form of annals (historia) that they have no history in the form of transactions (res gestae); that is, no growth expanding into a veritable political condition." (163)

It is true, however that the Hindoos have certain historical data. For instance, they have a fixed Era from which they reckon events—that of Vicramaditya. It was at this time that Calidasa lived who was the author of the nationally famous and beloved drama, Sacontala. There are also long lists of the names of kings but these are found to be contradictory. They show that there has been a prevailing confusion of historical matters and also a continual struggle which does not arrive at any settled condition that would further development either national or individual. Hegel endeavors to go through these dynasties with painstaking thoroughness in the hope of throwing light on all aspects of Indian history and life. However, for the present purpose, this must be, at best, an over-all picture which will but emphasize those characteristics that bear on the general subject of India's place in the evolution of the races toward the consciousness of subjective freedom. Hegel summarizes his findings in the following manner. "If then, in conclusion, we once more take a general view of the comparative condition of India and China, we shall see that China was characterized by a thoroughly unimaginative Understanding; a prosaic life amid firm and definite reality: while in the Indian world there is, so to speak, no object that can be regarded as real, and firmly defined—none that was not at its first apprehension perverted by the imagination to the very opposite of what it presents to an intelligent consciousness. In China it is the Moral which constitutes the substance of the laws, and which is embodied in external strictly determinate relations; while over all hovers the patriarchal providence of the Emperor, who like a Father, cares impartially for the interest of his subjects. Among the Hindoos, on the contrary—instead of this Unity—Diversity is the fundamental characteristic. Religion, War, Handicraft, Trade, yes, even the most trivial occupations are parcelled out with rigid separation—constituting as they do the import of the one will which they involve, and whose various requirements they exhaust. With this is bound up a monstrous, irrational imagination, which attaches the moral value and character of man to an infinity of outward actions as empty in point of intellect as of feeling; sets aside all respect for the welfare of man, and even makes a duty of the cruelest and severest contravention of it. Those distinctions being rigidly maintained, nothing remains for the one universal will of the State but pure caprice, against whose omnipotence only the fixed caste-distinctions avail for protection. The Chinese in their prosaic rationality, reverence as the Highest, only the abstract supreme lord; and they exhibit a contemptibly superstitious respect for the fixed and definite. Among the Hindoos there is no such superstition so far as it presents an antithesis to Understanding; rather their whole life and ideas are one unbroken superstition, because among them all is revery and consequent enslavement. Annihilation—the abandonment of all reason, morality and subjectivity—can only come to a positive feeling and consciousness of itself, by extravagating in a boundlessly wild imagination; in which, like a desolate spirit, it finds no rest, no settled composure, though it can content itself in no other way; as a man who is quite reduced in body and spirit finds his existence altogether stupid and intolerable, and is driven to the creation of a dream-world and a delirious bliss in Opium." (167)

As Hegel's estimate of the religious consciousness of India may have been adequate at the beginning of the year 1800, at this time—a century and a half later—we can only be thankful for a unique picture which we can no longer see from our present day perspective. It may be true that because of the conditions then existing the appraisal that Hegel made was a fitting picture of the countenance of India at that time. Yet if one would know India's true contribution to the Eastern people and to the rest of the world—one must plumb deeper. Also it must be remembered that Hegel's purpose in this review was a special one. He was reviewing not one religion so much as the whole sweep of the various racial concepts as they moved in a synthesized historic process. This process according to Hegel was to unfold Subjective Freedom. That this is being accomplished the later conditions in India, China and the world at large fully demonstrate. The picture which was presented by these oldest civilizations, a hundred or more years ago, might easily have given Hegel grounds for the judgments that he made. India was under a cloud of adversity and disruption. While she was under this cloud the sun of civilization was traveling Westward. Here undreamed of phases of man's inherent power were to come forth into the light. This awakening of the West brought a challenge to India to show her own true values. Now the whole globe is being animated in a reciprocal awareness of West versus East and East versus West.

For the sake of all around justice and a better understanding we will take a look at a summary of India's religion and philosophy made at a date nearer our own time. It comes from an authoritative source and on an occasion that was of international importance. There will here be interpolated the following.

A Condensation of the Address on Hinduism
as delivered by
Swami Vivekananda
at
The World's Parliament of Religions
Chicago Columbian Exposition
1893

. . . The Hindus have received their religion through their revelation, the Vedas. They hold that the Vedas are without beginning and without end. It may sound ludicrous to this audience, how a book can be without beginning or end. But by the Vedas no books are meant. They mean the accumulated treasury of spiritual law discovered by different persons in different times. Just as the law of gravitation existed before its discovery, and would exist if all humanity forgot it, so with the laws that govern the spiritual world. The moral, ethical and spiritual relation between soul and souls and between individual spirits and the Father of all spirits were there before their discovery and would remain even if we forgot them.

The discoverers of these laws are called Rishis and we honor them as perfected beings, and I am glad to tell this audience that some of the very best of them were women.

. . . The Vedas teach us that creation is without beginning or end. Science has proved to us that the sum total of the cosmic energy is the same throughout all. . . If I may be allowed to apply a simile, creation and creator are two lives, without beginning, and without end, running parallel to each other, and God is power, an ever active providence, under whose power, systems after systems are being evolved out of chaos—made to run for a time and again destroyed. This is what the Hindu boy repeats every day with his *guru*. "The sun and moon, the Lord created after other suns and moons." And this agrees with science.

Here I stand, and if I shut my eyes and try to conceive my existence, I, I, I—what is the idea before me? The idea of a body. Am I, then, nothing but a combination of matter and material substances? The Vedas declare "No," I am a spirit living in a body. I am not the body. The body will die, but I will not die. Here I am in this body, and when it will fail, still I will go on living, and also I had a past. The soul was not created from nothing, for creation means a combination. . . . Why if they are all created does a just and merciful God create one happy and the other unhappy? . . . The cause of those peculiar tendencies in that soul have been caused by his past actions, and a soul with a certain tendency would go and take birth in a body which is the fittest instrument of the display of that tendency by the laws of affinity. And this is in perfect accord with science, for science wants to explain everything by habit, and habit is got through repetitions. So these repetitions are also necessary to explain the habits of a new born soul—and they were not got in this present life; therefore they must have come down from past lives.

But there is another suggestion; taking all these for granted—how is it that I do not remember anything of my past life?

. . . Verification is the perfect proof of a theory and here is the challenge thrown to the world by the Rishis. We have discovered precepts by which the very depths of the ocean of memory can be stirred up—try it and you would get a complete reminiscence of your past life.

So the Hindu believes that he is a spirit. Him the sword cannot pierce—him the fire cannot burn—him the water cannot melt—him the air cannot dry. And that every soul is a circle whose circumference is no where and whose center is located in a body, and death means the change of this center from body to body.

. . . But there is another question; is man a tiny boat in a tempest, raised one moment on the foaming crest of a billow and dashed down into a yawning chasm the next, rolling to and fro at the mercy of good and bad actions—a powerless, helpless wreck in an ever-raging, ever-rushing, uncompromising current of cause and effect. . . Is there no escape? was the cry that went up from the bottom of the heart of despair. . . A Vedic sage stood up before the world and in trumpet voice proclaimed "Hear ye children of immortal bliss even ye that reside in higher spheres. I have found the Ancient One, who is beyond all darkness, all delusion, and knowing him alone you shall be saved from death over again." Children of immortal bliss, . . . the Hindu refuses to call you sinners.

The Almighty and the All merciful—He is everywhere the pure and formless one. . . He reveals himself to the pure heart, and the pure and stainless man sees God, yea even in this life, and then, and then only all the crookedness of the heart is made straight. Then all doubt ceases. He is no more the freak of a terrible law of causation. So this is the very center, the very vital conception of Hinduism. The Hindu does not want to live upon words and theories—if there are existences beyond the ordinary sensual existence, he wants to come face to face with them. If there is a soul in him which is not matter, if there is an all merciful universal soul, he will go to him direct. He must see him, and that alone can destroy all doubts. So the best proof a Hindu sage gives about the soul, about God, is "I have seen the soul; I have seen God." And that is the only condition of perfection. The Hindu religion does not consist in struggles and attempts to believe a certain doctrine or dogma, but in realizing; not in believing, but in being and becoming.

So the whole struggle in this system is a constant struggle to become perfect, even as the Father in Heaven is perfect, constitutes the religion of the Hindus.

And what becomes of man when he becomes perfect? He lives a life of bliss, infinite. He enjoys infinite and perfect bliss, having obtained the only thing in which man ought to have pleasure, God, and enjoys the bliss with God. So far all the Hindus are agreed. This is the common religion of all the sects of India; but then the question comes, perfection is absolute, and the absolute cannot be two, or three. It cannot have any qualities. It cannot be an individual. And so when a soul becomes perfect and absolute it must become one with

Brahma, and he would only realize the Lord as the perfection, the reality, of his own nature and existence, the existence absolute, knowledge absolute, and life absolute. We have often and often read about this being called the losing of Individuality, as becoming a stick, or a stone. "He jests at scars who never felt a wound."

I tell you it is nothing of the kind. It is happiness to enjoy the consciousness of this small body, it must be more happiness to enjoy the consciousness of two bodies, so three, four, five; and the aim, the ultimate of happiness would be reached when it would become a universal consciousness. Therefore, to gain this infinite universal individuality, this miserable little prison individuality must go. Then alone can death cease when I am one with life, then alone can misery cease, when I am one with happiness itself; then alone can all errors cease when I am one with knowledge itself; and it is the necessary scientific conclusion, science has proved to me that physical individuality is a delusion, that really my body is one little continuously changing body, in an unbroken ocean of matter, and the Adwaitam is the necessary conclusion with my other counterpart, mind.

Science is nothing but the finding of unity, and as my science can reach the perfect unity, it would stop from further progress, because it would reach the goal, thus chemistry cannot progress further when it would discover one element out of which all others could be made. Physics would stop when it would be able to fulfill its services in discovering one energy of which all the others are but the manifestations, and the science of religion became perfect when it discovered Him who is the one life in a universe of death; Him who is the constant basis of an everchanging world; One who is the only Soul of which all souls are but delusive manifestations. Thus was it, through multiplicity and duality, the ultimate unity was reached, and religion can go no farther. . .

All science is bound to come to this conclusion in the long run. . . . Descend we now from the aspirations of philosophy to the religion of the ignorant. On the outset, I may tell you that there is no polytheism in India. In every temple, if one stands and listens, he will find the worshipers applying all the attributes of God, including omnipresence, to these images. It is not polytheism. . .

. . . Why does a Christian go to church, why is the cross holy, why is the face turned towards the sky in prayer? Why are there so many images in the Catholic Church, why are there so many images in the minds of Protestants, when they pray? My brethren, we can no more think about anything without a material image than it is profitable for us to live without breathing. And by the law of association the material image calls the mental idea up and *vice versa.* Omnipotent, to almost the whole world, means nothing. Has God superficial area? If not, when we repeat the word we think of the extended earth; that is all.

As we find that somehow or other, by the laws of our constitution, we have got to associate our ideas of infinity with the idea of a blue sky or a sea; the omnipresence covering the idea of holiness with an idol of a church or a mosque, or a cross; so the Hindus have associated the ideas of holiness, purity, truth, omnipresence with different images and forms. But with this difference: upon certain actions some are drawn their whole lives to their idol of a church and never rise higher, because with them religion means an intellectual assent to certain doctrines and doing good to their fellows. The whole religion of the Hindus is centered in realization. Man is to become divine, and, therefore, idol, or temple, or church, or books, are only the supporters, the helps of his spiritual childhood, but on and on he must progress.

But if a man can realize his divine nature with the help of an image, would it be right to call it a sin. Nor ever when he has passed that stage that he should call it an error. To the Hindu, man is not traveling from error to truth but from truth to truth, from lower to higher truth. To him all the religions from the lowest fetishism to the highest absolutism means so many attempts of the human soul to grasp and realize the Infinite, determined by the conditions of its birth and association, and each of these marks a stage of progress, and every soul is a child eagle soaring higher and higher; gathering more and more strength till it reaches the glorious sun. . . .

. . . The Hindu might have failed to carry out all of his plans, but if there is to be ever a universal religion, it must be one which would hold no location in place or time, which would be infinite like the God it would preach, whose sun shines upon the followers of Krishna or Christ; saints or sinners alike; which in its catholicity would embrace in its infinite arms and formulate a place for every human being, from the lowest groveling man who is scarcely removed in intellectuality from the brute, to the highest mind, towering almost above humanity, and who makes society stand in awe and doubt his human nature. It would be a religion which would have no place for persecution or intolerance in its polity, and would recognize a divinity in every man or woman, and whose whole scope, whose whole force would be centered in aiding humanity to realize its divine nature. . .

May He who is the Brahma of the Hindus, the Ahura Mazda of the Zoroastrians, the Buddha of the Buddhists, the Jehovah of the Jews, the Father in Heaven of the Christians, give strength to you to carry out your noble idea. The star arose in the East; it traveled steadily toward the West, sometimes dimmed and sometimes effulgent, till it made a circuit of the world, and now it is again rising on the very horizon of the East, the borders of the Tasifu, a thousand-fold more effulgent than it ever was before. Hail Columbia, mother-land of liberty! It has been given to thee, who never dipped her hand in her neighbor's blood, who never found out that the shortest way of becoming rich was by robbing one's neighbor, it has been given to thee to march on at the vanguard of civilization with the flag of harmony.

THE ORIENT CONTINUED

The summary of the conditions in China and India is followed by reviews of the other countries comprising the remainder of the Orient, namely Ceylon, Farther India, Burma, Siam, Anam, Tibet, Mongolia, and the land of the Tartars. The contemplative temperament characterizing the Hindoo Spirit revelling through natural and spiritual forms and comprising at the same time ordinary sensuality and the profoundest thought, gives way here and we have a Dream-life *unconstrained*. It is of a ruder form and has not advanced so far as to make distinctions in its modes of life, but for that very reason has not succumbed to the binding force which this entails. Life is more free, more independent and more firmly established in itself. It also expresses itself in simpler conceptions and the political conditions are more calm and settled. The religion found here is Buddhism. It appears in two forms, the negative and the positive form. Of the former Hegel says: "The Religion of these people is *Buddhism,* which is the most widely extended religion on our globe. In China Buddha is reverenced as *Fo*; in Ceylon as *Gautama*; in Thibet and among the Mongols this religion has assumed the phase of Lamaism. In China—where the religion of Fo early received a great extension, and introduced a monastic life—it occupies the position of an integrant element of the Chinese principle. As the Substantial form of Spirit which characterizes China, develops itself only to a unity of *secular* national life, which degrades individuals to a position of constant dependence, religion also remains in a state of dependence. The element of freedom is wanting to it; for its object is the principle of Nature in general—Heaven—Universal Matter. But the (compensating) truth of this alienated form of Spirit (Nature occupying the place of the Absolute Spirit) is *ideal* Unity; the elevation above the limitation of Nature and of existence at large;—the return of consciousness into the soul. This element, which is contained in Buddhism, has made its way in China, to that extent to which the Chinese have become aware of the unspirituality of their condition, and the limitation that hampers their consciousness.—In this religion—which may be generally described as the religion of self-involvement (undeveloped Unity)—the elevation of that unspiritual condition to subjectivity, takes place in two ways; one of which is of a negative, the other of an affirmative kind." (168)

"The *negative* form of this elevation is the concentration of Spirit to the Infinite, and must first present itself under theological conditions. It is contained in the fundamental dogma, that Nothingness is the principle of all things—that all proceeded from and returns to, Nothingness. The various forms in the World are only modifications of procession (thence). If an analysis of these various forms were attempted, they would lose their quality; for in themselves all things are one and the same inseparable essence, and this essence is Nothingness. The connection of this with the Metempsychosis can be thus explained: All that we see is but a change of Form. The inherent infinity of Spirit—infinite concrete self-dependence—is entirely separate from this Universe of phenomena. Abstract Nothingness is properly that which lies beyond Finite Existence—what we may call the Supreme Being. This real principle of the Universe is, it is said, in eternal repose, and in itself unchangeable. Its essence consists in the absence of activity and volition. For Nothingness is abstract Unity with itself. To obtain happiness, therefore, man must seek to assimilate himself to this principle by continual victories over himself; and for the sake of this, do nothing, wish nothing, desire nothing. In this condition of happiness, therefore, Vice or Virtue is out of the question; for the true blessedness is Union with Nothingness. The more man frees himself from all speciality of existence, the nearer does he approach perfection; and in the annihilation of all activity—in pure passivity—he attains complete resemblance to Fo. The abstract Unity in question is not a mere Futurity—a Spiritual sphere existing beyond our own; it has to do with the present; it is truth for man (as he is), and ought to be realized in him. In Ceylon and the Burman Empire—where this Buddhistic Faith has its roots—there prevails an idea, that man can attain by mediation, to exemption from sickness, old age and death." (169)

"But while this is the *negative* form of the elevation of Spirit from immersion in the Objective to a subjective realization of itself, this Religion also advances to the consciousness of an *affirmative* form. Spirit is the Absolute. Yet in comprehending Spirit it is a point of essential importance in what determinate form Spirit is conceived. When we speak of Spirit as universal, we know that for us it exists only in an inward conception; but to attain this point of view—to appreciate Spirit in the pure subjectivity of Thought and conception—is the result of a longer process of culture. At that point in history at which we have now arrived, the form of Spirit is not advanced beyond Immediateness (the idea of it is not yet refined by reflection and abstraction). God is conceived in an immediate, unreflected form; not in the form of Thought—objectivity. But his immediate Form is that of humanity. The Sun, the Stars do not come up to the idea of Spirit; but Man seems to realize it; and he, as *Buddha, Gautama, Fo*—in the form of a departed teacher, and in the living form of the Grand Lama—receives divine worship." (170)

Now in this worship of the Godman it must be understood that it is not the individuality that is worshipped but the universal in him—the man being but the form in which the Spirit manifests itself. Nor does the Godman hold this Spiritual Essence as his particular property. He is only partaking of it; whereas in China the Imperial dignity was supposed to hold power over Nature, there is no such idea in the case of the Lama. It is the Mongols who have especially developed

Buddhism to this form of a living man in divine estate—for formerly the idea was affixed only to a deceased person. The Mongols, in adopting these different expressions of Buddhism, have to a great extent supplanted the older Shaman Religion —formerly prevalent in northern Mongolia and Siberia. This Shaman Religion was a religion of sorcery and superstition; and since Buddhism and Lamaism have taken the place of it the life of the Mongols has been simplified and moves along patriarchal patterns. In concluding this part of the treatise, Hegel writes: "Where they take any part in history we find them occasioning impulses that have only been the groundwork of historical development. There is therefore little to be said about the political administration of the Lamas. A Vizier has charge of the secular dominion and reports everything to the Lama: the government is simple and lenient; and the veneration which the Mongols pay to the Lama, expresses itself chiefly in their asking counsel of him in political affairs." (172)

THE PERSIAN EMPIRE

After the consideration of the Countries of the Orient—where people know only that One is free—we pass to the study of the nations constituting the Persian Empire. This loose confederation of many races, showing great variety of life and restless shifting, forms the transition to the Greek World where people know that Some are free. Of it Hegel says: "With the Persian Empire we first enter on continuous History. The Persians are the first Historical People; Persia was the first Empire that passed away. While China and India remain stationary, and perpetuate a natural vegetative existence even to the present time, this land has been subject to those developments and revolutions, which alone manifest a historical condition. The Chinese and the Indian Empire assert a place in the historical series only on their own account and for us (not for neighbors and successors). But here in Persia first arises that light which shines itself, and illuminates what is around; for *Zoroaster's* "Light" belongs to the World of Consciousness—to Spirit as a relation to something distinct from itself. We see in the Persian World a pure exalted Unity, as the essence which leaves the special existences that inhere in it, free;—as the Light, which only manifests what bodies are in themselves;—a Unity which governs individuals only to excite them to become powerful for themselves—to develop and assert their individuality. Light makes no distinctions: The Sun shines on the righteous and the unrighteous, on high and low, and confers on all the same benefit and prosperity. Light is vitalizing only in so far as it is brought to bear on something distinct from itself, operating upon and developing that. It holds a position of antithesis to Darkness, and this antithetical relation opens out to us the principle of activity and life. The principle of development begins with the history of Persia. This therefore constitutes strictly the beginning of World-History; for the grand interest of Spirit in History, is to attain an unlimited immanence of subjectivity —by an absolute antithesis to attain complete harmony." (174)

"Thus the transition which we have to make, is only in the sphere of the Idea, not in the external historical connection. The principle of this transition is that the Universal Essence, which we recognized in Brahm, now becomes perceptible to consciousness—becomes an object and acquires a positive import for man. Brahm is not worshipped by the Hindoos: he is nothing more than a condition of the Individual, a religious feeling, a non-objective existence—a relation, which for concrete vitality is that of annihilation. But in becoming objective, this Universal Essence acquires a positive nature: man becomes free, and thus occupies a position face to face as it were with the Highest Being, the latter being made objective for him. This form of Universality we see exhibited in Persia, involving a separation of man from the Universal essence; while at the same time the individual recognizes himself as identical with (a partaker in), that essence. In the Chinese and Indian principle, this distinction was not made. We found only a unit of the Spiritual and the Natural. But Spirit still involved in Nature has to solve the problem of freeing itself from the latter. Rights and Duties in India are intimately connected with special classes, and are therefore only peculiarities attaching to man by the arrangement of Nature. In China this unity presents itself under the conditions of *paternal* government. Man is not free there; he possesses no moral element, since he is identical with the external command (obedience is purely *natural*, as in the filial relation—not the result of reflection and principle). In the Persian principle, Unity first elevates itself to the distinction from the merely natural; we have the negation of that unreflecting relation which allowed no exercise of mind to intervene between the mandate and its adoption by the will.

In the Persian principle this unity is manifested as Light, which in this case is not simply light as such, the most universal physical element, but at the same time also *spiritual* purity—the Good. Speciality—the involvement with *limited* Nature—is consequently abolished. Light, in a physical and spiritual sense, imparts, therefore, elevation—freedom from the merely natural. Man sustains a relation to Light—to the Abstract Good—as to something objective, which is acknowledged, reverenced, and evoked to activity by his Will. If we look back once more—and we cannot do so too frequently—on the phases which we have traversed in arriving at this point, we perceive in China the totality of a moral Whole, but excluding subjectivity;—this totality divided into members, but without independence in its various portions. We found only an external arrangement of this political Unity. In India, on the contrary, distinctions made themselves prominent; but the *principle* of separation was unspiritual. We found incipient subjectivity, but hampered with the condition, that the separation in question is insurmountable; and that Spirit remains involved in the limitations of Nature, and is therefore a self-contradiction. Above this purity of Castes is that purity of Light which we observe in Persia; that Abstract Good, to which all are equally able to approach, and in which all equally may be hallowed. The Unity recognized therefore, now first becomes a principle, not an external bond of soulless order. The fact that everyone has a share in that principle, secures to him personal dignity." (175)

The formal religion of Persia, as well as Media, is the religion of Zoroaster. The canonical books are the *Zend Books,* written in the Zend language which is connected with Sanscrit. We find here the doctrine of Zoroaster in which Ormuzd is The Lord of Light. He creates the beautiful world in the kingdom of the Sun whose physical light clothes a spiritual essence. This spiritual essence, or spiritual light, the Persians think of as the Divine; of this light they may partake. This Divine Being—Ormuzd, speaks and says: "I am the Maintainer of the Universe; I am Free Will; I am Wisdom and

Science; I am Fullness of Blessedness and The Destroyer of the Ills of the World." These ills are said to arise in darkness —whose being is named Ahriman. To overcome this darkness, there is necessity for prayer, purity, and evermore light.

It is around this general conception—this Being of Light and its antithesis, Darkness, that the simple laws and institutions of the Persians are built. These people have no castes, but they are divided into four classes—the Priests, the Warriors, the Agriculturists and the Craftsmen. The society does not exhibit a political element. A trading class is not designated but later there is one developed. Regarding the philosophical import of their religion, Hegel says: "This people, attained to the consciousness, that absolute Truth must have the form of Universality—of Unity. This Universal, Eternal, Infinite Essence is not recognized at first, as conditioned in any way; it is Unlimited Identity. This is properly (and we have already frequently repeated it) also the character of Brahm. But this Universal Being became objective, and their Spirit became the consciousness of this its Essence; while on the contrary among the Hindoos this objectivity is only the *natural* one of the Brahmins, and is recognized as pure Universality only in the destruction of consciousness. Among the Persians this negative assertion has become a positive one; and man has a relation to Universal Being of such a kind that he remains positive in sustaining it. This One, Universal Being, is indeed not yet recognized as the free Unity of Thought; not yet "worshipped in Spirit and in Truth;" but is still clothed with a form—that of Light. But Light is not a Lama, a Brahmin, a Mountain, a brute—this or that particular existence—but sensuous Universality itself; simple manifestation. The Persian Religion is therefore no idol-worship; it does not adore individual natural objects, but the Universal itself. Light admits, moreover, the signification of the Spiritual; it is the form of the Good and True—the substantiality of knowledge and volition as well as of all natural things. Light puts man in a position to be able to exercise choice; and he can only choose when he has emerged from that which had absorbed him. But Light directly involves an Opposite, namely, Darkness; just as Evil is the antithesis of Good. As man could not appreciate Good, if Evil were not; and as he can be really good only when he has become acquainted with the contrary, so the Light does not exist without Darkness. Among the Persians, *Ormuzd* and *Ahriman* present the antithesis in question. Ormuzd is the Lord of the kingdom of Light—of Good; Ahriman that of Darkness—of Evil. But there is a still higher being from whom both proceeded—a Universal Being not affected by this antithesis, called *Zeruane-Akerene*—the Unlimited All. The All, i.e., is something abstract; it does not exist for itself, and Ormuzd and Ahriman have arisen from it. This Dualism is commonly brought as a reproach against Oriental thought; and, as far as the contradiction is regarded as absolute, that is certainly an irreligious understanding which remains satisfied with it. But the very nature of Spirit demands antithesis; the principle of Dualism belongs therefore to the idea of Spirit, which, in its concrete form, essentially involves distinction. Among the Persians, Purity and Impurity have both become subjects of consciousness; and Spirit, in order to comprehend itself, must of necessity place the Special and Negative existence in contrast with the Universal and Positive. Only by overcoming this antithesis is Spirit twice-born, regenerated. The deficiency in the Persian principle is only that the Unity of the antithesis is not completely recognized; for in that indefinite conception of the Uncreated All, whence Ormuzd and Ahriman proceeded, the Unity is only the absolutely *Primal* existence, and does not reduce the contradictory elements to harmony in itself. Ormuzd creates of his own free will; but also according to the decree of Zeruane-Akerene (the representation wavers); and the harmonizing of the contradiction is only to be found in the contest which Ormuzd carries on with Ahriman, and in which he will at last conquer." (178)

The principal concern of everyone in this religion is to keep himself pure and to spread purity around him. He must also help with the promotion of life, as such, which is a part of the positive realm of light. Therefore, the planting of a tree, or the digging of a well to bring water for plant and animal, is considered as a ministration to The Great Spirit of Light, Ormuzd. This zeal for Spiritual life is particularly characteristic of the Zend Race. The other peoples comprising the Persian Empire, notably the Assyrians and Babylonians put the emphasis rather on luxury, wealth and commerce. For it must be understood that we have here in the Persian Empire a great family of nations constituting the Near East. There were beside the Persians, Assyrians and Babylonians, also the Medians, The Chaldeans—a mountainous people who joined with the Babylonians— and later there were the Phoenicians, the Jews and the Egyptians. The Phoenicians were conspicuous for their aid with navies when the Persians set out on one of their great expeditions. Of this Great Empire of Persia, Hegel has the following to say: "The Persian Empire is an Empire in the *modern* sense—like that which existed in Germany, and the great imperial realm under the sway of Napoleon; for we find it consisting of a number of states, which are indeed dependent, but which have retained their own individuality, their manners, and laws. The general enactments, binding upon all, did not infringe upon their political and social idiosyncrasies, but even protected and maintained them; so that each of the nations that constitute the whole, had its own form of Constitution. As light illuminates everything—imparting to each object a peculiar vitality —so the Persian Empire extends over a multitude of nations, and leaves to each one its particular character. Some have even kings of their own; each one its distinct language, arms, way of life, and customs. All this diversity coexists harmoniously under the impartial dominion of Light. The Persian Empire comprehends all the three geographical elements, which we classified as distinct. First, the Uplands of Persia and Media; next, the Valley-plains of the Euphrates and Tigris, whose inhabitants are found united in a developed form of civilization, with Egypt—the Valley-plain of the Nile —where agriculture, industrial arts and sciences flourished;

and lastly a third element, viz. the nations who encounter the perils of the sea—the Syrians, the Phoenicians, the inhabitants of the Greek colonies and Greek Maritime states in Asia Minor. Persia thus united in itself the three natural principles, while China and India remained foreign to the sea. We find here neither that consolidated totality which China presents, nor that Hindoo life, in which an anarchy of caprice is prevalent everywhere. In Persia, the government, though joining all in a central unity, is but a combination of peoples —leaving each of them free. Thereby a stop is put to that barbarism and ferocity with which the nations had been wont to carry on their destructive feuds, and which the Book of Kings and the Book of Samuel sufficiently attest. The lamentations of the Prophets and their imprecations upon the state of things before the conquest, show the misery, wickedness and disorder that prevailed among them, and the happiness which Cyrus diffused over the region of Anterior Asia. It was not given to the Asiatics to unite self-dependence, freedom and substantial vigor of mind, with culture, i.e., an interest for diverse pursuits and an acquaintance with the conveniences of life. Military valor among them is consistent only with barbarity of manners. It is not the calm courage of order; and when their mind opens to a sympathy with various interests, it immediately passes into effeminacy; allows its energies to sink, and makes men the slaves of an enervated sensuality." (187-88)

"The Persians—a free mountain and nomad people— though ruling over richer, more civilized and fertile lands —retained on the whole the fundamental characteristics of their ancient mode of life. They stood with one foot on their ancestral territory, with the other on their foreign conquests. In his ancestral land the King was a friend among friends, and as if surrounded by equals. Outside of it he was the lord to whom all were subject, and bound to acknowledge their dependence by the payment of tribute. Faithful to the Zend religion, the Persians gave themselves to the pursuit of piety and pure worship of Ormuzd. The tombs of the Kings were in Persia Proper; and there the King sometimes visited his countrymen with whom he lived in relations of the greatest simplicity." (189)

These Persians made themselves illustrious for bravery. When the entire Persian host was to engage in an expedition a summons was sent to all the Asiatic countries and the affair was undertaken with characteristic nomadic restlessness. A number of different nations assembled—each accompanied by their families and marked by their national accoutrements of war. They went as a great migration and poured themselves *enmasse* upon the country to be conquered. In this manner did Persia invade Egypt, Scythia, Thrace and lastly Greece. Here in Greece the old despotic power that had ruled the East comes face to face with the new born spirit of the West—the Spirit of Democracy—and threatens its very life. It is to the immortal glory of Greece that in the strength of this new Spirit she was able to see her course clearly, to stand her ground firmly, and finally to win the victory over the foe against incalculable odds. Hegel has lengthy descriptions of all of the various people constituting this vast community of nations—The Persian Empire. Each one played a particular part and each one made its own peculiar contribution in tribute, as a dependent, towards the wealth and the maintainence of the whole. After this acquaintance with the inhabitants of the inland countries belonging to Persia, we move to the coast and take up the consideration of the early navigators there in the land of the Syrians and Phoenicians. Their commerce lay principally in the direction of the Mediterranean Sea and from there far to the West. On account of this intercourse with many nations, Syria soon acquired a high degree of culture. She advanced in skills such as weaving, dyeing, and fabricating in metal and precious stones. She attained proficiency in glass-making and building. Great Cities grew up along her coast and a written language was developed. Concerning them Hegel speaks in the following manner: "The Phoenicians discovered and first navigated the Atlantic Ocean. They had settlements in Cyprus and Crete.

In the remote island of Thasos, they worked gold mines. In the south and southwest of Spain they opened silver mines. In Africa they founded the colonies of Utica and Carthage. From Gades they sailed far down the African coast, and according to some, even circumnavigated Africa. From Britain they brought tin, and from the Baltic, Prussian amber. This opens to us an entirely new principle. Inactivity ceases, as also mere rude valor; in their place appears the activity of Industry, and that considerate courage which, while it dares the perils of the deep, rationally bethinks itself of the means of safety. Here everything depends on Man's activity, his courage, his intelligence; while the objects aimed at are also pursued in the interest of Man. Human will and activity here occupy the foreground, not Nature and its bounty. Babylonia had its determinate share of territory, and human subsistence was there dependent on the course of the sun and the process of Nature generally. But the sailor relies upon himself amid the fluctuations of the waves, and eye and heart must be always open. In like manner the principle of Industry involves the very opposite of what is received from Nature; for natural objects are worked up for use and ornament. In Industry Man is an object to himself, and treats Nature as something subject to him, on which he impresses the seal of his activity. Intelligence is the valor needed here, and ingenuity is better than mere natural courage. At this point we see the nations freed from the fear of Nature and its slavish bondage." (192)

In the matter of religion these diverse people manifested a nature at variance with the followers of Zoroaster. Here we find at first a rude idolatry, descriptions of which are furnished by the prophets. The worship took the form of a sensuous revelry, an emotional intoxication. The Gods represented the Powers of Nature—Astarte, Cybele, Diana of Ephesus. At a later period the Phoenicians established a worship of Hercules. He was known in connection with his twelve labors by virtue of which, through his own exertions—

the exertions of human spirit and valor—he makes himself a God. Farther along in the coast region there is also found the worship of Adonis. The feast of Adonis was similar to that of Osiris in Egypt—for Adonis dies, as does Osiris, and his death is commemorated. This brings a new phase to religious thought of which Hegel makes the following comments: "Here, human pain becomes an element of worship; in pain man realizes his subjectivity: it is expected of him—he may here indulge self-consciousness and the feeling of actual existence. Life here regains its value. A universality of pain is established: for death becomes immanent in the Divine, and the deity dies. Among the Persians we saw Light and Darkness struggling with each other, but here, both principles are united in one—the Absolute. The Negative is here, too, the merely Natural; but as the death of a *god,* it is not a limitation attaching to an individual object, but is pure Negativity itself. And this point is important, because the generic conception that has to be formed of Deity is Spirit; which involves its being concrete, and having in it the element of negativity. The qualities of wisdom and power are also concrete qualities, but only as predicates; so that God remains abstract substantial unity, in which differences themselves vanish, and do not become *organic* elements (Momente) of this unity. But here the Negative itself is a phase of Deity—the Natural—Death;—the worship appropriate to which is grief. It is in the celebration of the death of Adonis, and of his resurrection, that the concrete is made conscious. Adonis is a youth, who is torn from his parents by a too early death. In China, in the worship of ancestors, these latter enjoy divine honor. But parents in their decease only pay the debt of Nature. When a *youth* is snatched away by death, the occurrence is regarded as contrary to the proper order of things; and while affliction at the death of parents is no *just* affliction, in the case of youth death is a paradox. And this is the deeper element in the conception—that in the Divinity, Negativity—Antithesis—is manifested; and that the worship rendered to him involves both elements—the pain felt for the divinity snatched away, and the joy occasioned by his being found again." (194)

Next in this wide circle of nationalities, known as the Persian Empire, is the country of Judaea. It is conspicuous throughout the world for the association it bears to the founder of Christianity. There will therefore be particular interest attaching to this resume of the religion of the Jewish people in a philosophic light. Hegel speaks: "We find here, too, a canonical book—the *Old Testament;* in which the views of this people—whose principle is the exact opposite of the one just described—are exhibited. While among the Phoenician people the Spiritual was still limited by Nature, in the case of the Jews we find it entirely purified;—the pure product of Thought. Self-conception appears in the field of consciousness, and the Spiritual develops itself in sharp contrast to Nature and to union with it. It is true that we observed at an earlier stage the pure conception "Brahm"; but only as the universal being of Nature; and with this limitation, that Brahm is not himself an object of consciousness. Among the Persians we saw this abstract being become an object for consciousness, but it was that of sensuous intuition—as Light. But the idea of Light has at this stage advanced to that of "Jehovah"—the *purely One*. This forms the point of separation between the East and the West; Spirit descends into the depths of its own being, and recognizes the abstract fundamental principle as the Spiritual. Nature—which in the East is the primary and fundamental existence—is now depressed to the condition of a mere creature; and Spirit now occupies the first place. God is known as the creator of all men, as he is of all nature, and as absolute causality generally. But this great principle, as further conditioned, is *exclusive Unity*. This religion must necessarily possess the element of exclusiveness, which consists essentially in this—that only the One People which adopts it, recognizes the One God, and is acknowledged by him. The God of the Jewish People is the God only of

Abraham and of his seed: National individuality and a special local worship are involved in such a conception of deity. Before him all other gods are false: moreover the distinction between "true" and "false" is quite abstract; for as regards the false gods, not a ray of the Divine is supposed to shine into them." "But" continues Hegel, "every form of spiritual force, and *a fortiori* every religion is of such a nature, that whatever be its peculiar character, an affirmative element is necessarily contained in it. However erroneous a religion may be, it possesses truth, although in a mutilated phase. In every religion there is a divine presence, a divine relation; and a philosophy of History has to seek out the spiritual element even in the most imperfect forms. But it does not follow that because it is a religion, it is therefore *good*. We must not fall into the lax conception, that the content is of no importance, but only the form. This latitudinarian tolerance the Jewish religion does not admit, being absolutely exclusive." (195)

"The Spiritual speaks itself here absolutely free of the Sensuous, and Nature is reduced to something merely external and undivine. This is the true and proper estimate of Nature at this stage; for only at a more advanced phase can the Idea attain a reconciliation (recognize itself) in this its alien form. Its first utterances will be in opposition to Nature; for Spirit, which had been hitherto dishonored, now first attains its due dignity, while Nature resumes its proper position. Nature is conceived as having the ground of its existence in another—as something posited, created; and this idea, that God is the lord and creator of Nature, leads men to regard God as the Exalted One, while the whole of Nature is only his robe of glory, and is expended in his service. In contrast with this kind of exaltation, that which the Hindoo religion presents is only that of indefinitude. In virtue of the prevailing spirituality the Sensuous and Immoral are no longer privileged, but disparaged as ungodliness. Only the One—Spirit—the Nonsensuous is the Truth; Thought exists free for itself, and true morality and righteousness, and right-doing is "walking in the way of the Lord." With this is conjoined happiness, life and temporal prosperity as its reward; for it is said: "that thou mayest live long in the land."—Here too also we have the possibility of a *historical* view; for the understanding has become prosaic; putting the limited and circumscribed in its proper place, and comprehending it as the form proper to finite existence: Men are regarded as individuals, not as incarnations of God; Sun as Sun; Mountains as Mountains —not as possessing Spirit and Will." (196)

"We observe among this people a severe religious ceremonial expressing a relation to pure Thought. The individual as concrete does not become free, because the Absolute itself is not comprehended as *concrete* Spirit; since Spirit still appears posited as non-spiritual—destitute of its proper characteristics. It is true that subjective feeling is manifest—the pure heart, repentance, devotion; but the particular concrete individuality has not become objective to itself in the Absolute. It therefore remains closely bound to the observance of ceremonies and of the Law, the basis of which latter is pure freedom in its abstract form. The Jews possess that which makes them what they are, through the *One;* consequently the individual has no freedom for itself. Spinoza regards the code of Moses as having been given by God to the Jews for a punishment—a rod of correction. The individual never comes to the consciousness of independence; on that account we do not find among the Jews any belief in the immortality of the soul; for individuality does not exist in and for itself. But though in Judaism the *Individual* is not respected, the *Family* has inherent value; for the worship of Jehovah is attached to the Family, and it is consequently viewed as a substantial existence. But the State is an institution not consonant with the Judaistic principle, and it is alien to the legislation of Moses. In the idea of the Jews, Jehovah is the God of Abraham, of Isaac, and Jacob; who commanded them to depart out of Egypt, and gave them the land of Canaan. The accounts of the Patriarchs attract our interest. We see in this history the transition from the patriarchal nomadic condition of agriculture. On the whole the Jewish history exhibits grand features of character; but it is disfigured by an exclusive bearing (sanctioned in its religion), towards the genius of other nations (the destruction of the inhabitants of Canaan being even commanded)—by want of culture generally, and by the superstition arising from the idea of the high value of their peculiar nationality. Miracles, too, form a disturbing feature in this history—*as history;* for as far as concrete consciousness is not free, concrete perception is also not free; Nature is undeified, but not yet understood." (197)

In the Jewish people we see a family becoming a great nation. Through the conquest of Canaan there is a national country established with a Temple of Worship erected at Jerusalem. However, no permanent political union existed. It is true that later on Jewish Kings were chosen who rendered the Jews independent, but after a short period dissolution set in. Hegel says: "The One God could not be honored in different Temples, and there could not be two kingdoms attached to one religion. However spiritual may be the conception of God as objective, the subjective side—the honor rendered to him—is still very limited and unspiritual in character." (198)

"The two kingdoms, equally infelicitous in foreign and domestic warfare, were at last subjected to the Assyrians and Babylonians; through Cyrus the Great the Israelites obtained permission to return home and live according to their own laws." (198) This for our purposes is the picture of the jews in connection with the Empire of Persia—which is the phase of history under philosophical consideration. It must be understood that for this particular need of viewing the philosophical and religious content of a people, as they develop in the world process, it is only necessary to highlight the historic facts here and there in order to bring out enough regarding the external life to show forth the concepts that gave rise to them, or the phase of being that necessitated them. Hegel in this case groups these various nations of the Persian Empire as those that form the transition period to Western freedom. There is left but one other country of this contingency to be considered and this country is Egypt. All the rest of this vast Empire—then so powerful and wealthy—has passed away. The great cities that were the pride of their age are gone. Egypt alone has preserved something of herself for us of today.

EGYPT

It was under the Persian King Cambyses that an expedition was sent against Egypt. She was conquered and united to the Persian Empire. Egypt is characterized as the land of mystery, the land of marvels and the land of ruins. There are records left in architecture and hieroglyphics indicating the high intelligence of this civilization on the big and once dark continent of Africa. The understanding which the Egyptians had of themselves appears to us confusing. We find religious conceptions blended with historical facts and there are many contradictions. From the testimony given by Herodotus, after his visit to Egypt, the country was of great antiquity. He said she had possessed a deeper knowledge that was shrouded in mythology and symbolism. This was communicated to the historian but he declared that it could not be divulged because of its sacred nature. However, this trustworthy scholar gives accurate accounts of all other matters and conditions found by him. On these our writer draws freely. To quote Hegel: "Herodotus says that according to the statements of the priests, Gods had formerly ruled over Egypt.

That from the first human kingdom down to King Setho 341 generations, or 11,340 years, had passed away. The first human ruler was Menes (the resemblance of the name to the Greek Minos and the Hindoo Manu is striking)." (200) It may be further remarked parenthetically, that Egypt appears to be a country, like others in various parts of the world—whose antiquity is unaccounted for to date. This calls to mind a book, *The Faith of Ancient Egypt,* by Sidney G. P. Coryn, N.Y., 1913, which has the following: "Look for example at the great zodiac picture upon the ceiling of the temple at Denderah. The ideographs upon that zodiac and upon the papyri tell us that when that great picture was painted, the sun was in the sign of the Virgin, at the Spring Equinox, and that it had returned to that sign three times within the observation of their priests. The procession of the equinoctial points around the zodiacal circle occupies 25,920 years. When our calendar was formed, the sun at the Spring Equinox was in the sign Aries; and from Aries to Virgo is six signs. It is therefore fourteen thousand years since the sun was in Virgo at the equinox. But that was the third appearance of the sun in that sign, and for the sun to be three times in the sign of Virgo requires a period of at least 62,000 years, and at most 87,000. Taking the lowest calculation we find Denderah zodiac making practically the same claim as the Egyptain priest made to Solon." This concluding citation is a reference to a statement found in The Timaeus of Plato.

Yet, even in the days of Herodotus certain parts of Egypt, notably the upper part, were in a state of ruins. Hegel surmises that she might have derived her culture from Ethiopia, principally from the island Meroe. From these early beginnings Hegel traces the history through its triumphs and vicissitudes, kings and kingdoms. He stops along the way for descriptions of the life, manners and customs of these Egyptian people. For this historical data he must rely on contemporary writers and travelers, notably Herodotus, as there was no national work available. Ptolemy Philadelphus prompted the High Priest to write a history of Egypt. He it was who ordered also the sacred books of the Jews translated into Greek. The Egyptians, like some others of the ancient peoples, had their society divided into grades. There were the priests, warriors, agriculturists, artificers, seafarers and herdsmen. Although not included in these classes, there were also physicians and judges. But these divisions were not so rigidly fixed as they were in India. Each member went about the performance of the duties of his class and did not concern himself with matters pertaining to the state and its government. The king and his officials sufficed for this. We observe a condition quite different from the ones to be met in Greece and Rome. Here in Egypt there was a monarchy with certain limitations. The King's rule was supplemented by a court of justice administered by thirty judges who were nominated by the district. The king must be present at the judicial affairs each day. The land was under the control of the kings, priests and warriors. The court was conducted largely by means of written statements to prevent the undue influence of personality and oratory. It is evident that great intelligence was displayed in the legislative economy and we recognize the same in other matters. It was the Egyptians who divided the year into twelve months and each month into thirty days—the five additional days being interpolated at the end of the year. The same high grade of intelligence is shown in mechanics, arts and sciences. There is ample testimony to this in their gigantic edifices. These have been the wonder of the world. They excel all others in their solidity and size. It has been suggested that this proficiency was probably owing to the system of the hereditary transmission of teaching and developing of skills from father to son. Hegel says: "On account of its judicious economy, Egypt was regarded by the ancients as the pattern of a morally regulated condition of things—as an ideal such as Pythagoras realized in a limited select society, and Plato sketched on a larger scale. But in such ideals no account is taken of passion. A plan of society that is to be adopted and acted upon, as an absolutely complete one—in which everything has been considered, and especially the education and habituation to it, necessary to its becoming a second nature—is altogether opposed to the nature of Spirit, which makes contemporary life the object on which it acts; itself being the infinite impulse of activity to alter its forms. This impulse also expressed itself in Egypt in a peculiar way. It would appear at first as if a condition of things so regular, so determinate in every particular, contained nothing that had a peculiarity entirely its own. The introduction of a religious element would seem to be an affair of no critical moment, provided the highest necessities of men were satisfied; we should in fact rather expect that it would be introduced in a peaceful way and in accordance with the moral arrangement of things already mentioned. But in contemplating the *Religion* of the Egyptians, we are surprised by the strangest and most wonderful phenomena, and perceive that this calm order of things, bound fast by legislative enactment, is not like that of the Chinese, but that we have here to do with a Spirit entirely different—one full of stirring and urgent impulses, we have here the African element, in combination with Oriental massiveness, transplanted to the Mediterranean Sea, that grand *locale* of the display of nationalities; but in such a manner, that here there is no connection with foreign nations—this mode of stimulating intellect appearing superfluous; for we have here a prodigious urgent striving within the nationality itself, and which within its own circle shoots out into an objective realization of itself in the most monstrous productions. It is that African imprisonment of ideas combined with the infinite impulse of the spirit to realize itself objectively, which we find here. But Spirit has still, as it were, an iron band around its forehead; so that it cannot attain to the free consciousness of its existence, but produces this only as the problem, the enigma of its being." (207)

Egypt has been described at first as a vast sea of dust and sand, then a sea of fresh water, and lastly a sea of green growth. For the Egyptian there was the definite cycle caused by the yearly overflow of the Nile and its connection to the cycle of the sun. Many ascribe the religious figures in Egypt to these physical phenomenon. Others, notably the New Platonists, take a different view. Hegel says that each of these views is onesided. His explanation is this: "Natural and spiritual powers are regarded as most intimately united—(the free spiritual import, however, has *not* been developed at this stage of thought)—but in such a way, that the extremes of the antithesis were united in the harshest contrast. We have spoken of the Nile, of the Sun, and of the vegetation depending upon them. This limited view of Nature gives the principle of the religion, and its subject—matter is primarily a history.

The Nile and the Sun constitute the divinities, conceived under human forms; and the course of nature and the mythological history is the same. In the winter solstice the power of the sun has reached its minimum, and must be born anew. Thus also Osiris appears as born; but he is killed by Typhon—his brother and enemy—the burning wind of the desert. Isis, the Earth—from whom the aid of the Sun and of the Nile has been withdrawn—yearns after him: she gathers the scattered bones of Osiris, and raises her lamentation for him, and all Egypt bewails with her the death of Osiris, in a song which Herodotus calls Maneros. Maneros he reports to have been the only son of the first king of the Egyptians, and to have died prematurely; this song being also the Linus—Song of the Greeks, and the only song which the Egyptians have. Here again pain is regarded as something divine, and the same honor is assigned to it here as among the Phoenicians. Hermes then embalms Osiris; and his grave is shown in various places. Osiris is now judge of the dead, and lord of the kingdom of the Shades. These are the leading ideas. Osiris, the Sun, the Nile; this triplicity of being is united in one knot. The Sun is the symbol, in which Osiris and the history of that god are recognized, and the Nile is likewise such a symbol. The concrete Egyptian imagination also ascribes to Osiris and Isis the introduction of agriculture, the invention of the plough, the hoe, etc.; for Osiris gives not only the useful itself—the fertility of the earth—but, moreover, the means of making use of it. He also gives men laws, a civil order and a religious ritual; he thus places in men's hands the means of labor, and secures its result. Osiris is also the symbol of the seed which is placed in the earth, and then springs up—as also of the course of life. Thus we find this heterogeneous duality—the phenomena of Nature and the Spiritual—woven together into *one* knot." (209)

"The parallelism of the course of human life with the Nile, the Sun and Osiris, is not to be regarded as a mere allegory—as if the principle of birth, of increase in strength, of the culmination of vigor and fertility, of decline and weakness, exhibited itself in these different phenomena, in an equal or similar way; but in this variety imagination conceived only *one subject,* one vitality. This unity is, however, quite abstract: the heterogeneous element shows itself therein as pressing and urging, and in a confusion which sharply contrasts with Greek perspicuity. Osiris represents the Nile and the Sun: Sun and Nile are, on the other hand, symbols of human life—each one is signification and symbol at the same time: the symbol is changed into signification, and this latter becomes symbol of that symbol, which itself then becomes signification. None of these phases of existence is a Type without being at the same time a Signification; each is both; the one is explained by the other. Thus there arises one pregnant conception, composed of many conceptions, in which each fundamental nodus retains its individuality, so that they are not resolved into a general idea. The general idea—the thought itself, which forms the bond of analogy—does not present itself to the consciousness purely and freely as such, but remains concealed as an internal connection. We have a consolidated individuality, combining various phenomenal aspects; and which on the one hand is fanciful, on account of the combination of apparently disparate material, but on the other hand internally and essentially connected, because these various appearances are a particular prosaic matter of fact." (209)

One of the strange facts of the Egyptian Religion is Zoolatry. This fact of the existence of animals in their worship is significant of the union and bondage between the natural and the Spiritual which still existed in the Egyptian consciousness. It seems that here the two departments of the incomprehensible meet—man and animal. But here the reverence showed by man for these animals was carried to strange excess. Hegel has this to say: "It is in two departments that the so-called Incomprehensible meets us—in living Nature and in Spirit. But in very deed it is only in Nature that we have to encounter the Incomprehensible; for the being manifest to itself is the essence (supplies the very definition of),

Spirit: Spirit understands and comprehends Spirit. The obtuse self—consciousness of the Egyptians, therefore, to which the thought of human freedom is not yet revealed, worships the soul as still shut up within and dulled by the physical organization, and sympathizes with brute life. We find a veneration of mere vitality among other nations also: sometimes expressly, as among the Hindoos and all the Mongolians; sometimes in mere traces, as among the Jews: "Thou shalt not eat the blood of animals, for in it is the life of the animal." The Greeks and Romans also regarded birds as specially intelligent, believing that what in the human spirit was not revealed—the Incomprehensible and Higher—was to be found in them. But among the Egyptians this worship of beasts was carried to excess under the forms of a most stupid and nonhuman superstition. The worship of brutes was among them a matter of particular and detailed arrangement: each district had a brute deity of its own—a cat, an ibis, a crocodile, etc. Great establishments were provided for them; beautiful mates were assigned them; and, like human beings, they were embalmed after death. The bulls were buried, but with their horns protruding above their graves; the bulls embodying *Apis* had splendid monuments, and some of the pyramids must be looked upon as such. In one of those that have been opened, there was found in the most central apartment a beautiful alabaster coffin; and on closer examination it was found that the bones inclosed were those of the ox. This reverence for brutes was often carried to the most absurd excess of severity. If a man killed one designedly, he was punished with death; but even the undesigned killing of some animals might entail death. It is related, that once when a Roman in Alexandria killed a cat, an insurrection ensued, in which the Egyptians murdered the aggressor. They would let human beings perish by famine, rather than allow the sacred animals to be killed, or the provision made for them trenched upon. Still more than mere vitality, the universal *vis vitae* of productive nature was venerated in a Phallus—worship; which the Greeks also adopted into the rites paid by them to

Dionysus. With this worship the greatest excesses were connected." (212)

"The brute form is, on the other hand, turned into a symbol: it is also partly degraded to a mere hieroglyphical sign. I refer here to the innumerable figures on the Egyptian monuments, of sparrowhawks or falcons, dung—beetles, scarabaei, etc. It is not known what ideas such figures symbolized, and we can scarcely think that a satisfactory view of this very obscure subject is attainable. The dung-beetle is said to be the symbol of generation—of the sun and its course; the Ibis, that of the Nile's overflowing; birds of the hawk tribe, of prophecy—of the year—of pity. The strangeness of these combinations results from the circumstance that we have not, as in our idea of poetical invention, a general conception embodied in an image; conversely, we begin with a concept in the sphere of sense, and imagination conducts us into the same sphere again. But we observe the conception liberating itself from the direct animal form, and the continued contemplation of it; and that which was only surmised and aimed at in that form, advancing to comprehensibility and conceivableness. The hidden meaning—the Spiritual—emerges as a human face from the brute. The multiform sphinxes, with lions' bodies and virgins' heads—or as male sphinxes (ἀνδρόσφιγγες) with beards—are evidence supporting the view, that the meaning of the Spiritual is the problem which the Egyptians proposed to themselves; as the enigma generally is not the utterance of something unknown, but is the challenge to discover it—implying a wish to be revealed. But conversely, the human form is also disfigured by a brute face, with the view of giving it a specific and definite expression. The refined art of Greece is able to attain a specific expression through the spiritual character given to an image in the form of beauty, and does not need to deform the human face in order to be understood. The Egyptians appended an explanation to the human forms, even of the gods, by means of heads and masks of brutes; Anubis e.g. has a dog's head, Isis, a lion's head with bull's horns, etc. The priests, also, in performing their functions, are masked as falcons, jackals, bulls, etc.; in the same way the surgeon, who has taken out the bowels of the dead (represented as fleeing, for he has laid sacrilegious hands on an object once hallowed by life); so also the embalmers and the scribes. The sparrow-hawk, with a human head and outspread wings, denotes the soul flying through material space, in order to animate a new body. The Egyptian imagination also created new forms—combinations of different animals: serpents with bulls' and rams' heads, bodies of lions with rams' heads, etc." (213)

"We thus see Egypt intellectually confined by a narrow, involved, close view of Nature, but breaking through this; impelling it to self-contradiction, and proposing to itself the problem which that contradiction implies. The (Egyptian) principle does not remain satisfied with its primary conditions, but points to that other meaning and spirit which lies concealed beneath the surface." (214)

It is evident from the testimony of Herodotus that the Egyptians were believers in the immortality of the soul and were the first to express this thought. Hegel explains the fact in the following manner: "The proposition that the soul is immortal is intended to mean that it is something other than nature—that Spirit is inherently independent. The *ne plus ultra* of blessedness among the Hindoos, was the passing over into abstract unity—into Nothingness. On the other hand, subjectivity, when free, is inherently infinite: the Kingdom of free Spirit is therefore the Kingdom of the Invisible—such as Hades was conceived by the Greeks. This presents itself to men first as the empire of death—to the Egyptians as the Realm of the Dead." (215)

It is well known that the Egyptians embalmed their dead. So skillful were they in this art that many mummies are preserved to this day and show a permanence attesting to Egypt's proficiency.

Not only were the dead bodies preserved but elaborate sepulchres and monuments were built for them. These were of various kinds. Some of the subterranean vaults, passages and abodes for tombs are as large as the largest mining works of our times. Most prodigious of all these works were the Pyramids, which are known throughout the world. In modern times they have become the subject of scientific study. This study has brought to light remarkable facts regarding the geometrical relationships and astronomical significance of the proportions. Concerning these mighty works of art and the reason that caused the Egyptian consciousness to express itself in this way, Hegel has the following to say: "It is the distinguishing feature of the Egyptian Spirit, that it stands before us as this mighty taskmaster. It is not splendor, amusement, pleasure, or the like that it seeks. The force which urges it is the impulse of self—comprehension; and it has no other material or ground to work on, in order to teach itself what it is—to realize itself for itself—than this working out its thoughts in stone; and what it engraves on the stone are its enigmas—these hieroglyphs. They are of two kinds—hieroglyphs *proper,* designed rather to express language, and having reference to subjective conception; and a class of hieroglyphics of a different kind, viz. those enormous masses of architecture and sculpture, with which Egypt is covered. While among other nations history consists of a series of events—as, e.g. that of the Romans, who century after century, lived only with a view to conquest, and accomplished the subjugation of the world—the Egyptians raised an empire equally mighty—of achievements in works of art, whose ruins prove their indestructibility, and which are greater and more worthy of astonishment than all other works of ancient or modern time." (215)

The Egyptian hieroglyphs have also been a subject attracting the attention of modern scholars. They disclose the fact that after the man is dead, judgment is passed upon him. Osiris, with Isis beside him, stands ready with a balance which will weigh his attributes of good and evil. The soul of the deceased is thus pictured as being tried, while judgment is rendered by the living. Sometimes the honor of immortalization is refused; at other times it is granted. Says Hegel:

"The reception of the dead into the Kingdom of Osiris had also a profounder meaning, *viz.,* that the individual was united with Osiris. On the lids of the sarcophagi, therefore, the defunct is represented as having himself become Osiris; and in deciphering the hieroglyphs, the idea has been suggested that the kings are called gods. The human and the divine are thus exhibited as united." (218)

The Egyptians had a number of deities but among them Osiris holds the most exalted place. In him resides the Procreative Power; Isis constitutes the receptive fertility of Nature; Horos is the son, or power born of the union. Here we have the Spiritual characterized by intrinsic particularity. Such allusions are found permeating many conceptions of ancient civilizations.

Summarizing Egypt's position Hegel says: "If, in conclusion, we combine what has been said here of the peculiarities of the Egyptian Spirit in all its aspects, its pervading principle is found to be, that the two elements of reality—Spirit sunk in Nature, and the impulse to liberate it—are here held together inharmoniously as contending elements. We behold the antithesis of Nature and Spirit—not the primary Immediate Unity (As in the less advanced nations), nor the Concrete Unity, where Nature is posited only as a basis for the manifestation of Spirit (as in the more advanced); in contrast with the first and second of these Unities, the Egyptian Unity —combining contradictory elements—occupies a middle place. The two sides of this unity are held in abstract independence of each other, and their veritable union presented only as a problem. We have, therefore, on *one* side, prodigious confusion and limitation to the particular; barbarous sensuality with African hardness, Zoolatry, and sensual enjoyment . . . The *Other* side is the struggle of Spirit for liberation—fancy displayed in the forms created by art, together with the abstract understanding shown in the mechanical labors connected with their production. The same intelligence—the power of altering the form of individual existences; and that steadfast thoughtfulness which can rise above mere phenomena—shows itself in their policy and the mechanism of the State, in agricultural economy, etc.; and the contrast to this is the severity with which their customs bind them, and the superstition to which humanity among them is inexorably subject. With a clear understanding of the present, is connected the highest degree of impulsiveness, daring and turbulence. These features are combined in the stories which Herodotus relates to us of the Egyptians. They much resemble the tales of the Thousand and One Nights; and although these have Bagdad as the locality of their narration, their origin is no more limited to this luxurious court, than to the Arabian people, but must be partly traced to Egypt—as Von Hammer also thinks. The Arabian world is quite other than the fanciful and enchanted region there described; it has much more simple passions and interests. Love, Martial Daring, the Horse, the Sword, are the darling subjects of the poetry peculiar to the Arabians." (219)

"The Egyptian Spirit has shown itself to us as in all respects shut up within limits of particular conceptions, and, as it were, imbruted in them; but likewise stirring itself within these limits—passing restlessly from one particular form into another. This Spirit never rises to the Universal and Higher, for it seems to be blind to that; nor does it ever withdraw into itself: yet it symbolizes freely and boldly with particular existence, and has already mastered it. All that is now required is to posit that particular existence—which contains the germ of ideality—*as ideal,* and to comprehend Universality itself, which is already potentially liberated from the particulars involving it. It is the free, joyful Spirit of Greece that accomplishes this, and makes this its starting-point. An Egyptian priest is reported to have said, that the Greeks remain eternally children. We may say, on the contrary, that Egyptians are vigorous *boys*, eager for self-comprehension, who require nothing but clear understanding of themselves in an ideal form, in order to become *Young Men.* In the Oriental Spirit there remains as a basis the massive substantiality of Spirit immersed in Nature. To the Egyptian

Spirit it has become impossible—though it is still involved in infinite embarrassment—to remain contented with *that.* The rugged African nature disintegrated that primitive Unity, and lighted upon the problem whose solution is Free Spirit." (219)

"That the Spirit of the Egyptians presented itself to their consciousness in the form of a *problem,* is evident from the celebrated inscription in the sanctuary of the Goddess Neith at Sais: "*I am that which is, that which was, and that which will be; no one has lifted my veil.*" This inscription indicates the principle of the Egyptian Spirit; though the opinion has often been entertained, that its purport applies to all times." So ends our study of Egypt and its strange role in the Persian Empire. (220)

Our study is for the purpose of discerning that it was in the Great Empire of Persia that the transition was made to that principle of Free Spirit which we contrast with the former state of imprisonment in Nature. Does not this Spirit of Freedom connote movement and change? Henceforth the spirit will be seen to continually break up her forms and alter them whenever they become outgrown. This is an advance on the condition of duration found in China and India. In them we see a state of arrestment that contrasts strangely with the spirit of free movement first noticed in Persia. But this free spirit is destined to possess the human consciousness in ever greater degrees as it evolves into higher and more inward qualities along the march of the Historic Process. Finally it will arrive at Subjective Freedom for all mankind. For the first degree it is to the Greek World that we turn. It is in Greece that democracy receives its baptism. To this democratic freedom, Persia has led the way and made the transition.

THE GREEK WORLD

The Greek World is the fourth of the great world races reviewed by Hegel—namely China, India, Persia and Greece. The purpose is to watch the gradual birth of the subjective freedom of individuality in the consciousness of humanity. The first race considered was China. Here we saw subjective freedom completely nonexistent in a compact, prosaic, static unity. In the second country, India, subjective freedom is entirely unknown for reasons that are the direct opposite of those existing in China. There is no compact unity but movement and diversity. There is nothing prosaic but instead, consciousness dwells in the realm of an imaginative dream world. Solidarity gives way here to diverse social distinctions ranging from the princely Brahmin to the untouchable serfs. Yet in this land also there is no subjective freedom. There is unquestioning compliance to the Status quo which is abitrarily fixed by the natural decree of birth. The question of freedom is not admitted as an idea with reference to the individual reason and judgment—the highest principle being with the Indian Pure Abstraction. Thus two countries have not subjective freedom. The third great world development occurred in the Persian Empire. Here we leave the Far East which is distinctly Oriental and come into the Near East which is Occidental. It is made up chiefly of the Caucasian Race:—the Persians, Medians, Assyrians, Babylonians, Syrians, Lydians, Phoenicians and Egyptians. In this period the idea of light—in its spiritual and universal sense is born in the consciousness of man. There is also born the idea of a relationship between man and this light. It is the transition period for humanity from the submerged sense of individuality—existing in the East, to the rise of individuality existing in the West. The Great Persian

Empire, with its concourse of diverse peoples furnishes the stage for this transition. It is the period when a self that has been submerged, changes to a self that is recognized. It starts here in Persia, progresses further in Greece and Rome, then comes to maturity in The German Reformation. From Germany it is destined to spread gradually to all the individuals of the human race. We will therefore turn our attention to the fourth stage of the development—namely Greece.

Hegel designated the development that took place in The Greek World as that corresponding—in the life of the World's Spirit—to the period of adolescense. He sees in the Greek life an achievement full of the spirit of youth with two ideals portraying it—namely that of Achilles, the ideal youth of Homer's poetry and Alexander the Great, the ideal, free, fierce youth of reality. "Greece is (that form of) the Substantial (i.e. of Moral and Intellectual *Principle*), which is at the same time *individual*." (225)

The whole country of Greece with its broken mountain ranges, broken coast line, and general partitions into small divisions advances the development of individuality. There is no bond of nature that fosters solidarity. Here it is found necessary to originate development on independent grounds. Therefore, inherent distinctiveness of character soon manifests. The people that made up the Greek nation were first the nucleus of aboriginal stock, and then foreign settlers from all parts of the known world,—Egypt, Phoenicia, Lydia, Assyria, Babylonia, the Mediterranean and Aegean Coast lands and India. Of the multitude that finally became the Greek nation, it would be hard to determine the original Greeks. They are more properly the fusion of many different nationalities.

Through the early periods of Greek history there was much turbulence and insecure existence. But as Greece advanced in her development, wealthy and powerful foreigners were attracted to her shores and took up holdings with a view to their own personal aggrandizement. They soon found it necessary to fortify their acquisitions against enemies and free-booters. In times of dangers these fortified areas furnished a refuge for those living in the vicinity. As time went on they became the nucleus of cities and city states. In most cases the founders, or princes, had as much authority as they personally possessed and could assert. In this manner did the Greek nation come into existence and move forward in its expansion and national development. Yet even in the early periods there was manifest the spirit of liberalism that was to characterize these people. Of this Hegel says: "The various peoples do not fight as mercenaries of the prince in his battles, nor as a stupid serf-like herd driven to the contest, nor yet in their own interest; but as the companions of their honored chieftain —as witnesses of his exploits, and his defenders in peril. A perfect resemblance to these relations is also presented in the Greek Pantheon. Zeus is the Father of the Gods, but each one of them has his own will; Zeus respects them, and they him: he may sometimes scold and threaten them, and they then allow his will to prevail or retreat grumbling; but they do not permit matters to come to an extremity, and Zeus so arranges matters on the whole—by making this concession to one, that to another—as to produce satisfaction. In the terrestrial, as well as in the Olympian world, there is, therefore, only a lax bond of unity maintained; royalty has not yet become monarchy, for it is only in a more extensive society that the need of the latter is felt." (230)

"While this state of things prevailed, and social relations were such as have been described, that striking and great event took place—the union of the whole of Greece in a national undertaking, viz., the *Trojan War;* with which began that more extensive connection with Asia which had very important results for the Greeks. (The expedition of Jason to Colchis—also mentioned by the poets—and which bears an earlier date, was, as compared with the war of Troy, a very limited and isolated undertaking.) The occasion of that united expedition is said to have been the violation of the laws of hospitality by the son of an Asiatic prince, in carrying off the wife of his host. Agamemnon assembles the princes of Greece through the power and influence which he possesses. Thucydides ascribes his authority to his hereditary sovereignty, combined with naval power (Hom. II, ii, 108), in which he was far superior to the rest. It appears, however, that the combination was effected without external compulsion, and that the whole armament was convened simply on the strength of individual consent. The Hellenes were then brought to act unitedly, to an extent of which there is no subsequent example. The result of their exertions was the conquest and destruction of Troy, though they had no design of making it a permanent possession. No external result, therefore, in the way of settlement ensued, any more than an enduring political union, as the effect of the uniting of the nation in the accomplishment of this single achievement. But the poet supplied an imperishable portraiture of their youth and of their national spirit, to the imagination of the Greek people; and the picture of this beautiful human heroism hovered as a directing ideal before their whole development and culture." (231)

After the Trojan War many changes occurred and the royal houses gradually lost their power. By successive stages more democratic forms of government came into existence. Finally democracy superseded the monarchy. The towns and cities grew strong. There was trade, agricultural pursuits and many expeditions which resulted in extensive Greek colonization. Hegel names three distinct periods into which the life of these Greek people and their history falls. The first is that of the growth of real individuality; the second—to quote—"that of its independence and prosperity in external conquest (through contact with the previous World-historical people); and the third, the period of its decline and fall, in its encounter with the succeeding organ of World-history. The period from its origin to its internal completeness (that which enables a people to make head against its predecessor) includes its primary culture. If the nation has a basis—such as the Greek world has in the Oriental—a foreign culture enters as an element into its primary condition, and it has a double culture, one orignal, the other of foreign suggestion. The uniting of these two elements constitutes its training; and the first period ends with the combination of its forces to produce its real and proper vigor, which then turns against the very element that had been its basis. The second period is that of victory and prosperity. But while the nation directs its energies outwards, it becomes unfaithful to its principles at home, and internal dissension follows upon the ceasing of the external excitement. In Art and Science, too, this shows itself in the separation of the Ideal from the Real. Here is the point of decline. The third period is that of ruin, through contact with the nation that embodies a higher Spirit. The same process, it may be stated once and for all, will meet us in the life of every world-historical people." (224)

Having roughly outlined the first of these periods, let us now pass to the second one. It is not important to review all of the historical facts, although Hegel does go into the most important of these at some length. However, for the present purposes, let us rather give our attention to the nature and genesis of the Greek spirit which comes to efflorescence with the maturity of Greek national life. It is this feature that must particularily engage our attention. The object is to set forth the way in which the Greeks with the same world in which to live, the same sky overhead and the same sea surrounding, yet reacted in a manner that was distinctly their own and exhibited an individual freedom and creative ability in advance of their predecessors. Regarding this Hegel offers some interesting deductions. "Thus we see the Greeks—divided and separated from each other—thrown back upon their inner spirit and personal energy, yet at the same time most variously excited and cautiously circumspect. We behold them quite undetermined and irresolute in the presence of Nature, dependent on its contingencies, and listening anxiously to each signal from the external world; but, on the other hand, intelligently taking cognizance of and appropriating that outward existence, and showing boldness and independent vigor in contending with it. These are the simple elements of their culture and religion. In tracing up their mythological conceptions, we find natural objects forming the basis—not *en masse,* however; only in dissevered forms. The Diana of Ephesus (that is, Nature as the universal Mother), the Cybele and Astarte of Syria—such comprehensive conceptions remained Asiatic, and were not transmitted to Greece. For the Greeks only *watch* the objects of Nature, and form *Surmises* respecting them; inquiring, in the depth of their souls, for the hidden meaning. According to Aristotle's dictum, that Philosophy proceeds from Wonder, the Greek view of Nature also proceeds from wonder of this kind. Not that in their experience, Spirit meets something extraordinary, which it compares with the common order of things; for the intelligent view of a regular course of Nature, and the reference of phenomena to that standard, do not yet present themselves; but the Greek Spirit was excited to wonder at the *Natural* in Nature. It does not maintain the position of stupid indifference to it as something existing, and there an end of it; but regards it as something in the first instance foreign, in which, however, it has a presentiment of confidence, and the belief that it bears something within it which is friendly to the human Spirit, and to which it may be permitted to sustain a positive relation. This *Wonder,* and this *Presentiment,* are here the fundamental categories; though the Hellenes did not content themselves with these moods of feelings, but projected the hidden meaning, which was the subject of the surmise, into a distinct conception as an object of consciousness. The natural holds its place in their minds only after undergoing some transformation by Spirit—not immediately. Man regards Nature only as an excitement to his faculties, and only the Spiritual which he has evolved from it can have any influence over him. Nor is this commencement of the Spiritual apprehension of Nature to be regarded as an explanation suggested by *us;* it meets us in a multitude of conceptions formed by the Greeks themselves. The position of curious surmise, of attentive eagerness to catch the meaning of Nature, is indicated to us in the comprehensive idea of *Pan.* To the Greeks Pan did not represent the *objective* whole, but that indefinite neutral ground which involves the element of the *subjective*;

he embodies that thrill which pervades us in the silence of the forests; he was, therefore, especially worshipped in sylvan Arcadia: (a "panic terror" is the common expression for a groundless fright). Pan, this thrill-exciting being, is also represented as playing on the flute; we have not the bare internal presentiment, for Pan makes himself audible on the seven-reeded pipe. In what has been stated we have, on the one hand, the Indefinite, which, however, holds communication with man; on the other hand the fact, that such communication is only a subjective imagining—an explanation furnished by the percipient himself. On the same principle the Greeks listened to the murmuring of the fountains, and asking what might be thereby signified; but the signification which they were led to attach to it was not the objective meaning of the fountain, but the subjective—that of the subject itself, which further exalts the Naiad to a Muse. The Naiads, or Fountains, are the external, objective origin of the Muses. Yet the immortal songs of the Muses are not that which is heard in the murmuring of the fountains; they are the productions of the thoughtfully listening Spirit—*creative* while *observant*. The interpretation and explanation of Nature and its transformations—the indication of their sense and import—is the act of the subjective Spirit . . . That Nature answered the question which the Greek put to her, is in this converse sense true, that he obtained an answer to the Questions of Nature from his own Spirit. The insight of the Seer becomes thereby purely poetical; Spirit supplies the signification which the natural image expresses. Everywhere the Greeks desired a clear presentation and interpretation of the Natural. Homer tells us, in the last book of the Odyssey, that while the Greeks were overwhelmed with sorrow for Achilles, a violent agitation came over the sea: the Greeks were on the point of dispersing in terror, when the experienced Nestor arose and interpreted the phenomenon to them. Thetis, he said, was coming, with her nymphs, to lament for the death of her son. When a pestilence broke out in the camp of the Greeks, the Priest Calchas explained that Apollo was incensed at their not having restored the daughter of his priest Chryses when a ransom had been offered. The Oracle was originally interpreted exactly in this way. The oldest Oracle was at Dodona (in the district of the modern Janina). Herodotus says that the first priestesses of the temple there, were from Egypt; yet this temple is stated to be an ancient Greek one. The rustling of the leaves of the sacred oaks was the form of prognostication there. Bowls of metal were suspended in the grove. But the sounds of the bowls dashing against each other were quite indefinite, and had no objective sense; the sense—the signification—was imparted to the sounds only by the human beings who heard them." (236)

"In summing up the constituents of the *Greek Spirit,* we find its fundamental characteristic to be, that the freedom of Spirit is conditioned by and has an essential relation to some stimulus supplied by Nature. Greek freedom of thought is excited by an alien existence; but it is free because it transforms and virtually reproduces the stimulus by its own operation. This phase of Spirit is the medium between the loss of individuality on the part of man (such as we observe in the Asiatic principle, in which the Spiritual and Divine exists only under a Natural form), and Infinite Subjectivity as pure certainty of itself—the position that the Ego is the ground of all that can lay claim to substantial existence. The Greek Spirit as the medium between these two, begins with Nature, but transforms it into a mere objective form of its (Spirit's) own existence; Spirituality is therefore not yet absolutely free; not yet absolutely *self*-produced—is not self-stimulation. Setting out from surmise and wonder, the Greek Spirit advances to definite conceptions of the hidden meanings of Nature. In the subject itself too, the same harmony is produced. In Man, the side of his subjective existence which he owes to Nature, is the Heart, the Disposition, Passion, and Variety of Temperament; this side is then developed in a spiritual direction to free Individuality; so that the character is not placed in a relation to universally valid moral authorities, assuming the form of duties, but the Moral appears as a nature peculiar to the individual—an exertion of will, the result of disposition and individual constitution. This stamps the Greek character as that of *Individuality conditioned by Beauty,* which is produced by Spirit, transforming the merely Natural into an expression of its own being. The activity of Spirit does not yet possess in itself the material and organ of expression, but needs the excitement of Nature and the matter which Nature supplies: it is not free, self-determining Spirituality, but mere naturalness formed to Spirituality—Spiritual Individuality. The Greek Spirit is the plastic artist, forming the stone into a work of art. In this formative process the stone does not remain mere stone—the form being only superinduced from without; but it is made an expression of the Spiritual, even contrary to its nature, and thus *trans*formed. Conversely, the artist *needs* for his spiritual conceptions, stone, colors, sensuous forms to express his idea. Without such an element he can no more be conscious of the idea himself, than give it an objective form for the contemplation of others; since it cannot in Thought alone become an object to him. The Egyptian Spirit also was a similar laborer in Matter, but the Natural had not yet been subjected to the Spiritual. No advance was made beyond a struggle and contest with it; the Natural still took an independent position, and formed one side of the image, as in the body of the Sphinx. In Greek Beauty the Sensuous is only a sign, an expression, an envelope, in which Spirit manifests itself." (239)

"It must be added, that while the Greek Spirit is a transforming artist of this kind, it knows itself free in its production; for it is their creator, and they are what is called the "work of man." They are, however, not merely this, but Eternal Truth—the energizing Spirit in its innate Essence, and quite as really not created as created by man. He has a respect and veneration for these conceptions and images—this Olympian Zeus—this Pallas of the Acropolis—and in the same way for the laws, political and ethical, that guide his actions. But He, the human being, is the womb that conceived them, he the breast that suckled them, he the Spiritual to which their grandeur and purity are owing. Thus he feels himself calm in contemplating them, and not only free in himself, but possessing the consciousness of his freedom; thus the honor of the Human is swallowed up in the worship of the Divine. Men honor the Divine in and for itself, but at the same time as their deed, their production, their phenomenal existence; thus the Divine receives its honor through the respect paid to the Human and the Human in virtue of the honor paid to the Divine. Such are the qualities of the *Beautiful Individuality* which constitutes the center of the Greek character." (239)

The Greeks realized three accomplishments, They cultivated the individual in a rounded perfection of body, mind and spirit; next they gave material actuality to their realizations in drama, art and philosophy; and lastly, they evolved a political form of government that was a democracy. As the first of these, or the subjective development of man as body and spirit, and the second, or the objective release of this developed man of mental and spiritual power in objective form are the two parts of one whole, it will be well to hear Hegel's thoughts concerning them. First of the man, then of his works—says Hegel: "The exhilarating sense of personality, in contrast with sensuous subjection to nature, and the need, not of mere pleasure, but of the display of individual powers, in order thereby to gain special distinction and consequent enjoyment, constitute therefore the chief characteristic and principal occupation of the Greeks. Free as the bird singing in the sky, the individual only expresses what lies in his untrammeled human nature—(to give the world "assurance of a man")—to have his importance recognized. This is the *subjective* beginning of Greek Art—in which the human being elaborates his physical being, in free, beautiful movement and agile vigor, to a work of art. The Greeks first trained their own persons to beautiful configurations before they attempted the expression of such in marble and paintings. The innocuous contest of *games,* in which every one exhibits his powers, is of very ancient date.

Homer gives a noble description of the games conducted by Achilles, in honor of Patroclus; but in all his poems there is no notice of statues of the gods, though he mentions the sanctuary at Dodona, and the treasure-house of Apollo at Delphi. The games in Homer consist in wrestling and boxing, running, horse and chariot races, throwing the discus or javelin, and archery. With these exercises are united dance and song, to express and form part of the enjoyment of social exhilaration, and which arts likewise blossomed into beauty." (242)

"If the subject of Song as thus developed among the Greeks is made a question, we should say that its essential and absolute purport is *religious*. We have examined the Idea embodied in the Greek Spirit; and Religion is nothing else than this Idea made objective as the essence of being. According to that Idea, we shall observe also that the Divine involves the *vis naturae* only as an element suffering a process of transformation to spiritual power. Of this Natural Element, as its origin, nothing more remains than the accord of analogy involved in the representation they formed of Spiritual power; for the Greeks worshipped God as Spiritual. We cannot, therefore, regard the Greek divinity as similar to the Indian—some power of Nature for which the human shape supplies only an outward form. The essence is the Spiritual itself, and the Natural is only the point of departure. But on the other hand, it must be observed, that the divinity of the Greeks is not yet the *absolute,* free Spirit, but Spirit in a particular mode, fettered by the limitations of humanity—still dependent as a determinate individuality on external conditions. Individualities, objectively beautiful, are the gods of the Greeks. The divine Spirit is here so conditioned as to be not yet regarded as abstract Spirit, but has a *Specialized existence*— continues to manifest itself in sense; but so that the sensuous is not its *substance,* but is only an element of its manifestation. This must be our leading idea in the consideration of the Greek mythology, and we must have our attention fixed upon it so much the more firmly, as—partly through the influence of erudition, which has whelmed essential principles beneath an infinite amount of details, and partly through that destructive analysis which is the work of the abstract Understanding—this mythology, together with the more ancient periods of Greek history, has become a region of the greatest intellectual confusion." (244)

"In the Idea of the Greek Spirit we found the two elements, Nature and Spirit, in such a relation to each other, that Nature forms merely the point of departure. This degradation of Nature is in the Greek mythology the turning point of the whole—expressed as the War of the Gods, the overthrow of the Titans by the race of Zeus. The transition from the Oriental to the Occidental Spirit is therein represented, for the Titans are the merely Physical—natural existence, from whose grasp sovereignty is wrested. It is true that they continue to be venerated, but not as governing powers; for they are relegated to the verge (the limbus) of the world. The Titans are powers of Nature, Uranus, Gaea, Oceanus, Selene, Helios, etc. Chronos expresses the dominion of abstract Time, which devours its children. The unlimited power of reproduction is restrained, and Zeus appears as the head of the new divinities, who embody a spiritual import, and are themselves Spirit. It is not possible to express this transition more distinctly and naively than in this myth; the new dynasty of divinities proclaim their peculiar nature to be of a Spiritual order." (245)

"The second point is, that the new divinities retain natural elements, and consequently in themselves a determinate relation to the powers of Nature, as was previously shown. Zeus has his lightenings and clouds, and Hera is the creatress of the *Natural,* the producer of crescent vitality. Zeus is also the political god, the protector of morals and of hospitality. Oceanus, as such, is only the element of Nature which his name denotes. Poseidon has still the wildness of that element in his character; but he is also an ethical personage; to him is ascribed the building of walls and the production of the Horse. Helios is the sun as a natural element. This Light, according to the analogy of Spirit, has been transformed to self-consciousness, and Apollo has proceeded from Helios . . . Apollo was a herdsman in the employ of Admetus, but oxen not subjected to the yoke were sacred to Helios: his rays, represented as arrows, kill the Python. The idea of Light as the natural power constituting the basis of the representation, cannot be dissociated from this divinity: especially as the other predicates attached to it are easily united with it, and the explanations of Muller and others, who deny that basis, are much more arbitrary and far-fetched. For Apollo is the prophesying and discerning god—Light, that makes everything clear. He is, moreover, the healer and strengthener; as also the destroyer, for he kills men. He is the propitiating and purifying god, e.g., in contravention of the Eumenides—the ancient subterrene divinities—who exact hard, stern justice. He himself is pure, he has no wife, but only a sister, and is not involved in various disgusting adventures, like Zeus; moreover, he is the discerner and declarer, the singer and leader of the dances—as the sun leads the harmonious dance of stars.—In like manner the Naiads became the Muses. The mother of the gods, Cybele—continuing to be worshipped at Ephesus as Artemis—is scarcely to be recognized as the Artemis of the Greeks—the huntress and destroyer of wild beasts. Should it be said that this change of the Natural into the Spiritual is owing to our allegorizing, or that of the later Greeks, we may reply that this transformation of the Natural to the Spiritual is the Greek Spirit itself. The epigrams of the Greeks exhibit such advances from the Sensuous to the Spiritual. But the abstract Understanding cannot comprehend this blending of the Natural with the Spiritual." (246)

"It must be further observed, that the Greek gods are to be regarded as individualities—not abstractions, like "Knowledge," "Unity," "Time," "Necessity." Such abstractions do not form the substance of these divinities; they are no allegories, no abstract beings, to which various attributes are attached, like the Horatian "*Necessitas clavis trabalibus*." As little are the divinities symbols, for a symbol is only a sign, an adumbration of something else. The Greek gods express of themselves what they are. The eternal repose and clear intelligence that dignifies the head of Apollo, is not a symbol, but the expression in which Spirit manifests itself, and shows itself present. The gods are personalities, concrete individualities: an allegorical being has no qualities, but is itself one quality and no more. The gods are, moreover, special characters, since in each of them one peculiarity predominates as the characteristic one; but it would be vain to try to bring this circle of characters into a system. Zeus, perhaps, may be regarded as ruling the other gods, but not with substantial power; so that they are left free to their own idiosyncrasy. Since the whole range of spiritual and moral qualities was appropriated by the gods the unity, which stood above them all, necessarily remained abstract; it was therefore formless and unmeaning Fact, (the absolute constitution of things)—Necessity, whose oppressive character arises from the absence of the Spiritual in it; whereas the gods hold a friendly relation to men, for they are Spiritual natures. That higher thought, the knowledge of Unity as God—the One Spirit—lay beyond that grade of thought which the Greeks had attained." (246)

"But the Greek gods must not be regarded as more human than the Christian God. Christ is much more a *Man:* he lives, dies—suffers death on the cross—which is infinitely more human than the humanity of the Greek Idea of the Beautiful. But in referring to this common element of the Greek and the Christian religions, it must be said of both, that if a manifestation of God is to be supposed at all, his natural form must be that of Spirit, which for sensuous conception is essentially the human; for no other form can lay claim to spirituality. God appears indeed in the sun, in the mountains, in the trees, in everything that has life; but a natural appearance of this kind, is not the form proper to Spirit: here God is cognizable only in the mind of the percipient. If god himself is to be manifested in a corresponding expression, that can only be the human form: for from this the Spiritual beams forth. But if it were asked: Does God *necessarily* manifest himself? the question must be answered in the affirmative; for there is no essential existence that does not manifest itself. The defect of the Greek religion, as compared with the Christians, is, therefore, that in the former the *manifestation* constitutes the highest mode in which the Divine being is conceived to exist—the sum and substance of divinity; while in the Christian religion the manifestation is regarded only as a *temporary phase* of the Divine. Here the *manifested* God dies, and elevates himself to glory; only after death is Christ represented as sitting at the right hand of God. The Greek god, on the contrary, exists for his worshippers perennially *in the manifestation*— only in marble, in metal or wood, or as figured by the imagination. But why did God not appear to the Greeks in the flesh? Because man was not duly estimated, did not obtain honor and dignity, till he had more fully elaborated and developed himself in the attainment of the Freedom implicit in the aesthetic manifestation in question; the form and shaping of the divinity therefore continued to be the product of individual views, (not a general, impersonal one). One element in Spirit is, that it produces itself—*makes* itself what it is: and the other is, that it is originally free—that Freedom is its *nature* and its Idea. But the Greeks, since they had not attained an intellectual conception of themselves, did not yet realize Spirit in its Universality—had not the idea of man and the essential unity of the divine and human nature according to the Christian view. Only the self-reliant, truly subjective Spirit can bear to dispense with the phenomenal side, and can venture to assign the Divine Nature to Spirit alone. It then no longer needs to inweave the Natural into its idea of the Spiritual, in order to hold fast its conception of the Divine, and to have its unity with the Divine, externally visible; but while free Thought *thinks* the Phenomenal, it is content to leave it as it is; for it also *thinks* that union of the Finite and the Infinite, and recognizes it not as a mere accidental union, but as the Absolute—the eternal Idea itself. Since Subjectivity was not comprehended in all its depth by the Greek Spirit, the true reconciliation was not attained in it, and the human Spirit did not yet assert its true position. This defect showed itself in the fact of Fate as pure subjectivity appearing superior to the gods; it also shows itself in the fact, that men derive their resolves not yet from themselves, but from their Oracles. Neither human nor divine subjectivity, recognized as infinite, has as yet, absolutely decisive authority." (250)

"The State unites the two phases just considered, viz., the Subjective and the Objective Work of Art. In the State, Spirit is not a mere Object, like the deities, nor, on the other hand, is it merely subjectively developed to a beautiful physique. It is here a living, universal Spirit, but which is at the same time the self-conscious Spirit of the individuals composing the community." (249-250)

"The *Democratical* Constitution alone was adapted to the Spirit and political condition in question. In the East we recognized Despotism, developed in magnificent proportions, as a form of government strictly appropriate to the Dawn-Land of History. Not less adapted is the democratical form in Greece, to the part assigned to it in the same great drama. In Greece, viz., we have the freedom of the Individual, but it has not yet advanced to such a degree of abstraction, that the subjective unit is conscious of direct dependence on the (general) substantial principle—the State as such. In this grade of Freedom, the individual will is unfettered in the entire range of its vitality, and embodies that substantial principle (the bond of the political union), according to its particular idiosyncrasy. In Rome, on the other hand, we shall observe a harsh sovereignty dominating over the individual members of the State; as also in the German Empire a monarchy, in which the Individual is connected with and has *devoirs* to perform not only in regard to the monarch, but to the whole monarchical organization." (251)

This Democratic State in Greece rose gradually out of a long past. In the early days, in the time of the Kings, no political life as such existed. But after the Trojan War and in the interval between this and the coming of Cyrus the Great, political life arose in answer to the need of it. The first law givers were known as the Seven Sages. They were teachers of wisdom as well as practical politicians—among them was Thales of Miletus. Later the Athenians commissioned Solon to frame for them a constitution—which he did. Turning to Hegel at this point we have the following: "The main point in Democracy is moral disposition. *Virtue* is the basis of Democracy, remarks Montesquieu; and this sentiment is as important as it is true in reference to the idea of Democracy commonly entertained. The Substance, (the Principle) of Justice, the common weal, the general interest, is the main consideration; but it is so only as Custom, in the form of Objective Will, so that morality properly so called—subjective conviction and intention—has not yet manifested itself. Law exists, and is in point of substance, the Law of Freedom—rational (in its form and purport,) and valid *because it is Law, i.e.* without ulterior sanction. As in Beauty the Natural element—its sensuous coefficient—remains, so also in this customary morality, laws assume the form of a necessity of Nature. The Greeks occupy the middle ground of *Beauty* and have not yet attained the higher standpoint of Truth. While Custom and Wont is the form in which the Right is willed and done, that form is a stable one, and has not yet admitted into it the foe of (unreflected) immediacy—reflection and subjectivity of Will. The interest of the community may, therefore, continue to be intrusted to the will and resolve of the citizens—and this must be the basis of the Greek constitution; for no principle has as yet manifested itself, which can contravene such Choice conditioned by Custom, and hinder its realizing itself in action. The Democratic Constitution is here the only possible one: the citizens are still unconscious of particular interests, and therefore of a corrupting element: the Objective Will is in their case not disintegrated. Athene the goddess is Athens itself—*i.e.*, the real and concrete spirit of the citizens. The divinity ceases to inspire their life and conduct, only when the Will has retreated within itself—into the *adytum* of cognition and conscience—and has posited the infinite schism between the Subjective and the Objective. The above is the true position of the Democratic polity; its justification and absolute necessity rest on this still immanent Objective Morality. For the modern conception of Democracy this justification cannot be pleaded. These provide that the interests of the community, the affairs of State, shall be discussed and decided by the People; that the individual members of the community shall deliberate, urge their respective opinions, and give their votes; and this on the ground that the interests of the State and its concerns are the interests of such individual members. All this is very well; but the essential condition and distinction in regard to various phases of Democracy is: *What is the character of these* individual members? They are authorized to assume their position, only in as far as their will is still *Objective Will*—not one that wishes this or that, not mere "good" will. For good will is something particular —rests on the morality of individuals, on their conviction and subjective Feeling. That very subjective Freedom which constitutes the principle and determines the peculiar form of Freedom is *our* world—which forms the absolute basis of our political and religious life, could not manifest itself in Greece otherwise than as a *destructive* element. Subjectivity was a grade not greatly in advance of that occupied by the Greek Spirit; that phase must of necessity soon be attained: but it plunged the Greek world into ruin, for the polity which that world embodied was not calculated for this side of humanity—did not recognize this phase; since it had not made its appearance when that polity began to exist. Of the Greeks in the first and genuine form of their Freedom, we may assert, that they had no conscience; the habit of living for their country without further (analysis or) reflection, was the principle dominant among them. The consideration of the State in the abstract—which to our understanding is the essential point—was alien to them. Their grand object was their country in its living and real aspect;—*this actual* Athens, this Sparta, these Temples, these Altars, this form of social life, this union of fellow-citizens, these manners and customs. To the Greek his country was a necessary of life, without which existence was impossible. It was the Sophists—the "Teachers of Wisdom"—who first introduced subjective reflection, and the new doctrine that each man should act according to his own conviction. When reflection comes into play, the inquiry is started whether the Principles of Law (*das Recht*) cannot be improved. Instead of holding by the existing state of things, *internal* conviction is relied upon; and thus begins a subjective independent Freedom, in which the individual finds himself in a position to bring everything to the test of his own conscience, even in defiance of the existing constitution. Each one has his "principles," and that view which accords with his private judgment he regards as *practically* the best, and as claiming practical realization. This decay even Thucydides notices, when he speaks of every one's thinking that things are going badly when he has not a hand in the management." (253)

"To this state of things—in which every one presumes to have a judgment of his own—confidence in Great Men is antagonistic. When, in earlier times, the Athenians commission Solon to legislate for them, or when Lycurgus appears at Sparta as lawgiver and regulator of the State, it is evidently not supposed that the people in general think that they know best what is politically right. At a later time also, it was distinguished personages of plastic genius in whom the people placed their confidence: Cleisthenes, *e.g.* who made the constitution still more democratic than it had been—Miltiades, Themistocles, Aristides, and Cimon, who in the Median wars stand at the head of Athenian affairs—and Pericles, in whom Athenian glory centers as in its focus. But as soon as any of these great men had performed what was needed, envy intruded—*i.e.* the recoil of the sentiment of equality against conspicuous talent— and he was imprisoned or exiled. Finally, the Sycophants arose among the people, aspersing all individual greatness, and reviling those who took the lead in public affairs." (254)

Three other conditions in the Greek republics must be noted. The form of Government as it existed in Greece, had certain peculiar characteristics. One of these was the existence of *Oracles*. They formed a conspicuous part of public and private life. They demonstrated the fact that the Greeks were not yet in the entire command of their own volition. Another element that must receive comment was the fact of the existence of *Slavery*. Of this Hegel says, "Slavery does not cease until the Will has been infinitely self-reflective —until Right is conceived as appertaining to every freeman, and the term freeman is regarded as a synonym for man in his generic nature as endowed with Reason. But here we still occupy the standpoint of Morality as mere Wont and Custom, and therefore known only as a peculiarity attaching to a certain kind of existence (not as absolute and universal Law)." (255) The third point of comment on the Grecian Democracy concerns its size. Democratic life as practised in Greece was possible only in small states. Here the entire population was familiar with all the interests of the state, with its business and its critical stages, and community opinion was harmonized by means of persuasive oratory.

After the Greeks had been unified under the common danger of the war against Troy, and after the republic had been set up with its pliability to the distinct needs of the different Greek states, there came to Greece what Hegel designates as that event marking the second period of any nation—namely the contact with the preceding world-historical people. War with mighty Persia came to Greece. Some of Persia's colonies had revolted against her. In this revolt Greece had sympathized and given aid. After certain preliminaries, the Persian king arrived with a great army— which the Greeks at first, repulsed. Later Thrace, Macedon and Thessaly were subjugated. But at the Pass of Thermopylae a few hundred Greeks held the vast army at bay at the cost of their lives. Athens fell but the Greeks won a victory over the Persian fleet at Salamis and over the Persian land forces at Plataea. Of this Hegel writes: "Thus was Greece freed from the pressure which threatened to overwhelm it. Greater battles, unquestionably, have been fought; but these live immortal not in the historical records of Nations only, but also of Science and of Art—of the Noble and the Moral generally. For these are World-Historical victories; they were the salvation of culture and Spiritual vigor, and they rendered the Asiatic principle powerless. How often, on other occasions, have not men sacrificed everything for one grand object! How often have not warriors fallen for Duty and Country! But here we are called to admire not only valor, genius and spirit, but the purport of the contest—the effect, the result, which are unique in their kind. In all other battles a particular interest is predominant; but the immortal fame of the Greeks is none other than their due, in consideration of the noble cause for which deliverance was achieved. In the history of the world it is not the formal (subjective and individual) valor that has been displayed, not the so-called merit of the combatants, but the importance of the cause itself, that must decide the fame of the achievement. In the case before us, the interest of the World's History hung trembling in the balance. Oriental despotism—a world united under one lord and sovereign—on the one side, and separate states insignificant in extent and resources, but animated by free individuality—on the other side, stood front to front in array of battle. Never in History has the superiority of spiritual power over material bulk——and that of no contemptible amount—been made so gloriously manifest. This war, and the subsequent development of the states which took the lead in it, is the most brilliant period of Greece. Everything which the Greek principle involved, then reaches its perfect bloom and came into the light of day." (258)

"The Athenians continued their wars of conquest for a

considerable time, and thereby attained a high degree of prosperity; while the Lacedaemonians, who had no naval power, remained quiet. The antagonism of Athens and Sparta now commences." Regarding the rivalry that developed between the northern and southern halves of Greece—centered in Athens and Sparta, it must be first understood that their inherent natures were basically at variance. Athens had long been the asylum for the inhabitants of the various districts of Greece and she had a mixed population. Although she possessed a "vital equality of manners and customs" there existed also the greatest diversity of character and talents which gave rise in free expression to a number of different works. Pericles originated the production of those ornaments of sculpture which have been the wonder of posterity. It was before the Athenians that the dramas of Aeschylus, Sophocles and Euripides were performed. It was here that the orations of Pericles were delivered. Here were created the contributions of Aristophanes, Socrates, Plato and Thucydides. They constitute a galaxy of great geniuses whose productions have become classical. Indeed it may be said that although Athens paid attention to industry, she, in Hegel's words, "exhibited the spectacle of a state whose existence was essentially directed to realizing the Beautiful, and which had, beside this, a thoroughly cultivated consciousness respecting the serious side of public affairs and the interests of Man's Spirit and Life, and united with that consciousness hardy courage and practical ability." (262)

Athens and Sparta were bringing to light more and more the incongruity that existed between their temperaments. Sparta, contrary to Athens, had a rigid abstract virtue. Hers was a life devoted to the state. The Spartans were Dorians who had conquered the original Helots and enslaved them. A severe inhumanity and harshness characterized them. Although the constitution was based on democracy, it was in practise more nearly an Oligarchy. Little interest was shown for the individual, or for cultural pursuits. The state usurped the family life. The meals were served at a public state table;

the children of the Spartans were reared in a public State institution. Thus were the Spartans and the Athenians the antithesis of one another. The result was discord which brought on open antagonism. This culminated in the Peloponnesian War in which Athens was at last compelled to succumb to Sparta. In the meantime there was much treachery and contention among the various Greek states leading finally to the ruin of one and all. Of this period Hegel says: "Weakened and distracted, Greece could no longer find safety in itself, and needed an authoritative prop. In the towns there were incessant contests; the citizens were divided into factions, as in the Italian cities of the Middle Ages. The victory of one party entailed the banishment of the other; the latter then usually applied to the enemies of their native city, to obtain their aid in subjugating it by force of arms. The various States could no longer co-exist peaceably: they prepared ruin for each other, as well as for themselves." (267)

"We have, then, now to investigate the *corruption* of the Greek world in its profounder import, and may denote the principle of that corruption as *subjectivity obtaining emancipation for itself*. We see Subjectivity obtruding itself in various ways. Thought—the subjectively Universal—menaces the beautiful religion of Greece, while the passions of individuals and their caprice menace its political constitution. In short, Subjectivity, comprehending and manifesting itself, threatens the existing state of things in every department—characterized as that state of things is by Immediacy (a primitive, unreflecting simplicity). Thought, therefore, appears here as the principle of decay—decay, viz. of Substantial (prescriptive) morality; for it introduces an antithesis, and asserts essentially rational principles. In the Oriental states, in which there is no such antithesis, moral freedom cannot be realized, since the highest principle is (Pure) Abstraction. But when Thought recognizes its positive character, as in Greece, it establishes principles; and these bear to the real world the relation of Essence to Form.

For the concrete vitality found among the Greeks, is Customary Morality—a life for Religion, for the State, without analysis leading to abstract definitions, which must lead away from the concrete embodiment of them, and occupy an antithetical position to that embodiment. Law is part of the existing state of things, with Spirit *implicit* in it. But as soon as Thought arises, it investigates the various political constitutions: as the result of its investigation it forms for itself an idea of an improved state of society, and demands that this ideal should take the place of things as they are." (268)

"In the principle of Greek Freedom, inasmuch as it is Freedom, is involved the self-emancipation of Thought. We observed the dawn of Thought in the circle of men mentioned above under their well-known appellation of the Seven Sages. It was they who first uttered general propositions; though at that time wisdom consisted rather in a concrete insight (into things, than in the power of abstract conception). Parallel with the advance in the development of Religious Art and with political growth, we find a progressive strengthening of Thought, its enemy and destroyer; and at the time of the Peloponnesian War science was already developed. With the Sophists began the process of reflection on the existing state of things, and of ratiocination. That very diligence and activity which we observed among the Greeks in their practical life, and in the achievement of works of art, showed itself also in the turns and windings which these ideas took; so that, as material things are changed, worked up and used for other than their original purposes, similarly the essential being of Spirit—what is thought and known—is variously handled; it is made an object about which the mind can employ itself, and this occupation becomes an interest in and for itself. The movement of Thought—that which goes on within its sphere (without reference to an intrinsic object)—a process which had formerly no interest—acquires attractiveness on its own account. The cultivated Sophists, who were not erudite or scientific men, but masters of subtle turns of thought, excited the admiration of the Greeks. For all questions they had an answer; for all interests of a political or religious order they had general points of view; and in the ultimate development of their art, they claimed the ability to prove everything, to discover a justifiable side in every position. In a democracy it is a matter of the first importance, to be able to speak in popular assemblies—to urge one's opinions on public matters. Now this demands the power of duly presenting before them that point of view which we desire them to regard as essential. For such a purpose, intellectual culture is needed, and this discipline the Greeks acquired under their Sophists. This mental culture then became the means, in the hands of those who possessed it, of enforcing their views and interests on the Demos: the expert Sophist knew how to turn the subject of discussion this way or that way at pleasure, and thus the doors were thrown wide open to all human passions. A leading principle of the Sophists was, that "Man is the measure of all things"; but in this, as in all their apophthegms, lurks an ambiguity, since the term "Man" may denote Spirit in its depth and truth, or in the aspect of mere caprice and private interest. The Sophists meant Man simply as subjective, and intended in this dictum of theirs, that mere liking was the principle of Right, and that advantage to the individual was the ground of final appeal. This Sophistic principle appears again and again, though under different forms, in various periods of History; thus even in our own times subjective opinion of what is right—mere feeling—is made the ultimate ground of decision . . . And it was in *Socrates,* that at the beginning of the Peloponnesian War, the principle of subjectivity—of the absolute inherent independence of Thought—attained free expression. He taught that man has to discover and recognize in himself what is the Right and Good, and that this Right and Good is in its nature universal. Socrates is celebrated as a Teacher of Morality, but we should rather call him the *Inventor of Morality*. The Greeks had a *customary* morality; but Socrates undertook to teach them what moral virtues, duties, etc. were. The moral man is not he who merely wills and does that which is right—not the merely innocent man—but he who has the consciousness of what he is doing." (269)

"Socrates—in assigning to insight, to conviction, the determination of man's actions—posited the Individual as capable of a final moral decision, in contraposition to Country and to Customary Morality, and thus made himself an Oracle, in the Greek sense. He said that he had a Daemon within him, which counselled him what to do, and revealed to him what was advantageous to his friends. The rise of the inner world of Subjectivity was the rupture with the existing Reality. Though Socrates himself continued to perform his duties as a citizen, it was not the actual State and its religion, but the world of Thought that was his true home. Now the question of the existence and nature of the gods came to be discussed. The disciple of Socrates, Plato, banished from his ideal state, Homer and Hesiod, the originators of that mode of conceiving of religious objects which prevailed among the Greeks; for he desiderated a higher conception of what was to be reverenced as divine—one more in harmony with Thought. Many citizens now seceded from practical and political life, to live in the ideal world. The principle of Socrates manifests a revolutionary aspect towards the Athenian State; for the peculiarity of this State was, that Customary Morality was the form in which its existence was moulded, viz.—an inseparable connection of Thought with actual life. When Socrates wishes to induce his friends to reflection, the discourse has always a negative tone; he brings them to the consciousness that they do not know what the Right is. But when on account of the giving utterance to that principle which was advancing to recognition, Socrates is condemned to death, the sentence bears on the one hand the aspect of unimpeachable rectitude

—inasmuch as the Athenian people condemns its deadliest foe—but on the other hand, that of a deeply tragical character, inasmuch as the Athenians had to make the discovery, that what they reprobated in Socrates had already struck firm root among themselves, and that they must be pronounced guilty or innocent with him. With this feeling they condemned the accusers of Socrates, and declared him guiltless. In Athens that higher principle which proved the ruin of the Athenian state, advanced in its development without intermission. Spirit had acquired the propensity to gain satisfaction for itself—to reflect. Even in decay the Spirit of Athens appears majestic, because it manifests itself as the free, the liberal—exhibiting its successive phases in their pure idiosyncrasy—in that form in which they really exist. Amiable and cheerful even in the midst of tragedy is the light-heartedness and nonchalance with which the Athenians accompany their (national) morality to its grave. We recognize the higher interest of the new culture in the fact that the people made themselves merry over their own follies, and found great entertainment in the comedies of Aristophanes, which have the severest satire for their contents, while they bear the stamp of the most unbridled mirth." (271)

"In Sparta the same corruption is introduced, since the social unit seeks to assert his individuality against the moral life of the community: but there we have merely the isolated side of particular subjectivity—corruption in its undisguised form, blank immorality, vulgar selfishness and venality. All these passions manifest themselves in Sparta, especially in the persons of its generals, who, for the most part living at a distance from their country, obtain an opportunity of securing advantages at the expense of their own state as well as of those to whose assistance they are sent." (271)

After the fall of Athens, Sparta took the lead but selfishly misused her power and was universally hated. Then occurred clashes between Sparta, Thebes and the Phocians in which the latter stoops ignominiously to desecrating and plundering the temple at Delphi. "This deed," says Hegel, "completes the ruin of Greece; the sanctuary was desecrated, the god so to speak, killed; the last support of unity was thereby annihilated; reverence for that which in Greece had been, as it were, always the final arbiter—its monarchical principle—was displaced, insulted, and trodden under foot." (271)

The next step was that this dethroned power of the oracle was taken by another—a real authoritative human will—in the person of King Philip of Macedon. He entered in order to avenge the insult and soon made himself lord of Greece. At his death his son Alexander, who had been educated by Aristotle, took his place at the head of the Hellenes. His ambition of leading Greece into Asiatic conquests he soon executed—moving as far as to the northern provinces of India. Turning to Hegel at this point. "That he may stand before the eyes of posterity as a youth, an early death must hurry him away. Achilles, as remarked above, *begins* the Greek world, and his antitype Alexander *concludes* it: and these youths not only supply a picture of the fairest kind in their own persons, but at the same time afford a complete and perfect type of Hellenic existence. Alexander finished his work and completed his idea: and thus bequeathed to the world one of the noblest and most brilliant of visions, which our poor reflections only serve to obscure. For the great World-Historical form of Alexander, the modern standard applied by recent historical "Philistines"—that of virture or morality—will by no means suffice. And if it be alleged in depreciation of his merit, that he had no successor, and left behind no dynasty we may remark that the Greek Kingdoms that arose in Asia after him, are his dynasty." (273) Of these kingdoms Hegel mentions the Graeco-Bactrian lasting for two centuries and the fact that Greek dominion spead over northern India—even into China. It was finally ousted by the Indian, Chandraguptas. Other Greek kingdoms arose in Asia Minor, Babylonia, Armenia, Syria and Egypt. Here the city of

Alexandria became the chief center of commerce as well as of art and science. It formed the point of union between Eastern customs and traditions with Western civilization. "Besides these," says Hegel, "the Macedonian Kingdom, that of Thrace, stretching beyond the Danube, that of Illyria and that of Epirus, flourished under the sway of Greek princes." (274)

After the establishment of these several kingdoms—in the rule of which Alexander's generals took a noticeable part,—there was a certain glory still attached to the name of Greece. Hegel says "To some extent too the kings of the period reckoned it their greatest glory to render and to keep the Greek cities and states independent. The *Emancipation of Greece* had as it were, become the general watch-word; and it passed for a high title of fame to be called the *Deliverer of Greece*. However the real idea was to keep all in a state of dependency by means of separation and discord. We see here," writes Hegel, "an infinite involvement with the most manifold foreign interests—a subtle intermixture and play of parties, whose threads are continually being combined anew." (276) The third period of her destiny was upon Greece—that of succumbing to the weakness brought on by selfishness and debauchery. Hegel's appraisal is: "The third period of the history of Greece brings us to their contact with that people which was to play the next part on the theatre of the World's History; and the chief excuse for this contact was—as pretexts have previously been—the liberation of Greece. After Perseus the last Macedonian King, in the year 168 B.C. had been conquered by the Romans and brought in triumph to Rome, the Achaean league was attacked and broken up, and at last in the year 146 B.C. Corinth was destroyed. Looking at Greece as Polybius describes it, we see how a noble nature such as his, has nothing left for it but to despair at the state of affairs and to retreat into Philosophy; or if it attempts to act, can only die in the struggle. In deadly contraposition to the multiform variety of passion which Greece presents—that distracted condition which whelms good and evil in one common ruin—stands a blind fate—an iron power ready to show up that degraded condition in all its weakness, and to dash it to pieces in miserable ruin; for cure, amendment and consolation are impossible. And this crushing Destiny is the *Roman power*." (277)

THE ROMAN WORLD

We now enter upon the consideration of the Roman World. The part it played in the World Historical Process was an example, on a mighty scale, of the conception which the Greeks had of Destiny. Here that power will be named circumstance—the irresistible power of circumstance to mould human nature in accordance with the blue print for fulfillment. Because here, in the Roman World, mortals were cast into bonds by a Universal Dominion until nothing was left, as a way of escape, except a retreat inward to the subjective realm of spirit. Moreover Rome, this seat of Universal Dominion brought home to her Pantheon all the Gods, the Deities and Spirits, of the then known world. In her Pantheon she set them up—where finally they were to give way before the advance of a subjective consciousness as it came into the recognition of the Living Spirit and the eternal drama of the God-Man.

Hegel speaks of it in the following manner. "Through its being the aim of the State, that the social units in their moral life should be sacrificed to it, the world is sunk in melancholy: its heart is broken, and it is all over with the Natural side of Spirit, which has sunk into a feeling of unhappiness. Yet only from this feeling could arise the supersensuous, the free Spirit of Christianity." (278)

"In the Greek principle we have seen spiritual existence in its exhilaration—its cheerfulness and enjoyment: Spirit had not yet drawn back into abstraction; it was still involved with the Natural element—the idiosyncrasy of individuals;—on which account the virtues of individuals themselves became moral works of art. Abstract universal Personality had not yet appeared, for Spirit must first develop itself to that form of abstract Universality which exercised the severe discipline over humanity now under consideration. Here, in Rome, then, we find that free universality, that abstract Freedom, which on the one hand sets an abstract state, a political constitution and power, over *concrete* individuality; on the other side creates a personality in opposition to that universality—the inherent freedom of the *abstract* Ego, which must be distinguished from individual idiosyncrasy. For Personality constitutes the fundamental condition of legal Right: it appears chiefly in the category of Property, but it is indifferent to the concrete characteristics of the living Spirit with which individuality is concerned. These two elements, which constitute Rome—political Universality on the one hand, and the abstract freedom of the individual on the other—appear, in the first instance, in the form of Subjectivity. This Subjectivity—this retreating into one's self which we observed as the corruption of the Greek Spirit—becomes here the ground on which a new side of the World's History arises. In considering the Roman World, we have not to do with a concretely spiritual life, rich in itself; but the world-historical element in it is the *abstractum* of Universality, and the object which is pursued with soulless and heartless severity, is mere *dominion,* in order to enforce that *abstractum*." (278)

"In Greece, *Democracy* was the fundamental condition of political life, as in the East, *Despotism;* here we have *Aristocracy* of a rigid order, in a state of opposition to the people. In Greece also the Democracy was rent asunder, but only in the way of factions; in Rome it is principles that keep the entire community in a divided state—they occupy a hostile position towards, and struggle with each other: first the Aristocracy with the Kings, then the Plebs with the Aristocracy, till Democracy gets the upper hand; then first arise factions in which originated that later aristocracy of commanding individuals which subjugated the world. It is this dualism that, properly speaking, marks Rome's inmost being." (279)

The Roman World had its center in Italy, which, on account of its length and narrowness, its contour, its rivers and mountains is somewhat like the peninsula of Greece in that it does not present a natural unity. Its inhabitants were also drawn from various races. Strange to note, Rome itself arose outside recognized districts; nor was it formed from some ancient line; but from the start, in consonance with its character of universal harsh dominion, it owes its origin to artifice and violence. Situated between the borders of three different districts—those of the Latins, the Sabines and Etruscans (for many had been migrating to Italy since the time of the fall of Troy)—historians agree that it was roaming shepherds who first made the hills of Rome their camping ground. Later the community constituted itself a predatory state to which any were welcome. As time went on, the shepherd state became a refuge for the undesirable, or discontented, of the other districts. "The rabble of all the three districts, between which Rome lay," says Hegel, "was collected in the new city." This did not savor of respectability and Rome extending an invitation to her neighbors to celebrate certain religious festivals, the Sabines were the only ones who responded. They fared ill, however, for these shepherds and refugees were without women in their community. They thereupon captured and made away with the wives of their guests. So begins Mighty Rome—a conquering, dominating people from the commencement. Hegel writes: "The seizure of the Sabine women is a universally received historical fact. This circumstance involves a very characteristic feature, viz., that Religion is used as a means for furthering the purposes of the infant State. Another method of extension was the conveying to Rome of the inhabitants of neighboring and conquered towns. At a later date there was also a voluntary migration of foreigners to Rome; as in the case of the so celebrated family of the Claudii, bringing their whole clientela." (284)

"It is this peculiarity in the founding of the State which must be regarded as the essential basis of the idiosyncrasy of Rome. For it directly involves the severest discipline and self-sacrifice to the grand object of the union. A State which had first to form itself, and which is based on force, must be held together by force. It is not a moral, liberal connection, but a compulsory condition of subordination, that results from such an origin. The Roman *virtus* is valor; not, merely personal but that which is essentially connected with a union of associates; which union is regarded as the supreme interest, and may be combined with lawless violence of all kinds. While the Romans formed a union of this kind, they were not, indeed, like the Lacedaemonians, engaged in an internal contest with a conquered and subjugated people; but there arose a distinction and a struggle between *Patricians* and *Plebeians.* This distinction was mythically adumbrated in the hostile brothers, Romulus and Remus. Remus was buried on the Aventine mount; this is consecrated to the evil genii, and to it are directed the Secessions of the Plebs. The question comes, then, how this distinction originated? It has been already said, that Rome was formed by robber-herdsmen, and the concourse of rabble of all sorts. At a later date, the inhabitants of captured and destroyed towns were also conveyed thither. The weaker, the poorer, the later additions of population are naturally underrated by, and in a condition of dependence upon those who originally founded the state, and those who were distinguished by valor, and also by wealth. It is not necessary, therefore, to take refuge in a hypothesis which has recently been a favorite one—that the Patricians formed a particular race." (285)

"The dependence of the Plebeians on the Patricians is often represented as a perfectly legal relation—indeed, even a sacred one; since the Patricians had the *sacra* in their hands, while the plebs would have been godless, as it were, without them. The Plebeians left to the Patricians their hypocritical stuff (*ad decipiendam plebem,* Cic.) and cared nothing for their sacra and auguries; but in disjoining political rights from these ritual observances, and making good their claim to those rights, they were no more guilty of a presumptuous sacrilege than the Protestants, when they emancipated the political power of the State, and asserted the freedom of conscience"... (285)

"In the first predatory period of the state, every citizen was necessarily a soldier, for the state was based on war; this burden was oppressive, since every citizen was obligated to maintain himself in the field. This circumstance, therefore, gave rise to the contracting of enormous debts—the Patricians becoming the creditors of the Plebeians. With the introduction of laws, this arbitrary relation necessarily ceased; but only gradually, for the Patricians were far from being immediately inclined to release the plebs from the cliental relation; they rather strove to render it permanent. The laws of the Twelve Tables still contained much that was undefined; very much was still left to the arbitrary will of the judge—the Patricians alone being judges; the antithesis, therefore, between Patricians and Plebeians, continues till a much later period. Only by degrees do the Plebeians scale all the heights of official station, and attain those privileges which formerly belonged to the Patricians alone." (286)

The family life of the Romans bore the characteristics stamped upon it by its origin. It will be remembered that the fabulous twins, Romulus and Remus were left to the succor of a friendly mother wolf and the capture of the Sabine women did not show forth the nature of love and respect for those who were to be the mothers of the race. We therefore find family life harsh, stern and cold in all its aspects. The free life of love and feeling is replaced by a selfish severity excluding all the sensibilities of a natural refined relationship. Marriage bore the aspect of a mere contract. The husband possessed his wife and his daughters; also any property that came to them. The relation of sons was similar. A son could not possess property even if he were himself in office. When circumstances arose to sever children from the family, the connections ceased, as a rule, altogether. These same features characterize the larger life of the state.

Hegel has the following to say: "The immoral active severity of the Romans in this private side of character, necessarily finds its counterpart in the passive severity of their political union. For the severity which the Roman experienced from the State he was compensated by a severity, identical in nature, which he was allowed to indulge toward his family—a servant on the one side, a despot on the other. This constitutes the Roman greatness, whose peculiar characteristic was stern inflexibility in the union of individuals with the State, and with its law and mandate . . . It may be asked by what were such a disposition and character produced? Produced it cannot be, but it is essentially latent in the origination of the State from that primal robber—community, as also in the idiosyncrasy of the people who composed it, and lastly, in that phase of the World-Spirit which was just ready for development. The elements of the Roman people were Etruscan, Latin and Sabine; these must have contained an inborn natural adaptation to produce the Roman Spirit. Of the spirit, the character, and the life of the ancient Italian people we know very little—thanks to the non-intelligent character of the Roman historiography!—and that little, for the most part, from the Greek writers on Roman history. But of the general character of the Romans we may say that, in contrast with that primeval wild poetry and transmutation of the finite, which we observe in the East—in contrast with the beautiful, harmonious poetry, and well-balanced freedom of Spirit found among the Greeks, among the Romans, the *prose* of life makes its appearance—the self-consciousness of finiteness—the abstraction of the understanding and a rigorous principle of personality, which even in the Family does not expand itself to natural morality, but remains the unfeeling non-spiritual unit, and universality." (288) This abstract universality was the all powerful dominating sphere of the State. This was mighty Rome.

This prosaic, non-spiritual people set themselves the task of compiling a code of law which completed the separation between the mandates of the East and the juristic morality of the Greeks. They discovered a principle, not dependent on sentiment nor disposition,—a principle of right—which is external. They give it a form which has stood the test of time. Regarding the Roman law Hegel speaks the following: "While they have thus bestowed upon us a valuable gift, in point of *form*, we can use and enjoy it without becoming victims to that sterile Understanding—without regarding it as the *ne plus ultra* of Wisdom and Reason. They were its victims, living beneath its sway; but they thereby secured for others Freedom of Spirit—viz., that inward Freedom which has consequently become emancipated from the sphere of the Limited and the External. Spirit, Soul, Disposition, Religion have now no longer to fear being involved with that abstract juristical Understanding." (289)

The religion of the Romans carried with it the same characteristics as marked the other aspect of their life. It was a religion of formal constraint while among the Greeks it was cheer in the realm of fantasy. It is true that the use of the Gods was often similar to those of Greece. Some were identical; there was Jupiter, Juno and Minerva. But in the richly imaginative land of Greece, they represented concepts which were impossible to the Roman consciousness; to them the religious feeling of awe remained undeveloped. Yet the forms of religion occupied a prominent place. Every transaction was accompanied by a sacred ceremony. Turning to Hegel: "The knowledge of these *sacra* is utterly uninteresting and wearisome, affording fresh material for learned research as to whether they are of Etruscan, Sabine, or other origin. On their account the Roman people have been regarded as extremely pious, both in positive and negative observances; though it is ridiculous to hear recent writers speak with unction and respect of these *sacra*. The Patricians were especially fond of them; they have therefore been elevated in the judgment of some, to the dignity of sacerdotal families, and regarded as the sacred gentes—the possessors and conservators of Roman religion: the plebeians then became the godless element. On this head what is pertinent has already been said. The ancient kings were at the same time also *reges sacrorum*. After the royal dignity had been done away with, there still remained a *Rex Sacrorum;* but he, like all the other priests was subject to the *Pontifex Maximus*, who presided over all "sacra," and gave them such a rigidity and fixity as enabled the patricians to maintain their religious power so long." (291) It may be said, in connection with this subject, that the religion of the Romans did not expand to a free moral and spiritual comprehension; it remained a rigid formal ceremonial. It had for its establishment the figures of divinities as representing that to which they could turn for the fulfillment of private desires and selfish purposes. In Hegel's words, "The chief characteristic of Roman Religion is therefore a hard and dry contemplation of certain voluntary aims, which they regard as existing absolutely in their divinities, and whose accomplishment they desire of them as embodying absolute power. These purposes constitute that for the sake of which they worship the gods, and by which, in a constrained, limited way, they are bound to their deities. The Roman religion is therefore the entirely *prosaic* one of narrow aspirations, expediency, profit. The divinities peculiar to them are entirely prosaic; they are conditions (of mind or body), sensations, or useful arts, to which their dry fancy, having elevated them to independent power, gave objectivity; they are partly abstractions, which could only become rigid allegories—partly conditions of being which appear as bringing advantage or injury, and which were presented as objects of worship in their original bare limited form." (292)

"It was the Romans especially who introduced the practice of not merely supplementing the gods in time of need, and celebrating "lectisternia," but of also making solemn promises and vows to them. For help in difficulties they sent even into foreign countries, and imported foreign divinities and rites. The introduction of gods and most of the Roman temples thus arose from necessity—from a vow of some kind and an obligatory, not disinterested acknowledgment of favors. The Greeks, on the contrary, erected and instituted their beautiful temples, and statues, and rites, from love of beauty and divinity for their own sake." (292) The only side of the Roman religion that exhibited attractive elements were the festivals. They were related to pastoral and agricultural life. Of these the Saturnalia were the most renowned. At first held as religious ceremonials at the sowing and harvesting times, they later degenerated into mere buffoonery and even vulgarity.

Another feature of Roman life that must be mentioned, as indicative of their peculiarly harsh feelings, were the public games. Hegel describes these for us: "With increasing luxury the taste for the baiting of beasts and men became particularly keen. Hundreds of bears, lions, tigers, elephants, crocodiles and ostriches, were produced and slaughtered for mere amusement. A body consisting of hundreds, nay thousands of gladiators, when entering the amphitheatre of a certain festival to engage in a sham sea-fight, addressed the Emperor with the words: "Those who are devoted to death salute thee," to excite some compassion. In vain! the whole were devoted to mutual slaughter. In place of human sufferings in the depths of the soul and spirit, occasioned by the contradictions of life, and which find their solution in Destiny, the Romans instituted a cruel reality of corporeal suffering: blood in streams, the rattle in the throat which signals death, and the expiring gasp were the scenes that delighted them.—This cold negativity of naked murder exhibits at the same time that murder of all spiritual objective aim which had taken place in the soul. I need only mention, in addition, the auguries, auspices, and Sibylline books, to remind you how fettered the Romans were by superstitions of all kinds, and how they pursued exclusively their own aims in all the observances in question." (294)

The pleasure which the Romans derived from these cruel sports is indicative of the fact that their religion left them entirely free in all secular matters. Their sacred principles were a matter of ritual—a form to be pursued—this with impressive solemnity. To quote Hegel: "The Romans are invariably pious, whatever may be the substantial character of their actions. But as the sacred principle here is nothing but an empty form, it is exactly of such a kind that it can be an instrument in the power of the devotee; it is taken possession of by the individual, who seeks his private objects and interests; whereas the truly Divine possesses, on the contrary, a concrete power in itself. But where there is only a powerless form, the individual—the Will, possessing an independent concreteness able to make that form its own, and render it subservient to its views—stand above it. This happened in Rome on the part of the patricians. The possession of sovereignty by the patricians is thereby made firm, sacred, incommunicable, peculiar: the administration of government, and political privileges, receive the character of hallowed private property . . . The inequality which enters into the domain of sacred things forms the transition from religion to the bare reality of political life. The consecrated inequality of will and of private property constitutes the fundamental condition of the change. The Roman principle admits of *aristocracy* alone as the constitution proper to it, but which directly manifests itself only in an antithetical form—internal inequality. Only from necessity and the pressure of adverse circumstances is this contradiction momentarily smothered over; for it involves a duplicate power, the sternness and malevolent isolation of whose components can only be mastered and bound together by a still greater sternness, into a unity maintained by force." (295)

The history of the Romans has three periods. First the rule of the kings; then the Republic under Consuls; and finally the rule of the Emperors. The early periods of this history are mixed with fable. However it is fairly well established that seven kings ruled Rome. Romulus the founder of this community of freebooters, organized it into a state. Then came Numa who is said to have been the first to institute religious rituals. Here it is interesting to note that these religious rituals came after the political union had been effected and not before it, nor as a motive for it as is most often the case. The third king Tarquinius, gave his especial attention to the organization of society. He did this in such a way as to displease the Patricians. The Plebs could now have a share in the voting and part of their debts to the Patricians had been abolished. Tarquinius was followed by Tullus Hostilius while the next king, Ancus Martius, was the grandson of Numa. Tarquinius Priscus, who followed, was of a Corinthian line and Servius Tullius the next king came from the conquered town of Corniculum. The seventh and last of the Roman kings was Tarquinius Superbus, who was a descendant of Tarquinius Priscus. All of these men were of foreign origin.

By the time of Tarquinius Superbus, Rome had grown into a position of considerable importance. She had trade by land and sea. She possessed the art of writing, and had also a clear comprehension of mundane affairs as well as a method in recording them. She set down the principles of external law for which posterity still honors her. This last king however, had made himself so far independent of the senate and the Patricians that their displeasure finally took effect in action. When a pretext arose, in the form of the King's dishonoring a matron—he was deposed. Thus in the year 510 B.C. the royal sovereign of Rome was banished never to return. Hegel comments as follows: "The Kings were expelled by the patricians, not by the plebeians; if therefore the patricians are to be regarded as possessed of "divine right" as being a sacred race, it is worthy of note that we find them here contravening such legitimation; for the King was their High Priest. We observe on this occasion with what dignity the sanctity of marriage was invested in the eyes of the Romans. The principle of subjectivity and piety (pudor) was with them the religious and guarded element; and its violation becomes the occasion of the expulsion of the Kings, and later on of the Decemvirs too. We find monogamy therefore also looked upon by the Romans as an understood thing. It was not introduced by an express law; we have nothing but an incidental testimony in the Institutes, where it is said that marriages under certain conditions of relationship are not allowable, because a man may not have two wives. It is not until the reign of Diocletian that we find a law expressly determining that no one belonging to the Roman empire may have two wives, "since according to a pretorian edict also, infamy attaches to such a condition" . . . Monogamy therefore is regarded as naturally valid, and is based on the principle of subjectivity. Lastly, we must also observe that royalty was not abrogated here as in Greece by suicidal destruction on the part of the royal races, but was exterminated by hate. The King, himself the chief priest, had been guilty of the grossest profanation; the principle of subjectivity revolted against the deed, and the patricians thereby elevated to a sense of independence threw off the yoke of royalty. Possessed by the same feeling, the plebs at a later date rose against the patricians, and the Latins and Allies against the Romans; until the equality of the social units was restored through the whole Roman dominion (a multitude of slaves, too, being emancipated) and they were held together by simple Despotism." (299)

The most important changes that occurred in the government after royalty had been deposed were that the constitution became in *name* republican, and two Consuls, elected annually, took over the powers of the King. The expulsion of the kings had taken place to the advantage of the aristocracy. This fact soon became the cause of clashes between the two classes. There were also wars of defence against the attacking forces of the expelled king. The account is long and varied. Finally the king's armies were overcome and the class differences were relieved by certain measures. The plebeians were to receive, beside the right to landed property which they had previously won, new assignments of land. There was the institution of Tribunes of the People—two at first, ten later, who had power to veto degrees of the Senate. Finally these were replaced by the *Decemviri* at popular demand. By degrees the plebeians gained admittance to all public offices. This marked Rome's entrance into national maturity and now she was ready to turn her attention outward. Speaking of this period Hegel writes: "A period of satisfied absorption in the common interest ensues, and the citizens are weary of internal struggles. When after civil discords nations direct their energies outward, they appear in their greatest strength; for the previous excitement continues, and no longer having its object within, seeks for it without. This direction given to the Roman energies was able for a moment to conceal the defect of that union; equilibrium was restored, but without an essential centre of unity and support. The contradiction that existed could not but break out again fearfully at a later period; but previous to this time the greatness of Rome had to display itself in war and the conquest of the world." (304)

Rome's Expansion

Rome's first expansion was the one inside of Italy. Here war was carried on during hundreds of years with the Samnites, the Etruscans, the Umbrians, the Marsi, the Gauls, and the Bruttii. Finally they were all subjugated and the mastery of Italy was complete. The movement of expansion then went to the South. Sicily was occupied; then west to Sardinia, Corsica and Spain. These were likewise subjugated. This brought Rome into contact with Carthage and the mode of warfare was changed to include the naval aspect. In the first Punic War Rome had shown her power for dominion. Now came the Second Punic War and the clash not only with mighty Carthage, and her possessions in northern Africa and southern Spain, but to far wider fields in the East.

Hegel designates the Second Punic War as that event which marks Rome's entrance into the second period of her existence —that in which the national life is fully mature and there is the establishment of the new pattern of the World Historical Process,—in which the nation fixes her position as over against those who had preceded her on the theatre of this Process. After the subjugation of Carthage, Rome came into conflict with the king of Macedonia. Next Antiochus, king of Syria, was involved. He was beaten at Thermopylae. Then Magnesia and Asia Minor, as far as Taurus, were surrendered to Rome. In the third Punic War Carthage was reduced to ashes, Corinth was destroyed and Greece became a Roman province.

Rome was now the mistress of the Mediterranean and possessed of perfect security. During this period great personalities arose. "But," writes Hegel, "after the feeling of patriotism—the dominant instinct of Rome—had been satisfied, destruction immediately invades the state regarded *en masse*; the grandeur of *individual* character becomes stronger in intensity, and more vigorous in the use of means, on account of contrasting circumstances. We see the internal contradiction of Rome now beginning to manifest itself in another form; and the epoch which concludes the second period is also the second mediation of that contradiction. We observed that contradiction previously in the struggle of the patricians against the plebeians: now it assumes the form of private interest, contravening patriotic sentiment; and respect for the state no longer holds these opposites in the necessary equipoise. Rather, we observe now side by side with wars for conquest, plunder and glory, the fearful spectacle of civil discords in Rome and intestine wars. There does not follow, as among the Greeks after the Median wars, a period of brilliant splendor in culture, art and science, in which Spirit enjoys inwardly and ideally that which it had previously achieved in the world of action. If inward satisfaction was to follow the period of that external prosperity in war, the principle of Roman life must be more concrete. But if there were such a concrete life to evolve as an object of consiousness from the depths of their souls by imagination and thought, what would it have been! Their chief spectacles were triumphs, the treasures gained in war, and captives from all nations, unsparingly subjected to the yoke of abstract sovereignty. The concrete element, which the Romans actually find within themselves, is only this unspiritual unity, and any definite thought or feeling of a non-abstract kind, can lie only in the idiosyncrasy of individuals. The tension of virtue is now relaxed, because the danger is past. At the time of the first Punic War, necessity united the hearts of all for the saving of Rome. In the following wars too, with Macedonia, Syria, and the Gauls in Upper Italy, the existence of the entire state was still concerned. But after the danger from Carthage and Macedon was over, the subsequent wars were more and more the mere consequences of victories, and nothing else was needed than to gather in their fruits. The armies were used for particular expeditions, suggested by policy, or for the advantages of individuals—for acquiring wealth, glory, *sovereignty* in the abstract. The relation to other nations was purely that of force. The national individuality of peoples did not, as early as the time of the Romans, excite respect, as is the case in modern times. The various states had not yet recognized each other as legitimate, had not yet acknowledged each other as real essential existences. Equal right to existence entails a union of states, such as is found in modern Europe, or a condition like that of Greece, in which the states had an equal right to existence under the protection of the Delphic god. The Romans do not enter into such a relation to the other nations, for their god is only the *Jupiter Capitolinus;* neither do they respect the *sacra* of the other nations (any more than the plebeians those of the patricians); but as conquerors in the strict sense of the term, they plunder the Palladia of the nations. Rome kept standing armies in the conquered provinces, and proconsuls and propraetors were sent into them as viceroys. The Equites collected the taxes and tributes, which they farmed under the State. A net of such fiscal farmers *(publicani)* was thus drawn over the whole Roman world . . . The Roman principle thereby exhibits itself as the cold abstraction of sovereignty and power, as the pure egotism of the will in opposition to others, involving no moral element of determination, but appearing in a concrete form only in the shape of individual interests. Increase in the number of provinces issued in the aggrandizement of individuals within Rome itself, and the corruption thence arising. From Asia, luxury and debauchery were brought to Rome. Riches flowed in after the fashion of spoils in war, and were not the fruit of industry and honest activity; in the same way as the marine had arisen, not from the necessities of commerce, but with a warlike project. The Roman state, drawing its resources from rapine, came to be rent in sunder by quarrels about dividing the spoil." (309)

During this period certain noble Romans, among whom may be mentioned Tiberius and Caius Gracchus, made vain efforts to right the prevailing wrongs—wrongs which were beyond the power of any individual effort. Enormous corruption prevailed. This was accented by the war with Jugurtha. He had gained the Senate by bribery and then proceeded to commit crimes of the most atrocious nature. There were external troubles in the menacing position of the Cimbri and Teutons. They were quelled only after great exertion. About this time the Italians, who had been refused citizenship, revolted. Added to this, word came that Mithridates had put 80,000 Romans of Asia Minor to the sword. Sulla was sent against him and was merciless in his methods. After victory he returned and made himself master of Rome. Following this he instigated a wholesale massacre of the Roman senators and Knights. At the same time there began a revolt in Spain which lasted for eight years. Hegel writes;

"We thus see the most terrible and dangerous powers arising against Rome; yet the military force of this state is victorious over all. Great individuals now appear on the stage as during the times of the fall of Greece. The biographies of Plutarch are here also of the deepest interest. It was from the disruption of the state, which had no longer any consistency or firmness in itself that these colossal individualities arose instinctively impelled to restore that political unity which was no longer to be found in men's dispositions. It was their misfortune that they could not maintain a pure morality, for their course of action contravened things as they are, and was a series of transgressions. Even the noblest—the Gracchi—were not merely victims of injustice and violence from without, but were themselves involved in the corruption and wrong that universally prevailed. But that which these individuals purpose and accomplish has on its side the higher sanction of the World-Spirit, and must eventually triumph. The idea of an organization for the vast empire being altogether absent, the senate could not assert the authority of government. The sovereignty was made dependent on the people—that people which was now a mere mob, and was obliged to be supported by corn from the Roman provinces. We should refer to Cicero to see how all affairs of state were decided in riotous fashion, and with arms in hand, by the wealth and power of the grandees on the one side, and by a troop of rabble on the other. The Roman citizens attached themselves to individuals who flattered them, and who then became prominent in factions in order to make themselves masters of Rome. Thus we see in Pompey and Caesar the two foci of Rome's splendor coming into hostile opposition: on the one side, Pompey with the Senate, and therefore apparently the defender of the Republic—on the other, Caesar with his legions and a superiority of genius. This contest between the two most powerful individualities could not be decided at Rome in the Forum. Caesar made himself master in succession, of Italy, Spain and Greece, utterly routed his enemy at Pharsalia, forty-eight years before Christ, made himself sure of Asia, and so returned victor to Rome." (311)

"In this way the world wide sovereignty of Rome became the property of a single possessor. This important change must not be regarded as a thing of chance; it was *necessary*—postulated by the circumstances. The democratic constitution could no longer be really maintained in Rome, but only kept up in appearance. Cicero, who had procured himself great respect through his high oratorical talent, and whose learning acquired him considerable influence always attributes the corrupt state of the republic to individuals and their passions . . . But it was not the mere accident of Caesar's existence that destroyed the Republic—it was *Necessity*. *All* the tendencies of the Roman principle were to sovereignty and military force; it contained in it no spiritual center which it could make the object, occupation and enjoyment of its Spirit. The aim of patriotism—that of preserving the State—

ceases when lust of personal dominion becomes the impelling passion. The citizens were alienated from the state, for they found in it no objective satisfaction; and the interests of individuals did not take the same direction as among the Greeks, who could set against the incipient corruption of the practical world, the noblest works of art in painting, sculpture, and poetry, and especially a highly cultivated philosophy. Their works of art were only what they had collected from every part of Greece, and therefore not productions of their own; their riches were not the fruit of industry, as was the case in Athens, but the result of plunder. Elegance—Culture—was foreign to the Romans *per se*; they sought to obtain it from the Greeks, and for this purpose a vast number of Greek slaves were brought to Rome. Delos was the center of this slave trade, and it is said that sometimes on a single day, ten thousand slaves were purchased there. To the Romans, Greek slaves were their poets, their authors, the superintendents of the manufactories, the instructors of their children." (312)

"The Republic could no longer exist in Rome. We see especially from Cicero's writings, how all public affairs were decided by the private authority of the more eminent citizens—by their power, their wealth; and what tumultuary proceedings marked all political transactions. In the republic therefore, there was no longer any security; *that* could be looked for only in a single will. Caesar who may be adduced as a paragon of Roman adaptation of means to ends—who formed his resolves with the most unerring perspicuity and executed them with the greatest vigor and practical skill, without any superfluous excitement of mind—Caesar, judged by the great scope of history, did the Right; since he furnished a mediating element, and that kind of political bond which men's condition required. Caesar effected two objects: he calmed the internal strife and at the same time originated a new one outside the limits of empire. For the conquest of the world had reached hitherto only to the circle of the Alps, but Caesar opened a new scene of achievement: he founded the theatre which was on the point of becoming the center of History. He then achieved universal sovereignty by a struggle which was decided not in Rome itself, but by his conquest of the whole Roman World. His position was indeed hostile to the republic, but, properly speaking, only to its shadow; for all that remained of that republic was entirely powerless." (312)

This one individual who held the power became the Emperor of Rome. He united in his own person the princeps senatus, Censor, Consul and Tribune—also the military power. "Public business was indeed brought before the senate, and the Emperor appeared simply as one of its members; but the senate was obliged to obey, and who ever ventured to gainsay his will was punished with death and his property confiscated." Suicide was often resorted to, by which means the property, at least, was saved for the family. The choice of the senators and the constitution of the senate were left to the Emperor. He held in his person all power. This supreme power was at one end of the social scale and at the other were the people. They stood before him leveled to a powerless equality. Yet it must be remembered that it was the large army and the Pretorian body guard that made the Emperor's position possible. These legions soon became conscious of this fact. The next advance, in the affairs of Rome, is the arrogation to themselves of the disposal and choice of the imperial throne. The legions usurp this supreme power. By this means a number of diverse characters become the Emperors of Rome. Some of these were praiseworthy. Among such could be numbered Titus, Trajan and the Antonines. Others were coarse tyrants, as for instance Caracalla, Nero and Domitian. But the point to be noted in our connection is that whether these emperors were good or bad, in themselves, there was no change in the general features of existence in the Roman World. Over all there remained the fact of the emperor, with totality of power and the one supreme will,—against this there was the mass of people—all equal,—all equally powerless. It was absolute sovereignty on the one hand, absolute slavery on the other. This position of individuals must be noted. Hegel explains the situation in the following manner: "The second point which we have particularly to remark, is the position taken by individuals as *persons.* Individuals were perfectly equal (slavery made only a trifling distinction), and without any political right. As early as the termination of the Social War, the inhabitants of the whole of Italy were put on an equal footing with Roman citizens; and under Caracalla all distinction between the subjects of the entire Roman empire was abolished. Private Right developed and perfected this equality. The right of property had been previously limited by distinctions of various kinds, which were now abrogated. We observe the Romans proceeding from the principle of abstract Subjectivity, which now realizes itself as Personality in the recognition of Private Right. Private Right, *viz.*, is this, that the social unit as such enjoys consideration in the state, in the reality which he gives to himself—*viz.*, in property. The living political body—that Roman feeling which animated it as its soul—is now brought back to the isolation of a lifeless Private Right. As, when the physical body suffers dissolution, each point gains a life of its own, but which is only the miserable life of worms; so the political organism is here dissolved into atoms—viz., private persons. Such a condition is Roman life at this epoch: on the one side, Fate and the abstract universality of sovereignty; on the other, the *individual* abstraction. "Person," which involves the recognition of the independent dignity of the social unit—not on the ground of the display of the life which he possesses—in his complete individuality—but as the abstract individuum." (314-317)

"It is the pride of the social units to enjoy absolute importance as private persons; for the Ego is thus enabled to assert unbounded claims; but the substantial interest thus comprehended—the *meum*—is only of a superficial kind, and the development of private right, which this high principle introduced, involved the decay of political life. The Emperor domineered only, and could not be said to *rule*; for the equitable and moral medium between the sovereign and the subjects was wanting—the bond of a constitution and organization of independent recognition, exists in communities and provinces, which, devoting their energies to the general interest, exert an influence on the general government. There are indeed Curiae in the towns, but they are either destitute of weight, or used only as a means for oppressing individuals, and for systematic plunder. That, therefore, which was abidingly present to the minds of men was not their country, or such a moral unity as that supplies: the whole state of things urged them to yield themselves to fate, and to strive for a perfect indifference to life—an indifference which they sought either in freedom of thought or in directly sensuous enjoyment. Thus man was either at war with existence, or entirely given up to mere sensuous existence. He either recognized his destiny in the task of acquiring the means of enjoyment through the favor of the Emperor, or through violence, testamentary frauds, and cunning; or he sought repose in philosophy, which alone was still able to supply something firm and independent: for the systems of that time—Stoicism, Epicureanism, and Scepticism—although within their common sphere opposed to each other, had the same general purport, viz., rendering the soul absolutely indifferent to everything which the real world had to offer. These philosophies were therefore widely extended among the cultivated: they produced in man a self-reliant immobility as the result of Thought, i.e. of the activity which produces the Universal. But the inward reconciliation by means of philosophy was itself only an abstract one—in the pure principle of personality; for Thought, which, as perfectly refined, made itself its own object, and thus harmonized itself, was entirely destitute of a real object, and the immobility of Scepticism made aimlessness itself the object of the Will. This philosophy knew nothing but the negativity of all that assumed to be real, and was the counsel of despair to a world which no longer possessed anything stable. It could not satisfy the living Spirit, which longed after a higher reconciliation." (318)

CHRISTIANITY

A VERBATIM REPRODUCTION FROM HEGEL'S PHILOSOPHY OF HISTORY

It was in this world of the Roman Empire that Christianity took its rise. "It has been remarked," says Hegel, "that Caesar inaugurated the Modern World on the side of *reality*, while its spiritual and inward existence was unfolded under Augustus. At the beginning of that empire, whose principle we have recognized as finiteness and particular subjectivity exaggerated to infinitude, the salvation of the World had its birth in the same principle of subjectivity—viz., as a *particular person,* in abstract subjectivity, but in such a way that conversely, finiteness is only the *form* of his appearance, while infinity and absolutely independent existence constitute the essence and substantial being which it embodies. The Roman World, as it has been described—in its desperate condition and the pain of abandonment by God—came to an open rupture with reality, and made prominent the general desire for a satisfaction such as can only be attained in "the inner man," the Soul—thus preparing the ground for a higher Spiritual World. Rome was the Fate that crushed down the gods and all genial life in its hard service, while it was the power that purified the human heart from all speciality. Its entire condition is therefore analogous to a place of birth, and its pain is like the travail-throes of another and higher Spirit, which manifested itself in connection with the *Christian Religion.* This higher Spirit involves the reconciliation and emancipation of Spirit; while man obtains the consciousness of Spirit in its universality and infinity. The Absolute Object,

Truth, is Spirit; and as man himself is Spirit, he is present (is mirrored) to himself in that object, and thus in his Absolute Object has found Essential Being and *his own* essential being. But in order that the objectivity of Essential Being may be done away with, and Spirit be no longer alien to itself—may be *with* itself (self-harmonized)—the Naturalness of Spirit—that in virtue of which man is a special, empirical existence—must be removed; so that the alien element may be destroyed, and the reconciliation of Spirit be accomplished.

"God is thus recognized as *Spirit,* only when known as the Triune. This new principle is the axis on which the History of the World turns. This is *the goal* and the *starting point* of History. "When the fulness of time was come, God sent his Son," is the statement of the Bible. This means nothing else than that *self-consciousness* had reached the phases of development (Momente), whose resultant constitutes the Idea of Spirit, and had come to feel the necessity of comprehending those phases absolutely. This must now be more fully explained. We said of the Greeks, that the law for their Spirit was: "Man, know thyself." The Greek Spirit was a consciousness of Spirit, but under a limited form, having the element of Nature as an essential ingredient. Spirit may have had the upper hand, but the unity of the superior and the subordinate was itself still Natural. Spirit appeared as specialized in the idiosyncrasies of the genius of the several Greek nationalities and of their divinities, and was represented by *Art,* in whose sphere the Sensuous is elevated only to the middle ground of beautiful form and shape, but not to pure Thought. The element of Subjectivity that was wanting to the Greeks, we found among the Romans: but as it was merely formal and in itself indefinite, it took its material from passion and caprice;—even the most shameful degradations could be here connected with a divine dread (*vide* the declaration of Hispala respecting the Bacchanalia, Livy XXXIX. 13). This element of subjectivity is afterwards further realized as Personality of Individuals—a realization which is exactly adequate to the principle, and is equally abstract and formal. As such an Ego (such a personality), I am infinite to myself, and my phenomenal existence consists in the property recognized as mine, and the recognition of my personality. This inner existence goes no further; all the applications of the principle merge in this. Individuals are thereby posited as atoms; but they are at the same time subject to the severe rule of the *One,* which as *monas monadum* is a power over private persons (the connection between the ruler and the ruled is not mediated by the claim of Divine or of Constitutional Right, or any general principle, but is direct and individual, the Emperor being the immediate lord of each subject in the Empire). That Private Right is therefore, *ipso facto,* a nullity, an ignoring of the personality; and the supposed condition of Right turns out to be an absolute destitution of it. This contradiction is the misery of the Roman World. Each person is, according to the principle of his personality, entitled only to possession, while the Person of Persons lays claim to the possession of all these individuals, so that the right assumed by the social unit is at once abrogated and robbed of validity. But the misery of this contradiction is the *Discipline of the World.* "Zucht" (discipline) is derived from "Ziehen" (to draw). This "drawing" must be towards something; there must be some fixed unity in the background in whose direction that drawing takes place, and for which the subject of it is being trained, in order that the standard of attainment may be reached. A renunciation, a disaccustoming, is the means of leading to an absolute basis of existence. That contradiction which afflicts the Roman World is the very state of things which constitutes such a discipline—the discipline of that culture which compels personality to display its nothingness. But it is reserved for us of a later period to regard this as a training to those who are thus trained (*traines,* dragged), it seems a blind destiny, to which they submit in the stupor of suffering. The higher condition, in which the soul itself feels pain and longing—in which man is not only "drawn," but feels that the drawing is into himself (into his own inmost nature)—is still absent.

What has been reflection on our part must arise in the mind of the subject of this discipline in the form of a consciousness that in himself he is miserable and null. Outward suffering must, as already said, be merged in a sorrow of the inner man. He must feel himself as the negation of himself; he must see that his misery is the misery of his nature—that he is in himself a divided and discordant being. This state of mind, this self-chastening, this pain occasioned by our individual nothingness—the wretchedness of our (isolated) self, and the longing to transcend this condition of soul—must be looked for elsewhere than in the properly Roman World. It is this which gives to the *Jewish People* their World-Historical importance and weight; for from this state of mind arose that higher phase in which Spirit came to absolute self-consciousness—passing from that alien form of being which is its discord and pain, and mirroring itself in its own essence. That state of feeling in question we find expressed most purely and beautifully in the Psalms of David, and in the Prophets; the chief burden of whose utterances is the thirst of the soul after God, its profound sorrow for its transgressions, and the desire for righteousness and holiness. Of this Spirit we have the mythical representation at the very beginning of the Jewish canonical books, in the account of the Fall. Man, created in the image of God, lost, it is said, his state of absolute contentment, by eating of the Tree of Knowledge of Good and Evil. Sin consists here only in Knowledge: this is the sinful element, and by it man is stated to have trifled away his Natural happiness. This is a deep truth, that evil lies in consciousness: for the brutes are neither evil nor good; the merely Natural Man quite as little. Consciousness occasions the separation of the Ego, in its boundless freedom as arbitrary choice, from the pure essence of the Will—*i.e.* from the Good. Knowledge, as the disannulling of the unity of mere Nature, in the "Fall," which is no casual conception, but the eternal history of Spirit. For the state of innocence, the paradisaical condition, is that of the brute. Paradise is a park, where only brutes, not men, can remain. For the brute is one with God only implicitly (not consciously). Only Man's Spirit (that is) has a self-cognizant existence. This existence for self, this consciousness, is at the same time separation from the Universal and Divine Spirit. If I hold to my abstract Freedom, in contraposition to the Good, I adopt the standpoint of Evil. The Fall is therefore the eternal Mythus of Man—in fact, the very transition by which he becomes man. Persistence in this standpoint is, however, Evil, and the feeling of pain at such a condition, and of longing to transcend it, we find in David, when he says: "Lord, create for me a pure heart, a new *steadfast* Spirit." This feeling we observe even in the account of the Fall; though an announcement of Reconciliation is not made there, but rather one of continuance in misery. Yet we have in this narrative the *prediction* of reconciliation in the sentence, "The serpent's head shall be bruised"; but still more profoundly expressed where it is stated that when God saw that Adam had eaten of that tree, he said, "Behold Adam is become as one of us, knowing Good and Evil." God confirms the words of the Serpent. Implicitly and explicitly, then, we have the truth, that man through Spirit—through cognition of the Universal and the Particular—comprehends God Himself. But it is only God that declares this—not man: the latter remains, on the contrary, in a state of internal discord. The joy of reconciliation is still distant from humanity; the absolute and final repose of his whole being is not yet discovered to man. It exists, in the first instance, only for God. As far as the present is concerned, the feeling of pain at his condition is regarded as a final award. The satisfaction which man enjoys at first, consists in the finite and temporal blessings conferred on the Chosen Family and the possession of the Land of Canaan. His repose is not found in God. Sacrifices are, it is true, offered to Him in the Temple, and atonement made by outward offerings and inward penitence. But that mundane satisfaction in the Chosen Family, and its possession of Canaan, was taken from the Jewish people in the chastisement inflicted by the Roman Empire. The Syrian kings did indeed oppress it, but it was left for the Romans to annul its individuality. The Temple of Zion is destroyed; the God-serving nation is scattered to the winds. Here every source of satisfaction is taken away, and the nation is driven back to the standpoint of that primeval mythus—the standpoint of that painful feeling which humanity experiences when thrown upon itself. Opposed to the universal *Fatum* of the Roman World, we have here the consciousness of Evil and the direction of the mind Godwards. All that remains to be done, is that this fundamental idea should be expanded to an objective universal sense, and be taken as the concrete existence of man—as the completion of his nature. Formerly the Land of Canaan and themselves as the people of God had been regarded by the Jews as that concrete and complete existence. But this basis of satisfaction is now lost, and thence arises the sense of misery and failure of hope in God, with whom that happy reality had been essentially connected. Here, then, misery is not the stupid immersion in a blind Fate, but a boundless energy of longing. Stoicism taught only that the Negative *is not*—that pain must not be recognized as a veritable existence; but *Jewish* feeling persists in acknowledging Reality and desires harmony and reconciliation within its sphere; for that feeling is based on the Oriental Unity of Nature—*i.e.*, the unity of Reality, of Subjectivity, with the substance of the One Essential Being. Through the loss of mere outward reality Spirit is driven back within itself; the side of reality is thus refined to Universality, through the reference of it to the One. The Oriental antithesis of Light and Darkness is transferred to Spirit, and the Darkness becomes Sin. For the abnegation of reality there is no compensation but Subjectivity itself—the Human Will as intrinsically universal; and thereby alone does reconciliation become possible. Sin is the discerning of Good and Evil as separation; but this discerning likewise heals the ancient hurt, and is the fountain of infinite reconciliation. The discerning in question brings with it the destruction of that which is external and alien in consciousness, and is consequently the return of Subjectivity into itself. This, then, adopted into the actual self-consciousness of the World is the *Reconciliation* (atonement) *of the World.* From that unrest of infinite sorrow—in which the two sides of the antithesis stand related to each other—is developed the unity of God with Reality (which latter had been posited as negative) *i.e.,* with Subjectivity which had been separated from Him. The infinite loss is counterbalanced only by its infinity, and thereby becomes infinite gain. The recognition of the identity of the Subject and God was introduced into the World when the *fulness of Time was come*: the consciousness of this identity is the recognition of God in his true essence. The material of Truth is *Spirit* itself—inherent vital movement. The nature of God as pure Spirit, is manifested to man *in the Christian Religion.*

But what is Spirit? It is the one immutable homogeneous Infinite—pure Identity—which in its second phase separates itself from itself and makes this second aspect its own polar opposite, viz. as existence for and in self as contrasted with the Universal. But this separation is annulled by the fact that atomistic Subjectivity, as simple relation to itself (as occupied with self alone) is itself the Universal, the Identical with self. If Spirit be defined as absolute reflection within itself in virtue of its absolute duality—Love on the one hand as comprehending the Emotional (Empfindung), Knowledge on the other hand as Spirit (including the penetrative and active faculties, as opposed to the receptive)—it is recognized as *Triune*: the "Father" and the "Son," and that duality which essentially characterizes it as "Spirit." It must further be observed, that *in* this truth, the relation of man *to* this truth is also posited. For Spirit makes itself its own (polar) opposite—and is the return from this opposite into itself. Comprehended in pure ideality, that antithetic form of Spirit is the Son of God; reduced to limited and particular conceptions, it is the World-Nature and Finite Spirit: Finite Spirit itself therefore is posited as a constituent element

(Moment) in the Divine Being. Man himself therefore is comprehended in the Idea of God, and this comprehension may be thus expressed—that the unity of Man with God is posited in the Christian Religion. But this unity must not be superficially conceived, as if God were only Man, and Man, without further condition, were God. Man, on the contrary, is God only in so far as he annuls the merely Natural and Limited in his Spirit and elevates himself to God. That is to say, it is obligatory on him who is a partaker of the truth, and knows that he himself is a constituent (Moment) of the Divine Idea, to give up his merely natural being: for the Natural is the Unspiritual. In this Idea of God, then, is to be found also the *Reconciliation* that heals the pain and inward suffering of man. For Suffering itself is henceforth recognized as an instrument necessary for producing the unity of man with God. This implicit unity exists in the first place only for the thinking speculative consciousness; but it must also exist for the sensuous, representative consciousness—it must become an object for the World—it must *appear,* and that in the sensuous form appropriate to Spirit, which is the human. *Christ has appeared*—a Man who is God—God who is Man; and thereby peace and reconciliation have accrued to the World. Our thoughts naturally revert to the Greek anthropomorphism, of which we affirmed that it did not go far enough. For that natural elation of soul which characterized the Greeks did not rise to the Subjective Freedom of the Ego itself—to the inwardness that belongs to the Christian Religion—to the recognition of Spirit as a *definite positive being.*—The appearance of the Christian God involves further its being *unique* in its kind; it can occur only once, for God is realized as Subject, and as manifested Subjectivity is exclusively One Individual. The Lamas are ever and anon chosen anew; because God is known in the East as Substance, whose infinity of form is recognized merely in an unlimited multeity of outward and particular manifestations. But subjectivity as infinite relation to self, has its form *in itself,* and as manifested, must be a unity excluding all others.—Moreover, the sensuous existence in which Spirit is embodied is only a transitional phase. Christ dies; only as dead, is he exalted to Heaven and sits at the right hand of God; only thus is he Spirit. He himself says: "When I am no longer with you, the Spirit will guide you into all truth." Not till the Feast of Pentecost were the Apostles filled with the Holy Ghost. To the Apostles, Christ as living, was not that which he was to them subsequently as the Spirit of the Church in which he became to them for the first time an object for their truly spiritual consciousness. On the same principle, we do not adopt the right point of view in thinking of Christ only as a historical bygone personality. So regarded, the question is asked, What are we to make of his birth, his Father and Mother, his early domestic relations, his miracles, etc.?—*i.e.* What is he unspiritually regarded? Considered only in respect of his talents, character and morality—as a Teacher and so forth—we place him in the same category with Socrates and others, though his morality may be ranked higher. But excellence of character, morality, etc.—all this is not the *ne plus ultra* in the requirements of Spirit—does not enable man to gain the speculative idea of Spirit for his conceptive faculty. If Christ is to be looked upon only as an excellent, even impeccable individual, and nothing more, the conception of the Speculative Idea, of Absolute Truth is ignored. But this is the desideratum, the point from which we have to start. Make of Christ what you will, exegetically, critically, historically—demonstrate as you please, how the doctrines of the Church were established by Councils; attained currency as the result of this or that episcopal interest or passion, or originated in this or that quarter;—let all such circumstances have been what they might—the only concerning question is: What is the Idea or the Truth in and for itself?

Further, the real attestation of the Divinity of Christ is the witness of one's own Spirit—not Miracles; for only Spirit recognizes Spirit. The miracles may lead the way to such recognition. A miracle implies that the natural course of things is interrupted: but it is very much a question of relation what we call the "natural course"; and the phenomena of the magnet might under cover of this definition, be reckoned miraculous. Nor does the miracle of the Divine Mission of Christ prove anything; for Socrates likewise introduced a new self-consciousness on the part of Spirit, diverse from the traditional tenor of men's conceptions. The main question is not his Divine Mission but the revelation made in Christ and the purport of his mission. Christ himself blames the Pharisees for desiring miracles of him, and speaks of false prophets who will perform miracles.

We have next to consider how the Christian view resulted in the formation of the Church. To pursue the rationale of its development from the Idea of Christianity would lead us too far, and we have here to indicate only the general phases which the process assumed. The first phase is the founding of the Christian religion, in which its principle is expressed with unrestrained energy, but in the first instance abstractly. This we find in the Gospels, where the infinity of Spirit—its elevation into the spiritual world (as the exclusively true and authorized existence)—is the main theme. With transcendent boldness does Christ stand forth among the Jewish people. "Blessed are the pure in heart, for they shall see God," he proclaims in the Sermon on the Mount—a dictum of the noblest simplicity and pregnant with an elastic energy of rebound against all the adventitious appliances with which the human soul can be burdened. The pure heart is the domain in which God is present to man: he who is imbued with the spirit of this apophthegm is armed against all alien bonds and superstitions. The other utterances are of the same tenor: "Blessed are the peacemakers: for they shall be called the children of God"; and, "Blessed are they which are persecuted for righteousness' sake: for theirs is the kingdom of heaven"; and, "Be ye perfect, even as your Father which is in heaven is perfect." Christ enforces here a completely unmistakable requirement. The infinite exaltation of Spirit to absolute purity is placed at the beginning as the foundation of all. The form of the instrumentality by which that result is to be accomplished is not yet given, but the result itself is the subject of an absolute command. As regards the relation of this standpoint of Spirit to secular existence, we find that spiritual purity presented as the substantial basis. "Seek ye first the kingdom of God and his righteousness, and all things shall be added unto you"; and, "The sufferings of this present time are not worthy to be compared with that glory." Here Christ says that outward sufferings, as such, are not to be feared or fled from, for they are nothing as compared with that glory. Further on, this doctrine, as the natural consequence of its appearing in an abstract form, assumes a *polemical* direction. "If thy right eye offend thee, pluck it out and cast it from thee: if thy right hand offend thee, cut it off and cast it from thee. It is better that one of thy members should perish, and not that thy whole body should be cast into hell." Whatever might disturb the purity of the soul, should be destroyed. So in reference to property and worldly gain, it is said: "Care not for your life, what ye shall eat and drink, nor for your body, what ye shall put on. Is not the life more than meat, and the body more than raiment? Behold the fowls of the air: for they sow not, neither do they reap, nor gather into barns; yet your heavenly Father feedeth them. Are ye not much better than they?" Labor for subsistence is thus reprobated: "Wilt thou be perfect, go and sell what thou hast, and give it to the poor, so shalt thou have a treasure in heaven, and come, follow me." Were this precept directly complied with, a social revolution must take place; the poor would become the rich. Of such supreme moment, it is implied, is the doctrine of Christ, that all duties and moral bonds are unimportant as compared with it. To a youth who wishes to delay the duties of discipleship till he has buried his father, Christ says: "Let the dead bury their dead—follow thou me." "He that loveth father or mother more than me is not worthy of me." He said: "Who is my mother? and who are my brethren? and stretched his hand out over his disciples and said, Behold my mother and my brethren! For he that doeth the will of my Father in heaven, the same is my brother, and sister and mother." Yes, it is even said: "*Think not that I am come to send peace on the Earth. I am not come to send peace but the sword. For I am come to set a man against his father, and the daughter against her mother, and the mother-in-law against her daughter-in-law.*" Here then is an abstraction from all that belongs to reality, even from moral ties. We may say that nowhere are to be found such revolutionary utterances as in the Gospels; for everything that had been respected, is treated as a matter of indifference —as worthy of no regard.

The next point is the development of this principle; and the whole sequel of History is the history of its development. Its first realization is the formation by the friends of Christ, of a Society—a Church. It has been already remarked that only after the death of Christ could the Spirit come upon his friends; that only then were they able to conceive the true idea of God, viz., that in Christ man is redeemed and reconciled: for in him the idea of eternal truth is recognized, the essence of man acknowledged to be Spirit, and the fact proclaimed that only by stripping himself of his finiteness and surrendering himself to pure self-consciousness, does he attain the truth. Christ—man as man—in whom the unity of God and man has appeared, has in his death, and his history generally, himself presented the eternal history of Spirit—a history which every man has to accomplish in himself, in order to exist as Spirit, or to become a child of God, a citizen of his kingdom. The followers of Christ, who combine on this principle and live in the spiritual life as their aim, form the *Church,* which is the Kingdom of God. "Where two or three are gathered together in my name" (i.e., "in the character of partakers in my being") says Christ, "there am I in the midst of them." The Church is a real present life in the Spirit of Christ.

It is important that the Christian religion be not limited to the teachings of Christ himself: it is in the Apostles that the completed and developed truth is first exhibited. This complex of thought unfolded itself in the Christian community. That community, in its first experiences, found itself sustaining a double relation—first, a relation to the Roman World, and secondly, to the truth whose development was its aim. We will pursue these different relations separately.

The Christian community found itself in the Roman world, and in this world the extension of the Christian religion was to take place. That community must therefore keep itself removed from all activity in the State—constitute itself a separate company, and not react against the decrees, views, and transactions of the state. But as it was secluded from the state, and consequently did not hold the Emperor for its absolute sovereign, it was the object of persecution and hate. Then was manifested that infinite inward liberty which it enjoyed, in the great steadfastness with which sufferings and sorrows were patiently borne for the sake of the highest truth. It was less the miracles of the Apostles that gave to Christianity its outward extension and inward strength, than the substance, the truth of the doctrine itself. Christ himself says: "Many will say to me at that day: Lord, Lord! have we not prophesied in thy name, have we not cast out devils in thy name, have we not in thy name done many wonderful deeds? Then will I profess unto them: I never knew you, depart from me all ye workers of iniquity."

As regards its other relation, viz., that to the Truth, it is especially important to remark that the *Dogma*—the Theoretical—was already matured within the Roman World, while we find the development of the State from that principle, a much later growth. The Fathers of the Church and the Councils constituted the dogma; but a chief element in this constitution was supplied by the previous development of *philosophy*. Let us examine more closely how the philosophy of the time stood related to religion. It has already been remarked that the Roman inwardness and subjectivity, which presented itself only abstractly, as soulless personality in the exclusive position assumed by the Ego, was refined by the philosophy of Stoicism and Scepticism to the form of Universality. The ground of Thought was thereby reached, and God was known in Thought as the One Infinite. The Universal stands here only as an unimportant predicate—not itself a Subject, but requiring a concrete particular application to make it such. But the One and Universal, the Illimitable conceived by fancy, is essentially Oriental; for measureless conceptions, carrying all limited existence beyond its proper bounds, are indigenous to the East. Presented in the domain of Thought itself, the Oriental *One* is the invisible and non-sensuous God of the Israelitish people, but whom they also make an object of conception as a person. This principle became World-Historical with Christianity.—In the Roman World, the union of the East and West had taken place in the first instance by means of conquest: it took place now inwardly, psychologically, also;—the Spirit of the East spreading over the West. The worship of Isis and that of Mithra had been extended through the whole Roman World; Spirit, lost in the outward and in limited aims, yearned after an Infinite. But the West desired a deeper, purely inward Universality—an Infinite possessed at the same time of positive qualities. Again, it was in Egypt—in Alexandria, viz., the centre of communication between the East and the West—that the problem of the age was proposed for Thought; and the solution now found was—Spirit. There the two principles came into scientific contact, and were scientifically worked out. It is especially remarkable to observe there, learned Jews such as Philo, connecting abstract forms of the concrete, which they derived from Plato and Aristotle, with their conception of the Infinite, and recognizing God according to the more concrete idea of Spirit, under the definition of the λόγος. So, also, did the profound thinkers of Alexandria comprehend the unity of the Platonic and Aristotelian Philosophy; and their speculative thinking attained those abstract ideas which were likewise the fundamental purport of the Christian religion. The application, by way of postulate, to the pagan religion, of ideas recognized as true, was a direction which philosophy had already taken among the heathen. Plato had altogether repudiated the current mythology, and, with his followers, was accused of Atheism. The Alexandrians, on the contrary, endeavored to demonstrate a speculative truth in the Greek conceptions of the gods: and the Emperor Julian the Apostate resumed the attempt, asserting that the pagan ceremonials had a strict connection with rationality. The heathens felt, as it were, obliged to give to their divinities the semblance of something higher than sensuous conceptions; they therefore attempted to spiritualize them. This much is also certain, that the Greek religion contains a degree of Reason; for the substance of Spirit is Reason, and its product must be something Rational. It makes a difference, however, whether Reason is explicitly developed in Religion, or merely adumbrated by it, as constituting its hidden basis. And while the Greeks thus spiritualized their sensuous divinities, the Christians also, on their side, sought for a profounder sense in the historical part of their religion. Just as Philo found a deeper import shadowed forth in the Mosaic record, and idealized what he considered the bare shell of the narrative, so also did the Christians treat their records—partly with a polemic view, but still more largely from a free and spontaneous interest in the process. But the instrumentality of philosophy in introducing these dogmas into the Christian Religion, is no sufficient ground for asserting that they were foreign to Christianity and had nothing to do with it. It is a matter of perfect indifference where a thing originated; the only question is: "Is it true in and for itself?" Many think that by pronouncing the doctrine to be Neo-Platonic, they have *ipso facto* banished it from Christianity. Whether a Christian doctrine stands exactly thus or thus in the Bible—the point to which the exegetical scholars of modern times devote all their attention—is not the only question. The Letter kills, the Spirit makes alive: this they say themselves, yet pervert the sentiment by taking the *Understanding* for the *Spirit*. It was the Church that recognized and established the doctrines in question—*i.e.* the Spirit of the Church; and it is itself an Article of Doctrine: "I believe in a Holy Church"; as Christ himself also said: "The Spirit will guide you into all truth." In the Nicene Council (A.D. 325), was ultimately established a fixed confession of faith, to which we still adhere: this confession had not, indeed, a speculative *form*, but the profoundly speculative is most intimately inwoven with the manifestation of Christ himself. Even in John we see the commencement of a profounder comprehension.* The profoundest thought is connected with the personality of Christ—with the historical and external; and it is the very grandeur of the Christian religion that, with all this profundity, it is easy of comprehension by our consciousness in its outward aspect, while, at the same time, it summons us to penetrate deeper. It is thus adapted to every grade of culture, and yet satisfies the highest requirements.

Having spoken of the relation of the Christian community to the Roman world on the one side, and to the truth contained in its doctrines on the other side, we come to the third point—in which both doctrine and the external world are concerned—the Church. The Christian community is the Kingdom of Christ—its influencing present Spirit being Christ: for this kingdom has an actual existence, not a merely future one. This spiritual actuality has, therefore, also a phenomenal existence; and that, not only as contrasted with heathenism, but with secular existence generally. For the Church, as presenting this outward existence, is not merely a *religion* as opposed to another religion, but is at the same time a particular form of secular existence, occupying a place side by side with other secular existence. The religious existence of the Church is governed by Christ; the secular side of its government is left to the free choice of the members themselves. Into this kingdom of God an organization must be introduced. In the first instance, all the members

* (ἐυ ἀρχῇ ἦν ὁ λόγος, καὶ ὁ λογος ἦν πρὸς τὸν θεου, καὶ θεὸς ἦν ὁ λογος)

know themselves filled with the Spirit; the whole community perceives the truth and gives expression to it; yet, together with this common participation of spiritual influence, arises the necessity of a presidency of guidance and teaching—a body distinct from the community at large. Those are chosen as presidents who are distinguished for talents, character, fervor of piety, a holy life, learning, and culture generally. The presidents—those who have a superior acquaintance with that substantial Life of which all are partakers, and who are instructors in that Life—those who establish what is truth, and those who dispense its enjoyment—are distinguished from the community at large, as persons endowed with knowledge and governing power are from the governed. To the intelligent presiding body, the Spirit comes in a fully revealed and *explicit* form; in the mass of the community that Spirit is only *implicit*. While, therefore, in the presiding body, the Spirit exists as self-appreciating and self-cognizant, it becomes an authority in spiritual as well as in secular matters—an authority for the truth and for the relation of each individual to the truth, determining how he should conduct himself so as to act in accordance with the Truth. This distinction occasions the rise of an *Ecclesiastical Kingdom* in the Kingdom of God. Such a distinction is inevitable; but the existence of an authoritative government for the Spiritual, when closely examined, shows that human subjectivity in its proper form has not yet developed itself. In the heart, indeed, the evil will is surrendered, but the will, as human, is not yet interpenetrated by the Deity; the human will is emancipated only abstractly—not in its concrete reality—for the whole sequel of History is occupied with the realization of this concrete Freedom. Up to this point, finite Freedom has been only annulled, to make way for infinite Freedom. The latter has not yet penetrated secular existence with its rays. Subjective Freedom has not yet attained validity as such: Insight (speculative conviction) does not yet rest on a basis of its own, but is content to inhere in the spirit of an extrinsic authority. That *Spiritual* (geistig) kingdom has, therefore, assumed the shape of an *Ecclesiastical* (geistlich) one, as the relation of the substantial being and essence of Spirit to human Freedom. Besides the interior organization already mentioned, we find the Christian community assuming also a definite external position, and becoming the possessor of property of its own. As property belonging to the spiritual world, it is presumed to enjoy special protection; and the immediate inference from this is, that the Church has no dues to pay to the state, and that ecclesiastical persons are not amenable to the jurisdiction of the secular courts. This entails the government by the Church itself of ecclesiastical property and ecclesiastical persons. Thus there originates with the Church the contrasted spectacle of a body consisting only of private persons and the power of the Emperor on the secular side;—on the other side, the perfect democracy of the spiritual community, choosing its own president. Priestly consecration, however, soon changes this democracy into aristocracy;—though the further development of the Church does not belong to the period now under consideration, but must be referred to the world of a later date.

It was then through the Christian Religion that the Absolute Idea of God, in its true conception, attained consciousness. Here Man, too, finds himself comprehended in his true nature, given in the specific conception of "the Son." Man, finite when regarded *for himself,* is yet at the same time the Image of God and a fountain of infinity *in himself.* He is the object of his own existence—has in himself an infinite value, an eternal destiny. Consequently he has his true home in a supersensuous world—an infinite subjectivity, gained only by a rupture with mere Natural existence and volition, and by his labor to break their power within him. This is religious self-consciousness. But in order to enter the sphere and display the active vitality of that religious life, humanity must become capable of it. . . . What therefore remains to be considered is, those conditions of humanity which are the necessary corollary to the consideration that Man is Absolute Self-consciousness—his Spiritual nature being the starting-point and presupposition. These conditions are themselves not yet of a concrete order, but simply the first *abstract principles,* which are won by the instrumentality of the Christian Religion for the *secular State.* First, under Christianity Slavery is impossible; for man is man—in the abstract essence of his nature—is contemplated in God; each unit of mankind is an object of the grace of God and of the Divine purpose: "God will have *all* men to be saved." Utterly excluding all speciality, therefore, man, in and for himself—in his simple quality of man—has infinite value; and this infinite value abolishes, *ipso facto,* all particularity attaching to birth or country. The other, the second principle, regards the subjectivity of man in its bearing on the Fortuitous—on Chance. Humanity has this sphere of free Spirituality in and for itself, and everything else must proceed from it. The place appropriated to the abode and presence of the Divine Spirit—the sphere in question—is Spiritual Subjectivity, and is constituted the place to which all contingency is amenable. It follows thence, that what we observed among the Greeks as a form of Customary Morality, cannot maintain its position in the Christian world. For *that* morality is spontaneous unreflected Wont; while the Christian principle is independent subjectivity—the soil on which grows the True. Now an unreflected morality cannot continue to hold its ground against the principle of Subjective Freedom. Greek Freedom was that of Hap and "Genius"; it was still conditioned by Slaves and Oracles; but now the principle of absolute Freedom in God makes its appearance. Man now no longer sustains the relation of Dependence, but of Love—in the consciousness that he is a partaker in the Divine existence. In regard to particular aims (such as the Greeks referred to oracular decision), man now forms his own determinations and recognizes himself as plenipotentiary in regard to all finite existence. All that is special retreats into the background before that Spiritual sphere of subjectivity, which takes a secondary position only in presence of the Divine

Spirit. The superstition of oracles and auspices is thereby entirely abrogated: Man is recognized as the absolute authority in crises of decision.

It is the two principles just treated of, that now attach to Spirit in this its self-contained phase. The Inner shrine of man is designed, on the one hand, to train the citizen of the religious life to bring himself into harmony with the Spirit of God; on the other hand, this is the *point de départ for* determining secular relations, and its condition is the theme of Christian History. The change which piety effects must not remain concealed in the recesses of the heart, but must become an actual, present world, complying with the conditions prescribed by that Absolute Spirit. Piety of heart does not, *per se,* involve the submission of the subjective will, in its external relations, to that piety. On the contrary we see all passions increasingly rampant in the sphere of reality, because that sphere is looked down upon with contempt, from the lofty position attained by the world of mind, as one destitute of all claim and value. The problem to be solved is therefore the imbuing of the sphere of (ordinary) unreflected Spiritual existence, with the *Idea* of Spirit. A general observation here suggests itself. From time immemorial it has been customary to assume an opposition between Reason and Religion, as also between *Religion and the World*; but on investigation this turns out to be only a *distinction.* Reason in general is the Positive Existence (Wesen) of Spirit, divine as well as human. The distinction between Religion and the World is only this—that Religion as such, is Reason in the soul and heart—that it is a temple in which Truth and Freedom in God are presented to the conceptive faculty: the State, on the other hand, regulated by the selfsame Reason, is a temple of Human Freedom concerned with the perception and volition of a reality, whose purport may itself be called divine. Thus Freedom in the State is preserved and established by Religion, since moral rectitude in the State is only the carrying out of that which constitutes the fundamental principle of Religion. The process displayed in

History is only the manifestation of Religion as Human Reason—the production of the religious principle which dwells in the heart of man, under the form of Secular Freedom. Thus the discord between the inner life of the heart and the actual world is removed. To realize this is, however, the vocation of another people—or other peoples— viz., the *German*. In ancient Rome itself, Christianity cannot find a ground on which it may become actual, and develop an empire." (318-336)

THE GERMAN WORLD

After the Roman Empire, in which came the birth of Christianity, we take up the consideration of the German World in which was born the consciousness of Subjective Freedom. It was in Germany that this concept came to birth for the whole human race. Hegel declares of the German Spirit that it is the Spirit of the New World and that "its aim is the realization of absolute Truth as the unlimited self-determination of Freedom—*that* Freedom which has its own absolute form itself as its purport." He says further: "The destiny of the German people is, to be the bearers of the Christian principle. The principle of Spiritual Freedom—of Reconciliation (of the Objective and Subjective), was introduced into the still simple unformed minds of those peoples; and the part assigned them in the service of the World-Spirit was that of not merely possessing the Idea of Freedom as the substratum of their religious conceptions, but of producing it in free and spontaneous developments from their subjective self-consciousness." (341)

The races whose cycle of development was prior to that of the Germans were races that had had relations with earlier people who had gone before them on the stage of history and also relations with a people who were to come after them. To these two there existed connections. They received cultural ideas from the former which they further developed—transmuting these cultures in conformity with the idiosyncrasies of their own national spirit. These were then diffused and passed on to those who were to succeed them in the Historic Process. There were therefore three distinct periods noted in the histories of Persia, Greece and Rome. In the case of Germany there is a different pattern. Here we see something quite the contrary to the course that history followed in the case of the Greeks and Romans. For these had reached maturity within themselves before their energies were directed outward. In consideration of this Hegel writes: "The Germans, on the contrary, began with self-diffusion—deluging the world, and overpowering in their course the inwardly rotten, hollow political fabrics of the civilized nations. Only then did their *development* begin, kindled by a foreign culture, a foreign religion, polity and legislation. The process of culture they underwent consisted in taking up foreign elements and reductively amalgamating them with their own national life. Thus their history presents an introversion—the attraction of alien forms of life and the bringing those to bear upon their own. In the Crusades, indeed, and in the discovery of America, the Western World directed its energies outwards. But it was not thus brought in contact with a World-Historical people that had preceded it; it did not dispossess a principle that had previously governed the world. The relation to an extraneous principle here only *accompanies* (does not constitute) the history—does not bring with it essential changes in the nature of those conditions which characterize the peoples in question, but rather wears the aspect of internal evolution.—the relation to other countries and periods is thus entirely different from that sustained by the Greeks and Romans. For the Christian world is the world of completion; the grand principle of being is realized, consequently the end of days is fully come. The Idea can discover in Christianity no point in the aspirations of Spirit that is not satisfied. For its individual members, the Church is, it is true, a preparation for an eternal state as something future; since the units who compose it, in their isolated and several capacity, occupy a position of particularity: but the Church has also the Spirit of God actually present in it, it forgives the sinner and is a present kingdom of heaven. Thus the Christian World has no absolute existence outside its sphere, but only a relative one which is already implicitly vanquished, and in respect to which its only concern is to make it apparent that this conquest has taken place. Hence it follows that an external reference ceases to be the characteristic element determining the epochs of the modern world. We have therefore to look for another principle of division." (342)

"The German World took up the Roman culture and religion in their completed form. There was indeed a German and Northern religion, but it had by no means taken deep root in the soul; Tacitus therefore calls the Germans: "Securi adversus Deos." The Christian Religion which they adopted, had received from Councils and Fathers of the Church, who possessed the whole culture, and in particular, the philosophy of the Greek and Roman World, a perfected dogmatic system; the Church, too, had a completely developed hierarchy. To the native tongue of the Germans, the Church likewise opposed one perfectly developed—the Latin. In art and philosophy a similar alien influence predominated. What of Alexandrian and of formal Aristotelian philosophy was still preserved in the writings of Boethius and elsewhere, became the fixed basis of speculative thought in the West for many centuries. The same principle holds in regard to the form of the secular sovereignty. Gothic and other chiefs gave themselves the name of Roman Patricians, and at a later date the Roman Empire was restored. Thus the German world appears, superficially, to be only a continuation of the Roman. But there lived in it an entirely *new Spirit,* through which the World was to be regenerated—the free Spirit, viz., which reposes on itself—the absolute self-determination (Eigensinn) of subjectivity. To this self-involved subjectivity, the corresponding objectivity (Inhalt) stands opposed as absolutely alien. The distinction and antithesis which is evolved from these principles, is that of *Church* and *State.* On the one side, the Church develops itself, as the embodiment of absolute Truth; for it is the consciousness of this truth, and at the same time the agency for rendering the Individual harmonious with it. On the other side stands secular consciousness, which, with its aims, occupies the world of Limitation—the *State,* based on Heart (emotional and thence *social* affections) or mutual confidence and subjectivity generally. European history is the exhibition of the growth of each of these principles severally, in Church and State; then of an antithesis on the part of both—not only of the one to the other, but appearing within the sphere of each of these bodies themselves (since each of them is itself a totality); lastly, of the harmonizing of the antithesis." (343)

The History of the German World will therefore be treated in three periods. The first period begins with the appearance of the Teutonic people as they are contacted by the Romans and finally made a part of the Roman Empire. It extends to the time of Charlemagne. This world appears as one consolidated Christendom with the secular and spiritual forms as but the different aspects of one homogeneous whole.

In the second period these aspects evolve their characters more definitely. The church becomes a *Theocracy*. The secular aspect develops itself and becomes *A Feudal Monarchy*. About this time Charlemagne formed an alliance with the Holy See which gave promise of a spiritual kingdom on earth. But now the inward spiritual kingdom begins to turn outward and leaves its proper spiritual sphere. The Christian Freedom is perverted and there develops between church and state an antithesis. The third period falls in the reign of Charles V. It begins in the first half of the sixteenth century when secular consciousness gradually grows into an awareness of its own intrinsic worth. It does this as it expands through the ordeal of culture. This third period culminates in the German Reformation and extends onward into the modern era. During this period there is a fuller awakening and a deeper self-realization. To quote Hegel: "The consciousness of independent validity is aroused through the restoration of Christian Freedom. The Christian principle has now passed through the terrible discipline of culture, and it first attains truth and reality through the Reformation. This third period of the German World extends from the Reformation to our own times. The principle of Free Spirit is here made the banner of the World, and from this principle are evolved the universal axioms of Reason. Formal Thought—the Understanding—had been already developed; but Thought received its true material first with the Reformation, through the reviviscent concrete consciousness of Free Spirit. From that epoch Thought began to gain a culture properly its own: principles were derived from it which were to be the norm for the constitution of the State. Political life was now to be consciously regulated by Reason. Customary morality, traditional usage lost its validity; the various claims insisted upon, must prove their legitimacy as based on rational principles. Not till this era is the Freedom of Spirit realized." (345) Hegel continues:

"We may distinguish these periods as Kingdoms of the Father, the Son, and the Spirit. The Kingdom of the Father is the consolidated, undistinguished mass, presenting a half-repeating cycle, mere change—like that sovereignty of Chronos engulfing his offspring. The Kingdom of the Son is the manifestation of God merely in a *relation* to secular existence—shining upon it as upon an alien object. The Kingdom of the Spirit is the harmonizing of the antithesis." (345)

Relative to this third period of the German World, which culminates in the German Reformation and extends through the modern era, Hegel has something more to say. In Hegel's words: "The third epoch may be compared with the Roman World. The unity of a universal principle is here quite as decidedly present, yet not as the unity of abstract universal sovereignty, but as the Hegemony of self-cognizant Thought. The authority of Rational Aim is acknowledged, and privileges and particularities melt away before the common object of the State. People will the Right in and for itself; regard is not had exclusively to particular conventions between nations, but principles enter into the considerations with which democracy is occupied. As little can Religion maintain itself apart from Thought, but either advances to the comprehension of the Idea, or, compelled by thought itself, becomes intensive believe—or lastly, from despair of finding itself at home in Thought, flees back from it in pious horror, and becomes Superstition." (396) These thoughts of Hegel's serve to amplify his conception of this third period. It is the period that establishes thought in its self-cognizant rôle and advances with it into our modern world. For a one-sentence summary of these three periods we have,—first: The Teutonic people—as converts to Christianity—forming Medieval Christendom with the Spiritual and Secular as aspects of one world. Second, we have these aspects developing into the two sides of an antithesis,—the church as a Theocracy, the secular as a Feudal Monarchy—becoming the Feudal System—hence the Church and State. Third we have the birth of Subjective Freedom in which consciousness arrives at self-cognizant Thought enthroning Rational Aim whose object is the State. This third period reaches into our modern era.

Starting now with the first period we shall trace the history which was to unfold the above mentioned principles. The first period Hegel describes in detail. There is mention of the tribes that composed it, their origins, their migratory expeditions and their histories. There were German tribes that remained near their ancient habitations and other German tribes that spread themselves over the Roman Empire—many joining the Roman Armies. The Eastern Goths and the Western Goths were such Teutonic families. The Vandals and Suevi were the first settlers in Spain and Portugal. Later they were overrun by the Visigoths and a kingdom was established there. It was the object, with all of these migrating tribes, to find suitable country which they could possess as a home-land. Another Kingdom that had come into existence was that of the Franks, situated between the Rhine and Weser, and composed of Istaevonian races. They next possessed themselves of the land between the Moselle and the Scheldt and under their leader, Clovis, moved into Gaul and extended their territory as far as the Loire. Later on Clovis conquered the Franks on the Lower Rhine, the Alemanni on the Upper Rhine, while the Thuringians and Burgundians were subjugated by the sons of Clovis. These kingdoms were to develop into the nations of modern Europe. A third consolidated possession was that of the Ostrogoths founded by Theodoric in Italy. It was later subdued by the Byzantines under Belisarius and Narses. The far away Normans came to Southern Italy and took up residence there. The Angles and Saxons entered Britain and remained to dominate it. These countries had all been a part of the Roman Empire. There is noticeable a dual characteristic of Roman and Teutonic stocks which shows itself particularly in language. The Romance languages comprised those of Italy, Spain, Portugal and France; and the Teutonic comprised those of Germany, Scandinavia and to some extent England. In Eastern Europe were the great Sclavonii nations who settled on the Elbe and Danube. The Magyars were between them, while in Moldavia, Wallachia, and northern Greece appeared the Bulgarians, Servians and Albanians of Asiatic origin. They drop out of consideration for the present.

Germany itself was from the first characterized by a sense of National totality. A heart-felt loyalty was manifest to the idea of home—in its individual as well as in its national aspect.

From the earliest times it had been free confederation that constituted the social nuclei. To quote Hegel: "The connection in this case was that of *Fidelity*; for Fidelity is the second watchword of the Germans as Freedom was the first. Individuals attach themselves with free choice to an individual, and without external prompting make this relation an inviolable one. This we find neither among the Greeks nor the Romans. The relation of Agamemnon and the princes who accompanied him was not that of feudal suit and service: it was a free Association merely for a *particular purpose*—a Hegemony. But the German confederations have their being not in a relation to a mere external aim or cause, but in a relation to the spiritual self—the subjective inmost personality. Heart, disposition, the concrete subjective in its integrity, which does not attach itself to any abstract bearing of an object, but regards the whole of it as a condition of attachment—

making itself dependent on the person *and* the cause—renders this relation a compound of fidelity to a person and obedience to a principle." (353)

"The union of the two relations—of individual freedom in the community, and of the bond implied in association—is the main point in the formation of the State. In this, duties and rights are no longer left to arbitrary choice, but are determined as fixed relations;—involving, moreover, the condition that the state be the soul of the entire body, and remain its sovereign—that from it should be derived particular aims and the authorization both of political acts and political agents—the generic character and interest of the community constituting the permanent basis of the whole. But here we have the peculiarity of the German States, that contrary to the view thus presented, social relations do not assume the character of general definitions and laws, but are entirely split up into *private* rights and *private* obligations. They perhaps exhibit a social or communal mould or stamp, but nothing *universal;* the laws are absolutely particular and the Rights are Privileges. Thus the state was a patchwork of private rights, and a rational political life was the tardy issue of wearisome struggles and convulsions." (354)

"We have said, that the Germans were predestined to be the bearers of the Christian principle, and to carry out the Idea as the absolutely Rational aim. In the first instance we have only vague volition, in the background of which lies the True and Infinite. The True is present only as an unsolved problem, for their Soul is not yet purified. A long process is required to complete this purification so as to realize concrete Spirit. Religion comes forward with a challenge to the violence of the passions, and rouses them to madness. The excess of passions is aggravated by evil conscience, and heightened to an insane rage; which perhaps would not have been the case, had that opposition been absent. We behold the terrible spectacle of the most fearful extravagance in all the royal houses of that period. Clovis, the founder of the Frank Monarchy, is stained with the blackest crimes. Barbarous harshness and cruelty characterize all the succeeding Merovingians; the same spectacle is repeated in the Thuringian and other royal houses. The Christian principle is certainly the problem implicit in their souls; but these are primarily still crude. The Will—potentially true—mistakes itself, and separates itself from the true and proper aim by particular, limited aims. Yet it is in this struggle with itself and contrariety to its bias, that it realizes its wishes; it contends against the object which it really desires, and thus accomplishes it; for implicitly, *potentially,* it is *reconciled.* The Spirit of God lives in the Church; it is the inward impelling Spirit. But it is in the World that Spirit is to be realized—in a material not yet brought into harmony with it. Now this material is the Subjective Will, which thus has a contradiction in itself. On the religious side, we often observe a change of this kind: a man who has all his life been fighting and hewing his way—who with all vehemence of character and passion, has struggled and revelled in secular occupations—on a sudden repudiates it all, to betake himself to religious seclusion. But in the World, secular business cannot be thus repudiated; it demands accomplishment, and ultimately this discovery is made, that Spirit finds the goal of its struggle and its harmonization, in that very sphere which it made the object of its resistance—it finds that *secular pursuits are a spiritual occupation.*" (354-355)

"We thus observe, that individuals and people regard that which is their misfortune, as their greatest happiness, and conversely, struggle against their happiness as their greatest misery. *La vérité, en la repoussant, on l'embrasse.* Europe comes to the truth while, and to the degree in which, she has repulsed it. It is in the agitation thus occasioned, that Providence especially exercises its sovereignty; realizing its absolute aim—its honor—as the result of unhappiness, sorrow, private aims and the unconscious will of the nations of the earth." (355)

"While, therefore, in the West this long process in the world's history—necessary to that purification by which

Spirit in the concrete is realized—is commencing, the purification requisite for developing *Spirit in the abstract* which we observe carried on contemporaneously in the East, is more quickly accomplished. The latter does not need a long process, and we see it produced rapidly, even suddenly, in the first half of the seventh century, in Mohametanism." (355)

MOHAMETANISM

While the nations of Europe were developing themselves in Christendom with emphasis on particularity, Mohametanism arose in the East to produce the balance of spiritual power. "It made the Abstract One the absolute object of attention and devotion . . . the only aim of reality." It made "the *Unconditioned*, the *condition* of existence." (356) Before this the Jews had proclaimed the principle of unity of the pure spiritual nature in Jehovah, but Jehovah was only the God of the Children of Abraham, Isaac and Jacob. It was with Abraham that God had made the covenant. Now in Mohametanism this speciality is done away with; no nationality, no class distinction, no claim of birth or possession is regarded—only man as the believer and the worshipper of Allah—whose prophet is Mohamet. It was a pure intellectual worship—no image or representation was allowed. "To adore the One, to believe in him, to fast—to remove the sense of speciality and consequent separation from the Infinite, arising from corporeal limitation—and to give alms—that is, to get rid of particular private possessions—this is the essence of Mohametan injunctions; but the highest need is to die for the Faith. He who perishes for it in battle is sure of Paradise." (357)

In this conquest by the sword, for the faith, Mohamet led the way. After his flight from Mecca, in the year 622, and later his death, the Arab successors fulfilled his designs of spreading the Faith. They first entered Syria and took

Damascus in 634. Then in rapid succession they conquered Persia, Egypt, North Africa, Spain and part of Southern France. Here they were halted by Charles Martel in the year 732. There were also further extensions of Mohametanism in Asia Minor. In these conquests it was understood that the converts immediately gained equal rights with all Mussulmen, while those who rejected the faith were slaughtered. Later on this last degree was changed for a payment of a yearly tax.

In this boundless enthusiasm for the establishment of an abstract worship there were set up dynasties and kingdoms but these were destitute of organic firmness and soon degenerated. Yet even in this limited period the Arts and Sciences found time to come to life and bloom. Indeed, science and Eastern knowledge—specially philosophy—came, by means of the Arabs, to the West—where it had much influence in the kindling of free imagination and noble fancy. But the East itself, when the zeal had cooled, sank back into its customary usages sanctioned by Mohametan doctrine.

THE EMPIRE OF CHARLEMAGNE

It was Clovis and his sons who founded and built up the empire of the Franks. The method was conquest after which the king parcelled out his freemen as princes of his realms and collected revenues. These holdings were not heritable but were given as personal benefits for which the warrior was personally obligated— and became a vassal of the sovereign. It was these vassals who formed the king's feudal array. The clergy of the realm were also united—the opulent Bishops constituting the King's Council—which was subordinate to him. A very important figure in these feudal set-ups was the man at the head of the feudal array—the Major Domus. These individuals managed, as time went on

—to get considerable power into their hands. Finally they assumed entire sovereignty, while the kings became mere puppets—who were satisfied to pose as the royal head, meanwhile devoting themselves to self-indulgent luxury. The Majores Domus, on the contrary were on the tide of ascendant fortune. Often, with the allegiance of the nobility they were able to usurp the royal crown. The Pope had paved the way for this when he released the Franks from their oath of allegiance to their king Childeric III—last of the Merovingian line. He entered a monastery. In gratitude for this help the Franks lent assistance to the Pope against the Lombards —sending Pepin to oppose them. In 800 Pepin's son, Charlemagne, succeeded him and was crowned Emperor by the Pope. There was established a strong bond between the Carlovingians and the Papal See. This was important because the Roman Empire continued to enjoy great prestige among the barbarians. It was the dispenser of law, religion and learning. Indeed Charlemagne made all of these to be living realities throughout his domain. He set to work to develop the institutions already existent and demanded of them an ever expanding efficiency. He stood as the King in very truth. He was master of the army, the landed proprietors and of the judicial power as well. The country itself was divided into provinces, over these were Dukes whose seats were in the large cities. There was the Duchy of Alsatia as also Lorraine, Trisia, Thuringia, Saxony, Rhaetia, Bavaria and Alamannia. The revenues were derived from the crownlands, fees in lieu of military service and judicial fines. There were no direct taxes and but few tolls on roads and rivers. The Judicial administration was in the hands of the king with the aid of royal tribunals. There were communal assemblies under the presidency of a Count. A spiritual and temporal envoy made circuits of the realm at certain times of the year to help with the hearing of complaints incident to the judicial administration.

In Charlemagne's time the ecclesiastical body had already

risen to considerable power. The great bishoprics and cathedrals were the seats of learning with seminaries and scholastic institutions attached to them. These were enhanced by rich gifts from pious souls who believed in good works as a means of earning salvation. So large did these ecclesiastical estates become that stewards and bailiffs had to be appointed to manage them. People often took refuge in these monasteries and churches as asylums—that is, inviolable sanctuaries against violence. The custom was beneficial as a protection, but it was perverted as a means of impunity for crime.

The deliberations of the imperial council on the general affairs of state were held as the opportunity for convening was made possible; for instance in the spring or at the time of the ecclesiastical councils. Custom required at least two meetings a year. It was then that the selection of officials for high secular offices took place as well as some of the ecclesiastical functionaries. The king held his court in the different provinces by turn and to these convocations the nobles were invited. They attended with their retinues in great state and were the guests of the prince who was most able, or for other reasons was assigned the honor of being host. These conventions were different from the Imperial Diets that developed later. In the latter the nobles held a position of more independence.

"Such was the state," writes Hegel, "of the Frank Empire—that first consolidation of Christianity into a political form proceeding from itself, the Roman empire having been swallowed up by Christianity. The constitution just described looks excellent; it introduced a firm military organization and provided for the administration of justice within the empire. Yet, after Charlemagne's death, it proved itself utterly powerless—externally defenceless against the invasions of the Normans, Hungarians, and Arabs, and internally inefficient in resisting lawlessness, spoliation and oppression of every kind. Thus we see, side by side with an excellent constitution, the most deplorable condition of things, and therefore confusion in all directions. Such political edifices need, for the very reason that they originate suddenly, the additional strengthening afforded by negativity evolved within themselves: they need reactions in every form, such as manifest themselves in the following period." (365) That is, in the Middle Ages.

THE MIDDLE AGES

In opening the review of the period known as the Middle Ages, Hegel has the following: "While the *first* period of the German World ends brilliantly with a mighty empire, the *second* is commenced by reaction resulting from the antithesis occasioned by that infinite falsehood which rules the destinies of the *Middle Ages* and constitutes their life and and spirit. This reaction is *first,* that of particular nationalities against the universal sovereignty of the Frank empire—manifesting itself in the splitting up of that great empire. The *second reaction* is that of individuals against legal authority and the executive power—against subordination, and the military and judicial arrangements of the constitution. This produced the *isolation* and therefore *defencelessness* of individuals. The universality of the power of the state disappeared through this reaction: individuals sought protection with the powerful, and the latter became oppressors. Thus was gradually introduced a condition of universal dependence, and the protecting relation is then systematized into the Feudal System. The *third reaction* is that of the Church—the reaction of the spiritual element against the existing order of things. Secular extravagances of passion were repressed and kept in check by the Church, but the latter was itself secularized in the process, and abandoned its proper position. From that moment begins the introversion of the secular principle. These relations and reactions all go to constitute the history of the Middle Ages, and the culminating point of this period is *The Crusades*; for with them arises a universal instability, but one through which the states of Christendom first attain internal and external independence." (366)

We have seen the first period of the German World end brilliantly with Christendom united as the mighty empire of Charlemagne. The second period of the German World is that of the reaction of the different nationalities which composed it against the sovereignty of the Franks. Charlemagne had been able to effect this universality by the dynamic force of his own personal genius. When that was withdrawn the national particularities began to manifest. The western Franks had united with the Gauls and these reacted against the German Franks. Other small sovereignties to develop were the Burgundies, also Normandy, Brittany, Lorraine, and the Kingdom of Italy. Those that remained as part of Germany were Eastern Franconia, Saxony, Thuringia, Bavaria, and Swabia. France Proper was more or less enclosed. In England the Normans had made frequent encroachments. There were seven dynasties of Anglo-Saxon Kings established at different times. Under Egbert they were united in the year 827. Next came the Danes whom Alfred the Great successfully resisted until King Canute, the Danish conqueror arrived. He completed the subjugation of England. Contemporary with these events was the invasion of France by the Normans. Added to this the Eastern side of the empire was invaded by the Magyars.

While these general reactions of particular nationalities against the sovereign universality were in progress, the second reaction—that of individuals against the prevailing authority set in. The authority of law, the duties of citizens, the decisions of judges were all disregarded in the confusion that accompanied the vanished power of a former day. Individuals found themselves in a defenseless position and were obliged to seek refuge with other individuals more powerful than themselves who were able to furnish protection. They committed their property to a Convent, a Lord, an Abbot, or a Bishop and therefore became encumbered with certain obligations as payment for the protection which was thus received. These agreements developed into The Feudal System. In every district arose castles and fortresses for the defense of private property. As individual authority was established the political totality was ignored. Turning to Hegel: "Only in a few towns where communities of freemen were independently strong enough to secure protection and safety, did relics of the ancient free constitution remain. With these exceptions the free communities entirely disappeared, and became subject to the prelates or to the Counts and Dukes, thenceforth known as seigneurs and princes. The imperial power was extolled in general terms, as something very great and exalted: the Emperor passed for the secular head of entire Christendom: but the more exalted the *ideal* dignity of the Emperors, the more limited was it in reality. France derived extraordinary advantage from the fact that it entirely repudiated this baseless assumption, while in Germany the advance of political development was hindered by that pretence of power. The kings and emperors were no longer chiefs of the *state,* but of the *princes,* who were indeed their vassals, but possessed sovereignty and territorial lordships of their own. The whole social condition therefore, being founded on individual sovereignties it might be supposed that the advance to a State would be possible only through the return of those individual sovereignties to an official relationship. But to accomplish this, a superior power would have been required, such as was not in existence; for the feudal lords themselves determined how far they were still dependent on the general constitution of the state. No authority of Law and Right is valid any longer; nothing but chance power—the crude caprice of particular as opposed to universally valid Right; and this struggles against equality of Rights and Laws. Inequality of political privileges—the allotment being the work of the purest haphazard—is the predominant feature. It is impossible that a Monarchy can arise from such a social condition through the subjugation of the several minor powers under the Chief of the State, as such. Reversely, the former were gradually transformed into Principalities (Fürstentümer), and became united with the Principality of the Chief; thus enabling the authority of the king and of the state to assert itself. While, therefore, the bond of political unity was still wanting, the several seigneuries attained their development independently." (372)

In France the powerful Hugh Capet, who was the Duke, became the King of France by proclamation. His title gave him no real power but later through marriage alliances, through the dying out of families and through considerations for the bestowal of protection on oppressed nobles, his wealth and influence were increased. The royal authority in France was made heritable at an early date. This had been the custom in the case of the fiefs. France was divided into the Duchy of Guienne, the Earldom of Toulouse, the Duchy of Burgundy, and Earldom of Vermandois, and Lorraine. The Normans made constant inroads on royal territory, so finally as a relief measure, Normandy was given to the Normans.

In 1066 Duke William of Normandy passed over into England and conquered it—establishing a feudal system there. Germany was made up of the duchies of Saxony, Swabia, Bavaria, Carinthia, the Margraviate of Thuringia and several bishoprics and archbishoprics. Here the princes retained their power. Germany had no dominant family at the head of affairs. The Emperors were curtailed by conditions imposed at each election. In Italy the general situation was similar. The German Emperors had pretensions to overlordship in Italy but there were individual dukedoms, earldoms, seigneuries and bishoprics which stood for their own individual rights and desires against the sovereign authority. Throughout Christendom we see the picture of individual Might turning against the power of universal sovereignty. Rational legislation vanished. In this state of affairs there gradually came into human consciousness a new urge. It was that which Hegel names the third reaction—the reaction of universality against the real world now split up into particularity where it found itself powerless in a futile separativeness.

In consideration of the forces at work and their effects Hegel gives the following: "This reaction proceeded from below upwards—from that condition of isolated possession itself; and was then promoted chiefly by the church. A sense of the *nothingness* of its condition seized on the world as it were universally. In that condition of utter isolation, where only the unsanctioned might of individuals had any validity (where the State was non-existent), men could find no repose, and Christendom was, so to speak, agitated by the tremor of an evil conscience. In the eleventh century, the fear of the approaching final judgment and the belief in the speedy dissolution of the world, spread through all Europe. This dismay of soul impelled men to the most irrational proceedings. Some bestowed the whole of their possessions on the Church, and passed their lives in continual penance; the majority dissipated their worldly wealth in riotous debauchery. The Church alone increased its riches by the hallucinations, through donations and bequests.—About the same time too, terrible famines swept away their victims: human flesh was sold in open market. During this state of things, lawlessness, brutal lust, the most barbarous caprice, deceit and cunning, were the prevailing moral features. Italy, the centre of Christendom, presented the most revolting aspect. Every virtue was alien to the times in question; consequently *virtus* had lost its proper meaning: in common use it denoted only violence and oppression, sometimes even libidinous outrage. This corrupt state of things affected the clergy equally with the laity. Their own advowees had made themselves masters of the ecclesiastical estates intrusted to their keeping, and lived on them quite at their own pleasure, restricting the monks and clergy to a scanty pittance. Monasteries that refused to accept advowees were compelled to do so; the neighboring lords taking the office upon themselves or giving it to their sons. Only bishops and abbots maintained themselves in possession, being able to protect themselves partly by their own power, partly by means of their retainers; since they were, for the most part, of noble families . . .

"Nor did the Papal dignity fare any better. Through a long course of years the Counts of Tusculum near Rome conferred it on members of their own family, or on persons to whom they had sold it for large sums of money. The state of things became at last so intolerable, that laymen as well as ecclesiastics of energetic character opposed its continuance. The Emperor Henry III put an end to the strife of factions, by nominating the Popes himself, and supporting them by his authority in defiance of the opposition of the Roman nobility. Pope Nicholas II decided that the Popes should be chosen by the Cardinals; but as the latter partly belonged to dominant families, similar contests of factions continued to accompany their election. Gregory VII (already famous as Cardinal Hildebrand) sought to secure the independence of the church in this frightful condition of things, by two measures especially. *First,* he enforced the *celibacy of the clergy* . . . *His second* measure was directed against *simony, i.e.* the sale of or arbitrary appointment to bishoprics and to the Papal See itself. Ecclesiastical offices were thenceforth to be filled by the clergy, who were capable of administering them; an arrangement which necessarily brought the ecclesiastical body into violent collision with secular seigneurs." (375)

"These were the two grand measures by which Gregory purposed to emancipate the Church from its condition of dependence and exposure to secular violence. But Gregory made still further demands on the secular power. The transference of benefices to a new incumbent was to receive validity simply in virtue of his ordination by his ecclesiastical superior, and the Pope was to have exclusive control over the vast property of the ecclesiastical community. The Church as a divinely constituted power, laid claim to supremacy over secular authority—founding that claim on the abstract principle that the Divine is superior to the Secular.

The Emperor at his coronation—a ceremony which only the Pope could perform— was obliged to promise upon oath that he would always be obedient to the Pope and the Church. Whole countries and states, such as Naples, Portugal, England and Ireland came into a formal relation of vassalage to the Papal chair." (376)

"Thus the Church attained an independent position: the Bishops convoked synods in the various countries, and in these convocations the clergy found a permanent centre of unity and support. In this way the Church attained the most influential position in secular affairs. It arrogated to itself the award of princely crowns, and assumed the part of mediator between sovereign powers in war and peace. The contingencies which particularly favored such interventions on the part of the Church were the marriages of princes. It frequently happened that princes wished to be divorced from their wives; but for such a step they needed the permission of the Church. The latter did not let slip the opportunity of insisting upon the fulfillment of demands that might have been otherwise urged in vain, and thence advanced till it had obtained universal influence. In the chaotic state of the community generally, the intervention of the authority of the Church was felt as a necessity. By the introduction of the "Truce of God," feuds and private revenge were suspended for at least certain days in the week, or even for entire weeks; and the Church maintained this armistice by the use . . . of excommunication, interdict and other threats and penalties. The secular possessions of the Church brought it however into a relation to other secular princes and lords, which was alien to its proper nature; it constituted a formidable secular power in contraposition to them, and thus formed in the first instance a centre of opposition against violence and arbitrary wrong. It withstood especially the lordships of the Bishops; and on occasion of opposition on the part of vassals to the violence and caprice of princes, the former had the support of the Pope. But in these proceedings the Church brought to bear against opponents only a force and arbitrary resolve of the same kind as their own, and mixed up its secular interest with its interest as an ecclesiastical, *i.e.* a divinely substantial power. Sovereigns and peoples were by no means incapable of discriminating between the two, or of recognizing the worldy aims that were apt to intrude as motives for ecclesiastical intervention. They therefore stood by the Church as far as they deemed it their interest to do so; otherwise they showed no great dread of excommunication or other ghostly terrors. Italy was the country where the authority of the Popes was least respected; and the worst usage they experienced was from the Romans themselves. Thus what the Popes acquired in point of land and wealth and directed sovereignty, they lost in influence and consideration." (377)

"We have then to probe to its depths the *spiritual element* in the Church—the form of its power. The essence of the Christian principle has already been unfolded; it is the principle of Mediation. Man realizes his Spiritual essence only when he conquers the Natural that attaches to him. This conquest is possible only on the supposition that the human and the divine nature are essentially one, and that Man, so far as he is Spirit, also possesses the essentiality and substantiality that belong to the idea of Deity. The condition of the mediation in question is the consciousness of this unity; and the intuition of this unity was given to man in Christ. The object to be attained is therefore, that man should lay hold on this consciousness, and that it should be continually excited in him. This was the design of the *Mass*: in the *Host* Christ is set forth as actually present; the piece of bread consecrated by the priest is the present God, subjected to human contemplation and ever and anon offered up. One feature of this representation is correct, inasmuch as the sacrifice of Christ is here regarded as an actual and eternal transaction, Christ being not a mere sensuous and single, but a completely universal, *i.e.* divine, *individuum*; but on the other hand it involves the error of isolating the sensuous phase; for the Host is adored even apart from its being partaken of by the faithful, and the presence of Christ is not exclusively limited to mental vision and Spirit . . . The Holy as a mere thing has the character of externality; thus it is capable of being taken possession of by another to my exclusion: it may come into an alien hand, since the process of appropriating it is not one that takes place in Spirit, but is conditioned by its quality as an external object (Dingheit). The highest of human blessings is in the hands of others. Here arises *ipso facto* a separation between those who possess this blessing and those who have to receive it from others—between the Clergy and the Laity. The laity as such are alien to the Divine. This is the absolute schism in which the Church in the Middle Ages was involved: it arose from the recognition of the Holy as something external. The clergy imposed certain conditions, to which the laity must conform if they would be partakers of the Holy. The entire development of *doctrine,* spiritual insight and the knowledge of divine things, belonged exclusively to the Church: it has to ordain, and the laity have simply to believe: obedience is their duty—the obedience of faith, without insight on their part. This position of things rendered faith a matter of external legislation, and resulted in compulsion and the stake." (378)

"With this perversion is connected the absolute separation of the spiritual from the secular principle generally. There are two Divine Kingdoms—the intellectual in the heart and cognitive faculty, and the socially ethical whose element and sphere is secular existence. It is science alone that can comprehend the kingdom of God and the socially Moral world as one Idea, and that recognizes the fact that the course of Time has witnessed a process ever tending to the realization of this unity. But Piety (or Religious Feeling) as such, has nothing to do with the Secular: it may make its appearance in that sphere on a mission of mercy, but this stops short of a strict socially ethical connection with it—does not come up to the idea of Freedom. Religious Feeling is extraneous to History, and has no History; for History is rather the Empire of Spirit recognizing itself in its *Subjective* Freedom, as the economy of social morality (sittliches Reich) in the State. In the Middle Ages that embodying of the Divine in actual life was wanting; the antithesis was not harmonized. Social morality was represented as worthless, and that in its *three* most essential particulars." (380)

These three essential particulars were Love, Activity and Freedom. Those enforced by the church as its three cardinal requirements were: Poverty, Chastity and Obedience. By them, as practiced in the medieval church and later, Hegel declares that social morality was degraded and that the church had become an ecclesiastical power rather than a power ministering to spiritual freedom. "For," says he, "Subjective Spirit, although testifying to the Absolute is at the same time *limited* and definitely existing Spirit as Intelligence and Will." (381) From this it follows that this Intelligence and Will must be enriched and since the Spirit exists *in* Man, the Church as teacher and director must foster their enrichment and development. But an antithesis had arisen between that which is, and is not, truly of the Holy Spirit within man's consciousness. So great is this antithesis that it is only by means of its full alienation, bringing total rupture, that there is revealed the position that had been assumed. By this means it is able to attain true harmony again.

It was during the eleventh, twelfth, and thirteenth centuries that an impulse arose destined to effect this revaluation. It came about naturally and in various ways, particularly three: study, travel, and art. The fortresses and castles were no longer of prime importance. The incentive for building to the more worthy aim of religion, i.e. of churches for communal worship, was paramount. As time went on Great Cathedrals were erected; then Art was employed to embellish them. Meanwhile maritime commerce was bringing communities and their products closer; while men's minds were receiving an outer stimulus. The urge came to seek answers to the many questions suggested by the natural world around them. Over against this scientific endeavor there was Scholastic Philosophy. The church dogmas were examined and effort was made to interpret them and square them with the best that Aristotelian logic could supply. In various places schools and universities took on new activity. Law and medicine were studied. Towns came into existence as an aftergrowth of the feudal protectorates. Individuals who were in close relation by the soil they cultivated established themselves as confederations; a tower was erected in which was suspended a bell to serve as a signal for convocation. A militia was formed. Walls were erected and trenches dug to give communal defense. Trades and crafts began to flourish. By degrees the towns secured independent jurisdiction—freeing themselves from all obligation to the neighboring noblemen. The trading class divided itself into guilds or unions. Municipal government developed.

In the meantime there was a continual struggle going on between the Secular rulers and the Holy See—each contending for supremacy. There were a number of points of issue but that which held special importance was the matter of investiture. In regard to these matters we turn to Hegel: "The contest between the Emperors and the Popes regarding investitures was settled at the close of 1122 by Henry V and Pope Calixtus II on these terms: the Emperor was to invest with the sceptre; the Pope with the ring and crozier; the chapter was to elect the Bishops in the presence of the Emperor or of imperial commissioners; then the Emperor was to invest the Bishop as a secular feudatory with the *temporalia,* while the ecclesiastical investiture was reserved for the Pope. Thus the protracted contest between the secular and spiritual powers was at length set at rest." (398)

"The Church gained the victory in the struggle referred to . . . and in this way secured as decided a supremacy in Germany, as she did in other states of Europe by a calmer process. She made herself mistress of all the relations of life, and of science and art; and she was the permanent repository of spiritual treasures. Yet notwithstanding this full and complete development of ecclesiastical life, we find a deficiency and consequent craving manifesting itself in Christendom, and which drove it out of itself. To understand this want, we must revert to the nature of the Christian religion itself, and particularly to that aspect of it by which it has a footing in the Present in the consciousness of its votaries." (389)

"The objective doctrines of Christianity had been already so firmly settled by the Councils of the Church, that neither the medieval nor any other philosophy could develop them further, except in the way of exalting them intellectually, so that they might be satisfactory as presenting the *form* of Thought. And one essential point in this doctrine was the recognition of the Divine Nature as not in any sense an *other-world* existence (ein Jenseits), but as in unity with Human Nature in the Present and Actual. But this Presence is at the same time exclusively Spiritual Presence. Christ as a particular human personality has left the world; his *temporal* existence is only a past one— *i.e.*, it exists only in mental conception. And since the Divine existence on earth is essentially of a spiritual character, it cannot appear in the form of a Dalai-Lama. The Pope, however high his position as Head of Christendom and Vicar of Christ, calls himself only the Servant of Servants. How then did the Church realize Christ as a *definite and present existence*? The principal form of this realization was, as remarked above, the Holy Supper, in the form it presented as the Mass: in this the Life, Suffering, and Death of the actual Christ were verily present, as an eternal and daily repeated sacrifice. Christ appears as a definite and present existence in a sensuous form as the *Host*, consecrated by the Priest; so far all is satisfactory: that is to say, it is the Church, the Spirit of Christ, that attains in this ordinance direct and full assurance." (390)

But although the Church has a direct assurance of Christ in the Holy Communion and the Mass, this fact does not alter the other repellent realization that the place of Christ's death and resurrection—the Holy Sepulchre—and the Holy

Places of his earthly ministry were in the control of Infidels. This idea was brought to the consciousness of the period and began to assume magnified proportions as the feeling grew and spread. It formed itself into a motive that began to unite the whole of Christendom. The Infidel must be expelled from the Holy Land! Step by step there was conceived the plan of a crusade against this outrage. Turning to Hegel at this point for the amplification we find: "The West once more sallied forth in hostile array against the East. As in the expedition of the Greeks against Troy, so here the invading hosts were entirely composed of independent feudal lords and knights; though they were not united under a real individuality as were the Greeks under Agamemnon or Alexander. Christendom, on the contrary, was engaged in an undertaking whose object was the securing of the *definite and present existence* (of Deity)—the real culmination of Individuality. This object impelled the West against the East, and this is the essential interest of the Crusades." (391)

"The first and immediate commencement of the Crusades was made in the West itself. Many thousands of Jews were massacred, and their property seized; and after this terrible prelude Christendom began its march. The monk, Peter the Hermit of Amiens, led the way with an immense troop of rabble. This host passed in the greatest disorder through Hungary, and robbed and plundered as they went; but their numbers dwindled away, and only a few reached Constantinople. For rational considerations were out of the question; the mass of them believed that God would be their immediate guide and protector. The most striking proof that enthusiasm almost robbed the nations of Europe of their senses, is supplied by the fact that at a later time troops of children ran away from their parents, and went to Marseilles, there to take ship for the Holy Land. Few reached it; the rest were sold by the merchants to the Saracens as slaves." (392)

"At last, with much trouble and immense loss, more regular armies attained the desired object; they beheld themselves in possession of all the Holy Places of note—Bethlehem, Gethsemane, Golgotha, and even the *Holy Sepulchre.* In the whole expedition—in all the acts of the Christians—appeared that enormous contrast (a feature characteristic of the age)—the transition on the part of the Crusading host from the greatest excesses and outrages to the profoundest contrition and humiliation. Still dripping with the blood of the slaughtered inhabitants of Jerusalem, the Christians fell down on their faces at the tomb of the Redeemer, and directed their fervent supplications to him." (392)

"Thus did Christendom come into the possession of its highest good. Jerusalem was made a kingdom, and the entire feudal system was introduced there—a constitution which, in presence of the Saracens, was certainly the worst that could be adopted. Another crusade in the year 1204 resulted in the conquest of Constantinople and the establishment of a Latin Empire there. Christendom, therefore, had appeased its religious craving; it could now veritably walk unobstructed in the footsteps of the Savior. Whole shiploads of earth were brought from the Holy Land to Europe. Of Christ himself no corporal relics could be obtained, for he was arisen: the Sacred Handkerchief, the Cross, and lastly the Sepulchre, were the most venerated memorials. But in the Grave is found the real point of retroversion; it is in the grave that all the vanity of the Sensuous perishes. At the Holy Sepulchre the vanity of (the cherished) opinion passes away (the fancies by which the substance of truth has been obscured disappear); there all is seriousness. In the negation of that *definite and present embodiment—i.e.* of the Sensuous—it is that the turning-point in question is found, and those words have an application: "Thou wouldst not suffer thy Holy One to see corruption." Christendom was not to find its ultimatum of truth in the grave. At this sepulchre the Christian world received a second time the response given to the disciples when they sought the body of the Lord there: *"Why seek ye the living among the dead? He is not here, but is risen."* You must not look for the principle of your religion in the

Sensuous, in the grave among the dead, but in the living Spirit in yourselves. We have seen how the vast idea of the union of the Finite with the Infinite was perverted to such a degree as that men looked for a *definite embodiment* of the Infinite in a mere isolated outward object (the Host). Christendom found the empty Sepulchre, but not the union of the Secular and the Eternal; and so it lost the Holy Land. It was practically undeceived; and the result which it brought back with it was of a negative kind: viz., that the *definite embodiment* which it was seeking, was to be looked for in *Subjective Consciousness* alone, and in no external object; that the definite form in question, presenting the union of the Secular with the Eternal, is the Spiritual self-cognizant independence of the individual. Thus the world attains the conviction that man must look within himself for that *definite embodiment* of being which is of a divine nature: subjectivity thereby receives absolute authorization, and claims to determine for itself the relation (of all that exists) to the Divine. This then was the absolute result of the Crusades, and from them we may date the commencement of self-reliance and spontaneous activity. The West bade an eternal farewell to the East at the Holy Sepulchre, and gained a comprehension of its own principle of subjective infinite Freedom. Christendom never appeared again on the scene of history as *one* body." (393)

At the end of the crusades the church stood at the completion of her authority. Numerous monasteries were established to give a further enactment of what was recommended. Likewise there was a reverse movement for various heresies now arose. The development in the direction of science took on new vigor and Thought set itself the task of justifying the doctrines of the Church. All Europe presented the scene of intellect, and art advancing to new positions. Feudalism had become outworn. What had formerly been Nobles and Serfs gave way to One Monarch and no serfs. Those who had been vassals became, instead, officers of State. The State itself was established in one of three different ways. In the first of these, the lord gained mastery over his vassals and made himself sole ruler; or secondly, princes freed themselves from feudal relations and became the rulers of the occupied territory; or lastly, the lord united his vassals with their consent and a state, under one ruler, was set up by peaceful means. In Germany the situation was different. A number of predatory states had sprung up, but since the feudal constitution was no longer recognized, violence, injustice and plunder were the order of the day. After the Count of Hapsburg became Emperor, the cities began to form confederations. The object was resistance to the encroachments of the feudal lords. In more than one instance steel-clad nobles were beaten back by a band of citizens with clubs and iron-capped staffs. Then there came another ally, to further the cause, in the form of gunpower. This made the old methods of warfare of little avail.

Thus through the final establishment of cities and states the period of medieval feudalism passed gradually away while there arose the formation of the rudiments of national life. There was Italy which, in the same manner as Germany, had attained an independent position by means of isolated centers of power. There was France gaining strength and influence as a hereditary monarchy. England under its subjugation by William Duke of Normandy, was divided into fiefs—which had been given to Duke William's followers patterning after the custom of feudalism. As time went on these English barons gained power and were able, when the King's oppressions became too great, to withstand him. In the case of King John they exacted the Magna Charta.

Not only was each country well on the way toward national life, but the tranquility of a more settled political order beckoned the Soul to give expression to its realizations. Art was specially emphasized. Of this Hegel writes:—"Art spiritualizes—animates the mere outward form and material object of adoration with a form which expresses soul, sentiment, Spirit; so that piety has not a bare sensuous embodiment of the Infinite to contemplate, and does not lavish its devotion on a mere *Thing,* but on a higher element with which the material object is imbued—that expressive form with which *Spirit* has invested it." (408)

As free Spirit expanded, it continued to grapple with Thought, as such. Plato became widely studied and presented to the West an advanced view of human relations. Thought likewise entered the realm of scientific investigation. There was present, to mark the age, the Spirit of geographical exploration. It began with the discovery of America and then pressed outward in every direction. Turning to Hegel: "These three events—the so-called Revival of Learning, the flourishing of the Fine Arts and the discovery of America and of the passage to India by the Cape—may be compared with that *blush of dawn*, which after long storms betokens the return of a bright and glorious day. This day is the day of Universality, which breaks upon the world after the long, eventful and terrible night of the Middle Ages—a day which is distinguished by science, art and inventive impulse—that is, by the noblest and highest, and which Humanity, rendered free by Christianity and emancipated through the instrumentality of the Church, exhibits as the eternal and veritable substance of its being." (411)

"Humanity has now attained consciousness of a real internal harmonization of Spirit, and a good conscience in regard to actuality—to secular existence. The Human Spirit has come to stand on its own basis. In the self-consciousness to which man has thus advanced, there is no revolt against the Divine, but a manifestation of that better subjectivity, which recognizes the Divine in its own being; which is imbued with the Good and True, and which directs its activities to general and liberal objects bearing the stamp of rationality and beauty." (408)

The German Reformation has given birth in men's consciousness to the fact that infinite subjectivity establishes the true spirituality. That Christ, as essentially spiritual, is obtained, after being reconciled to God, in faith and spiritual realization. This does not mean mere belief, but rather, says

Hegel, "the subjective assurance of the Eternal, of Absolute Truth, the Truth of God." (415)

"And this subjectivity is the common property of *all mankind.* Each has to accomplish the work of reconciliation in his own soul.—Subjective Spirit has to receive the Spirit of Truth into itself, and give it a dwelling place there. Thus that absolute inwardness of soul which pertains to religion itself, and Freedom in the Church are both secured. Subjectivity therefore makes the objective purport of Christianity, *i.e.* the doctrine of the Church, its own . . . . The subjective feeling and the conviction of the individual is regarded as equally necessary with the objective side of Truth. Truth . . . is not a finished and complete thing; the subject himself must be imbued with Truth, surrendering his particular being in exchange for the substantial Truth, and making that Truth his own. Thus subjective Spirit gains emancipation in the Truth, abnegates its particularity and comes to itself in realizing the truth of its being. Thus Christian Freedom is actualized. If subjectivity be placed in feeling only, without the objective side, we have the stand-point of the merely Natural Will." (416)

"In the proclamation of these principles is unfurled the new, the latest standard round which the peoples rally—the banner of *Free Spirit,* independent, though finding its life in the Truth, and enjoying independence only in it. This is the banner under which we serve, and which we bear. Time, since that epoch, has had no other work to do than the formal imbuing of the world with this principle, in bringing the Reconciliation implicit (in Christianity) into objective and explicit realization. Culture is essentially concerned with Form; the work of Culture is the production of the Form of Universality, which is none other than Thought. Consequently Law, Property, Social Morality, Government, Constitutions, etc., must be conformed to general principles in order that they may accord with the idea of Free Will and be Rational. Thus only can the Spirit of Truth manifest itself in Subjective Will—in the particular shapes which the activity of the will assumes. In virtue of that degree of intensity which Subjective Free Spirit has attained elevating it to the form of Universality, Objective Spirit attains manifestation. This is the sense in which we must understand the State to be based on Religion. States and Laws are nothing else than Religion manifesting itself in the relations of the actual world." (417)

"This is the essence of the Reformation: Man is in his very nature destined to be free." (417)

"We spoke above of the relation *which the new doctrine sustained to secular life,* and now we have only to exhibit that relation in detail. The development and advance of Spirit from the time of the Reformation onwards consist in this, that Spirit, having now gained the consciousness of its Freedom, through that process of mediation which takes place between man and God—that is, in the full recognition of that objective process as the existence (the positive and definite manifestation) of the Divine essence—now takes it up and follows it out in building up the edifice of secular relations. That harmony (of Objective and Subjective Will) which has resulted from the painful struggles of History, involves the recognition of the Secular as capable of being an embodiment of Truth; whereas it had been formerly regarded as evil only, as incapable of Good—the latter being considered essentially ultramundane. It is now perceived that Morality and Justice in the State are also divine and commanded by God, and that in point of substance there is nothing higher or more sacred. One inference is that *Marriage* is no longer deemed less holy than *Celibacy*. . . . The Family introduces man to community—to the relation of interdependence in society; and this union is a moral one:" (422)

"Man himself has a conscience; consequently the subjection required of him is a free allegiance. This involves the possibility of a development of Reason and Freedom, and of their introduction into human relations; and Reason and the Divine commands are now synonymous. The Rational no longer meets with contradiction on the part of the religious conscience; it is permitted to develop itself in its own sphere without disturbance, without being compelled to resort to force in defending itself against an adverse power." (423) Formerly this adverse element had been sanctioned. The New Subjective Freedom brings into existence an understanding of the religious and secular life in relation to each other.

"This harmony between the State and the Church has now attained *immediate* realization. We have, as yet, no reconstruction of the State, of the system of jurisprudence, etc., for thought must first discover the essential principle of Right. The Laws of Freedom, had first to be expanded to a system as deduced from an absolute principle of Right. Spirit does not assume this complete form immediately after the Reformation; it limits itself at first to direct and simple changes, as *e.g.* the doing away with conventual establishments and episcopal jurisdiction, etc. The reconcilation between God and the World was limited in the first instance to an abstract form; it was not yet expanded into a system by which the moral world could be regulated." (424)

"In the first instance this reconciliation must take place in the individual soul, must be realized by feeling; the individual must gain the assurance that the Spirit dwells in him—that, in the language of the Church, a brokenness of heart has been experienced and that Divine grace has entered into the heart thus broken. By Nature man is not what he ought to be; only through a transforming process does he arrive at truth." (424)

The process of man's elevation from the Natural state to the state of Spiritual self-realization is a long one. It entails, in the case of mankind, many individuals showing various degrees of advance. But all of these constitute the eternal pilgrim, humanity, destined to arrive at the goal of full blown Spiritual maturity and destined to establish on global dimensions the Perfect State.

On this subject a few lines from Hegel. "The principle of *Development* involves also the existence of a latent germ of being—a capacity or potentiality striving to realize itself.

This formal conception finds actual existence in Spirit; which has the History of the World for its theatre, its possession, and the sphere of its realization. It is not of such a nature as to be tossed to and fro amid the superficial play of accidents, but is rather the absolute arbiter of things; entirely unmoved by contingencies, which, indeed, it applies and manages for its own purposes. Development, however, is also a property of organized natural objects. Their existence presents itself, not as an exclusively dependent one, subjected to external changes, but as one which expands itself in virtue of an internal unchangeable principle; a simple essence—whose existence, *i.e.,* as a germ, is primarily simple—but which subsequently develops a variety of parts, that become involved with other objects, and consequently live through a continuous process of changes—a process nevertheless, that results in the very contrary of change, and is even transformed into a *vis conservatrix* of the organic principle, and the form embodying it. Thus the organized individuum produces itself; it expands itself actually to what it was always *potentially.*—So Spirit is only that which it attains by its own efforts; it makes itself *actually* what it always was *potentially.* —That development (of *natural organisms)* takes place in a direct, unopposed, unhindered manner. Between the Idea and its realization—the essential constitution of the original germ and the conformity to it of the existence derived from it—no disturbing influence can intrude. But in relation to Spirit it is quite otherwise. The realization of its Idea is mediated by consciousness and will; these very faculties are, in the first instance, sunk in their primary *merely* natural life; the first object and goal of their striving is the realization of their merely natural destiny—but which, since it is Spirit that animates it, is possessed of vast attractions and displays great power and (moral) richness. Thus Spirit is at war with itself; it has to overcome itself as its most formidable obstacle. That development which in the sphere of Nature is a peaceful growth is, in that of spirit, a severe, a mighty conflict with itself. What Spirit really strives for is the realization of its

Ideal being; but in doing so, it hides that goal from its own vision, and is proud and well satisfied in this alienation from it." (55)

"Its expansion, therefore, does not present the harmless tranquillity of mere growth, as does that of organic life, but a stern reluctant working against itself. It exhibits, moreover, not the mere formal conception of development, but the attainment of a definite result. The goal of attainment we determined at the outset: it is Spirit in its *Completeness*, in its essential nature, *i.e.,* Freedom. This is the fundamental object, and therefore also the leading principle of the development—that whereby it receives meaning and importance.". . . (55)

"Universal History exhibits the *graduation* in the development of that principle whose substantial *purport* is the consciousness of Freedom. The analysis of the successive grades, in their abstract form, belongs to Logic; in their concrete aspect to the Philosophy of Spirit. Here it is sufficient to state that the first step in the process presents that immersion of Spirit in Nature which has been already referred to; the second shows it as advancing to the consciousness of its freedom. But this initial separation from Nature is imperfect and partial, since it is derived immediately from the merely natural state, is consequently related to it, and is still encumbered with it as an essentially connected element. The third step is the elevation of the soul from this still limited and special form of freedom to its pure universal form; that state in which the spiritual essence attains the consciousness and feeling of itself. These grades are the ground-principles of the general process; but how each of them on the other hand involves within *itself* a process of formation—constituting the links in a dialectic of transition—to particularize this must be reserved for the sequel." (57)

"Here we have only to indicate that Spirit begins with a germ of infinite possibility, but *only* possibility—containing its substantial existence in an undeveloped form, as the object and goal which it reaches only in its resultant—full reality. In actual existence Progress appears as an advancing from the imperfect to the more perfect; but the former must not be understood abstractly as *only* the imperfect, but as something which involves the very opposite of itself—the so-called perfect—as a *germ* or impulse. So—reflectively, at least—*possibility* points to something destined to become actual; the Aristotelian δύναμις is also *potentia,* power and might. Thus the Imperfect, as involving its opposite, is a contradiction, which certainly exists, but which is continually annulled and solved; the instinctive movement—the inherent impulse in the life of the soul—to break through the rind of mere nature, sensuousness, and that which is alien to it, and to attain the light of consciousness, *i.e.* to itself." (57)

It is this light of consciousness, involving the inward nature of man, that has now been realized. This realization bestows on every individual so realizing, a participation in the divine in the nature of regenerated life—a new inner realization. It involves Thought, as such, with all that is thereby connoted. Turning to Hegel concerning the light of consciousness as existing in Thought we find: "For in thinking we must elevate the object to Universality. This is utter and absolute Freedom, for the pure Ego, like pure Light, is with itself alone (is not involved with any alien principle); thus that which is diverse from itself, sensuous or spiritual, no longer presents an object of dread, for in contemplating such diversity it is inwardly free and can freely confront it. A practical interest makes use of, consumes the objects offered to it: a theoretical interest calmly contemplates them, assured that in themselves they present no alien element.—Consequently, the *ne plus ultra* of Inwardness, of Subjectiveness, is Thought. Man is not free, when he is not thinking; for except when thus engaged he sustains a relation to the world around him as to another, an alien form of being. This comprehension—the penetration of the Ego into and beyond other forms of being with the most profound self-certainty (the identity of subjective and objective Reason being recognized), directly involves the harmonization of Being: for it must be observed that the unity of Thought with its Object is already *implicitly* present (*i.e.* in the fundamental constitution of the Universe), for Reason is the substantial basis of Consciousness as well as of the External and Natural. Thus that which presents itself as the Object of Thought is no longer an absolutely distinct form of existence (ein Jenseits), not of an alien and grossly substantial (as opposed to intelligible) nature." (439)

"Thought is the grade to which Spirit has now advanced. It involves the Harmony of Being in its purest essence, challenging the external world to exhibit the same Reason which Subject (the Ego) possesses. Spirit perceives that Nature—the World—must also be an embodiment of Reason, for God created it on principles of Reason. An interest in the contemplation and comprehension of the present world became universal. Nature embodies Universality, inasmuch as it is nothing other than Sorts, Genera, Power, Gravitation, etc., phenomenally present. Thus *Experimental Science* became the science of the World; for experimental science involves on the one hand observation of phenomena, on the other hand also the discovery of the Law, the essential being, the hidden force that causes those phenomena—thus reducing the data supplied by observation to their simple principles. Intellectual consciousness was first extricated from that sophistry of thought, which unsettles everything, by *Descartes*. As it was the purely German nations among whom the principle of *Spirit* first manifested itself, so it was by the Romanic nations that the *abstract idea* (to which the character assigned them above—viz., that of internal schism, more readily conducted them) was first comprehended. Experimental science therefore very soon made its way among them (in common with the Protestant English), but especially among the Italians. It seemed to men as if God had but just created the moon and stars, plants and animals, as if the laws of the universe were now established for the first time; for only then did they feel a real interest in the universe, when they recognized their own Reason in the Reason which pervades it. The human eye became *clear,* perception quick, thought active and interpretative. The discovery of the laws of Nature enabled men to contend against the monstrous superstition of the time, as also against all notions of mighty alien powers which magic alone could conquer . . . The independent authority of Subjectivity was maintained against belief founded on authority, and the Laws of Nature were recognized as the only bond connecting phenomena with phenomena. Thus all miracles were disallowed: for Nature is a system of known and recognized Laws; Man is at home in it, and that only passes for truth in which he finds himself at home; he is free through the acquaintance he has gained with Nature. Nor was thought less vigorously directed to the Spiritual side of things: Right and (Social) Morality come to be looked upon as having their foundation in the actual present Will of man, whereas formerly it was referred only to the command of God enjoined *ab extra,* written in the Old and New Testament, or appearing in the form of particular Right (as opposed to that based on general principles) in old parchments, as *privilegia,* or in international compacts. What the nations acknowledge as international Right was deduced empirically from observation (as in the work of Grotius); then the source of the existing civil and political law was looked for, after Cicero's fashion, in those instincts of men which Nature has planted in their hearts—*e.g.,* the social instinct; next the principle of security for the person and property of the citizens, and of the advantage of the commonwealth—that which belongs to the class of "reasons of State." On these principles private rights were on the one hand despotically contravened, but on the other hand such contravention was the instrument of carrying out the general objects of the State in opposition to mere positive or prescriptive claims . . ." (441)

"These general conceptions, deduced from actual and present consciousness—the Laws of Nature and the substance of what is right and good, have received the name of *Reason.* The recognition of the validity of these laws were designated by the term *Éclaircissement (Aufklärung).* From France it passed over into Germany, and created a new world of ideas. The absolute criterion—taking the place of all authority based on religious belief and positive laws of Right (especially political Right)—is the verdict passed by Spirit itself on the character of that which is to be believed or obeyed. After a free investigation in open day . . . , there had been secured to mankind Spiritual Freedom and the Reconciliation (of the Objective and Subjective) in the concrete: there had been triumphantly established the position that man's eternal destiny (his spiritual and moral position) must be wrought out *in himself* (cannot be an *opus operatum,* a work performed *for him*). But the import of that which is to take place in him—what truth is to become vital in him, was taken for granted . . . as something already given, something revealed by religion. *Now,* the principle was set up that this import must be capable of actual investigation—something of which I (in this modern time) can gain an inward conviction—and that to this basis of inward demonstration every dogma must be referred." (442)

"This principle of thought makes its appearance in the first instance in a general and abstract form; and is based on the axiom of Contradiction and Identity. The results of thought as thus posited as finite, and the éclaircissement utterly banished and extirpated all that was speculative from things human and divine. Although it is of incalculable importance that the multiform complex of things should be reduced to its simplest conditions, and brought into the form of Universality, yet this still abstract principle does not satisfy the living Spirit, the concrete human soul." (442)

"Secular life is the positive and definite embodiment of the Spiritual Kingdom—the Kingdom of the *Will* manifesting itself in outward existence. Mere impulses are also forms in which the inner life realizes itself; but these are transient and disconnected; they are the ever-changing applications of volition. But that which is just and moral belongs to the essential, independent, intrinsically universal Will; and if we would know what Right really is, we must abstract from inclination, impulse and desire as the particular; *i.e.*, we must know what the Will is in itself. For benevolent, charitable, social impulses are nothing more than impulses—to which others of a different class are opposed. What the Will is in itself can be known only when these specific and contradictory forms of volition have been eliminated. Then Will appears as Will, in its abstract essence. The Will is Free only when it does not will anything alien, extrinsic, foreign to itself (for as long as it does so, it is dependent), but wills itself alone—wills the Will. This is absolute Will—the volition to be free. Will making itself its own object is the basis of all Right and Obligation—consequently of all statutory determination of Right, categorical imperatives, and enjoined obligations. The Freedom of the Will *per se,* is the principle and substantial basis of all Right—is itself absolute inherently eternal Right, and the Supreme Right in comparison with other specific Rights; nay, it is even that by which Man becomes Man, and is therefore the fundamental principle of Spirit. But the next question is: How does Will assume a definite form? For in willing itself, it is nothing but an identical reference to itself; but, in point of fact, it wills something specific; there *are,* we know, distinct and special Duties and Rights. A particular application, a definite form of Will, is desiderated; for pure Will is its own object, its own application, which, as far as this showing goes, is no object, no application. In fact, in this form it is nothing more than *formal* Will. But the metaphysical process by which this abstract Will develops itself, so as to attain a definite form of Freedom, and how Rights and Duties are evolved therefrom this is not the place to discuss. It may however be remarked that the same principle obtained speculative recognition in Germany, in the *Kantian* Philosophy. According to it the simple unity of Self-consciousness, the Ego, constitutes the absolutely independent Freedom, and is the fountain of all general conception—*i.e.* all conceptions elaborated by Thought—Theoretical Reason; and likewise of the highest of all practical determinations (or conceptions)—Practical Reason, as free and pure Will; and Rationality of Will is none other than the maintaining one's self in pure Freedom—willing this and this alone—Right purely for the sake of Right, Duty purely for the sake of Duty." (443)

"This absolute principle brings us to *the last stage in History, our world, our own time.*" (442)

SUBJECTIVE FREEDOM—REALIZATION OF SUBJECTIVE LIFE

"This is the point which consciousness has attained, and these are the principal phases of that form in which the principle of Freedom has realized itself;—for the History of the World is nothing but the development of the Idea of Freedom. But Objective Freedom—the laws of *real* Freedom—demand the subjugation of the mere contingent Will—for this is in its nature formal. If the Objective is in itself Rational, human insight and conviction must correspond with the Reason which it embodies, and then we have the other essential element—Subjective Freedom—also realized . . . Philosophy concerns itself only with the glory of the Idea mirroring itself in the History of the World. Philosophy escapes from the weary strife of passions that agitate the surface of society into the calm region of contemplation; that which interests it is the recognition of the process of development which the Idea has passed through in realizing itself—*i.e.* the Idea of Freedom, whose reality is the consciousness of Freedom and nothing short of it." (457)

Thus we see that subjective freedom has been born. After a long and terrible travail the brilliant sun of the *Day of Universality* has arisen. Like any day it belongs to a larger cycle—let us say, the year. The year in its turn has seasons and the seasons can be looked upon as signifying the stages of advance and retardation through which consciousness moves. For consciousness develops in a cyclic periodicity constituting a spiral that carries the Spirit onward towards its goal with many a new birth and many a retardation. We are witnessing the world in the manifestation of these cycles, which, like the seasons, get a new birth in their springtime, advance in their summer, culminate in their autumn and are arrested in a pralaya of winter—prior to each new advance. In this way is fulfilled the ever continuous drama of human consciousness as it makes actual in manifestations its latent potencies. In the field of psychology, in the field of the arts and sciences we perceive its intermittent advances. In the political field we share its travail as it strives with its ever recurring problems. The perfect state does not realize itself except after a long process. For says Hegel: "There must be institutions adapted, political machinery invented, accompanied by appropriate political arrangements—necessitating long struggles of the understanding before what is really appropriate can be discovered—involving, moreover, contentions with private interest and passions, and a tedious discipline of these latter, in order to bring about the desired harmony." (24)

In the case of the world today these cycles of development have attained different degrees of advancement in the different races of the earth yet are now to be caught up in the overall consciousness that has come to mankind—Subjective Freedom. It is the day that is to be lighted by the light that never was on land nor sea yet is the whole world's light—the day of Universality. Turning to Hegel:

"That the History of the World, with all the changing scenes which its annals present, is this process of development and the realization of Spirit—this is the true *Theodicaea,* the justification of God in History. Only this insight can reconcile Spirit with the History of the World—viz., that what has happened, and is happening every day, is not only not "without God," but is essentially His Work." (457)